NOT ALMS
BUT OPPORTUNITY

TOURÉ F. REED

NOT ALMS
BUT OPPORTUNITY

The Urban League & the Politics
of Racial Uplift, 1910-1950

The University of North Carolina Press

Chapel Hill

Designed by Heidi Perov

Set in Warnock with Champion Heavyweight and Univers
by Keystone Typesetting, Inc.

The paper in this book meets the guidelines for permanence
and durability of the Committee on Production Guidelines for
Book Longevity of the Council on Library Resources.

Library of Congress Cataloging-in-Publication Data

Reed, Touré F.

Not alms but opportunity : the Urban League and the politics of
racial uplift, 1910–1950 / Touré F. Reed.

p. cm.

Includes bibliographical references and index.

ISBN 978-0-8078-3223-3 (cloth: alk. paper)

ISBN 978-0-8078-5902-5 (pbk.: alk. paper)

1. National Urban League—History—20th century. 2. African Americans—
New York (State)—New York—Social conditions—20th century. 3. African
Americans—Illinois—Chicago—Social conditions—20th century. 4. Social
classes—New York (State)—New York—History—20th century. 5. Social
classes—Illinois—Chicago—History—20th century. 6. New York (N.Y.)—
Social conditions—20th century. 7. Chicago (Ill.)—Social conditions—20th
century. 8. African Americans—Social conditions—To 1964. 9. African
Americans—Economic conditions—20th century. I. Title.

E185.5.N33R44 2008

305.896'07307470904—dc22   2008007810

cloth   12 11 10 09 08   5 4 3 2 1

paper   12 11 10 09 08   5 4 3 2 1

To my father and friend

Contents

Illustrations

Preface

The origins of this study of the National, New York, and Chicago Urban
Leagues date back to work I first undertook in a research seminar with Professor Kenneth Jackson during my first year as a history graduate student at
Columbia University. Inspired by the work of scholars such as Ira Katznelson,
Michael Katz, and James Grossman, I entered graduate school hoping to
explore the ways in which race and class have shaped politics and social
relations of American cities. Like most first-year graduate students the questions that I grappled with were often unwieldy; however, over the course of my
first semester or so I refined my focus as I became interested in the class issues
informing black Progressive Era reformers. It is probably safe to say that, at the
time, no single concept influenced my thinking on this topic more than Evelyn
Brooks Higginbotham's "politics of respectability," advanced in her pioneering
Righteous Discontent. Higginbotham contends that Afro-American Baptist
women set out to counter white racists' allegation that blacks were unassimilable by encouraging Afro-Americans to embrace Victorian values of thrift,
industry, and sexual restraint. While this approach could have revealed a
pronounced middle-class bias, Higginbotham argues that racism, sexism, and
Christian humanism generally muted inegalitarian impulses among Afro-
American churchwomen who identified behavior, rather than mere wealth, as
both class marker and engine of racial uplift.

As a member of the black middle class myself, I was intrigued by the idea
that Afro-American activists, in contrast to their white counterparts, might
have developed political models driven by adherence to normative values that
mitigated their own particular class interests. Thus when I had an opportunity
to delve into archival research during my second semester in graduate school,
I set out to test some of the basic tenets of the "politics of respectability" by
examining the ideology and programs of a black middle-class social reform
organization—the New York Urban League (NYUL).

I chose the NYUL for both intellectual and practical reasons. Despite the
fact that New York had been home to the nation's largest urban black population for most of the twentieth century, the New York League had received
scant attention from scholars. At the time, I thought that the dearth of scholarship on the NYUL afforded an opportunity to make a significant contribu-

tion to the historiography on black New York. I had also assumed that the NYUL Papers were conveniently located at the Schomburg, which was a relatively short subway ride from Columbia. I imagined, moreover, that the records of the New York branch of one of the most important civil rights organizations were highly detailed and would therefore offer a wealth of information to play with. Though the study of the NYUL did offer new insights into black politics, I quickly discovered that the rest of my assumptions were off base. After reading the three histories of the National Urban League (NUL), I realized that the bulk of the NYUL's records were located not in New York but at the Library of Congress in Washington, D.C.—a less than convenient Amtrak ride for a poor graduate student. Once I was finally able to take a look at the NYUL Papers, I also learned that the New York League's holdings were shockingly spare. A combination of improper storage and inadequate record keeping meant that the NYUL's papers, like those of most local Leagues, suffered from major gaps.

Since my immediate goal was simply to write a forty-page seminar paper, the problems I experienced my first year in graduate school were hardly insurmountable. They would, however, prevent me from attempting to write a book-length monograph on the NYUL. Thus, when I decided to expand my research on the League, I chose to broaden my focus to include the New York, Chicago, and National Urban Leagues. This is not to suggest that this project's focus is purely utilitarian. My decision to examine the specific groups I have chosen to study here is rooted, at least in part, in my belief that this approach offers a clear window into black politics of the era. New York and Chicago were, of course, home to the nation's two largest urban black communities, ensuring the importance of these Urban League affiliates. Study of the National Urban League along with two of its locals also permits insights into ideological trends that might be obscured by a focus that is either too narrow or too broad, since the NUL guided, though it did not manage, its branches. The intellectual advantages of this approach notwithstanding, it is nonetheless a reflection on the problems posed by sources. Like all historians, my research strategies were and are necessarily shaped by extant sources. A multigroup approach allowed me to "fill in" some of the holes in the Urban League's records.

In a context of incomplete records, making sense of class implications of the League's ideology and programs is an inherently difficult task. As historian Nancy Weiss noted in her own groundbreaking and very useful study of the NUL, gaps in the Urban League Papers make it impossible to examine certain basic aspects of the League's operation. One cannot know, for example, whether policy decisions ultimately rested with the group's interracial board or its black executive secretaries. While this project is, by its nature, part institutional history, the ins and outs of backroom operations are of less concern here than the ways in which the Urban League's black leadership defined the group's mission. Funding and internal politics necessarily shaped the League's activities, but so too did the ideological matrix in which the Urban Leaguers operated.

It should, of course, be said that League histories by Nancy Weiss, Guichard Parris and Lester Brooks, Jesse T. Moore, and Arvarh Strickland have all touched upon the philosophical issues shaping the group's work. These authors' studies have, moreover, greatly enriched my own project. Still, perhaps with the exception of Jesse T. Moore's work, League historiography is less concerned with the ideological impulses shaping the group's work than with its institutional imperatives. By viewing the League's work through officials' writings and publications, *Not Alms but Opportunity* not only situates the Urban League's program within broader currents of progressive reform, but it also places the Leaguers themselves at the center of the story.

Who runs things?
in Race organisations?
Race members or allies?

Acknowledgments

Writing a book is a deeply personal and often solitary experience; even so, the frustrations and challenges presented by scholarly research ultimately preclude one from "going it alone." That said, I am grateful for the support I have received from a great many individuals and institutions.

As this study evolved into book form, I had the good fortune of working with a number of wonderful historians and social scientists. Over the years, I have benefited from the guidance and/or support of scholars such as Eric Foner, Alan Brinkley, Ira Katznelson, Kenneth Jackson, Francesca Poletta, Daryl Scott, Judith Stein, Jonathan Holloway, Preston Smith, Dean Robinson, Kenneth Warren, Adolph L. Reed Jr., Alice O'Connor, Subho Basu, Mohamad Tavakoli, Tony Adedze, C. Alvin Bowman, John Freed, and Roger Biles. Each of these individuals not only gave freely of their time but, at various stages of the project, offered constructive criticism that greatly enhanced my work.

Rebecca A. Lewis and Scarlett Weibull have also made valuable contributions to this book. Rebecca graciously offered her services as proofreader, "personal copyeditor," and regular sounding board. Her support has been indispensable. More to the point, Rebecca's diligence and intelligence have been an inspiration to me for nearly two decades of friendship.

Scarlett Weibull took on the role as my research assistant. Scarlett, who is one of the most talented students I have taught, not only took time away from her own life to track down photos and documents, but she is also responsible for the book's index. Scarlett's attention to detail, sharp analytical mind, and pitbull-like determination bode well for her own career as a scholar.

Since historians are only as good as the archivists who assist them, it probably goes without saying that I am indebted to a good many library staff around the country. While I cannot remember the names of all the librarians and archivists I've worked with over the years, this book benefited greatly from the efforts of library staff at the University of Illinois at Chicago, the Library of Congress, Columbia University, the University of Chicago, the Wisconsin Historical Society, and the Schomburg Center for Research in Black Life. The archivists at the University of Illinois, Chicago, and librarian T. J. Urbanski, formerly of Illinois State University, warrant special acknowledgment for their patience and professionalism.

Columbia University and Illinois State University provided crucial funding for my research. For most of my years in graduate school at Columbia, I was, as luck would have it, a George Edmund Haynes Fellow in History. Without the support I received from Columbia, I could not have pursued this project. ISU, my first employer out of graduate school, likewise provided valuable research assistance.

I must also thank the staff at UNC Press. My experience with Chapel Hill has been simply outstanding. I am especially appreciative of the efforts of Senior Editor Sian Hunter, who has been a fantastic resource.

Finally, to my friends and family, I am truly grateful for your understanding. Because of my own personality defects, I have often found it difficult to balance personal commitments and work. As all who know me will attest to, I have generally prioritized my work over all else. To you all—including Clarita M. Reed, Adolph L. Reed Jr., Kimberly Haley-Jackson, Kameron T. Jackson, Haley J. Jackson, Symone Jackson, Christopher J. Pappas, Cynthia Pappas, Deirdre Darnall, Nikol Alexander Floyd, Maria Diaz, David Hearn, and Andrew Hartman—thank you so much for your patience and tolerance.

Abbreviations

AA	Amalgamated Association of Iron and Steel Workers
AFL	American Federation of Labor
AMC	Amalgamated Meat Cutters and Butchers Union
ANLC	American Negro Labor Congress
BSCP	Brotherhood of Sleeping Car Porters
CAP	Community Action Programs
CCC	Civil Conservation Corps
CCRR	Chicago Commission on Race Relations
CIICN	Committee for Improving Industrial Conditions of Negroes in New York
CIO	Committee for Industrial Organizations (1935–38)
	Congress of Industrial Organizations (1938–55)
CPUSA	Communist Party of the United States
CUCAN	Committee on Urban Conditions Among Negroes
CUL	Chicago Urban League
CWA	Civil Works Administration
EAC	Emergency Advisory Councils
ERP	Employee Representation Plan
FEPC	Fair Employment Practices Committee
FHA	Federal Housing Administration
IEAC	Illinois Emergency Advisory Council
IIT	Illinois Institute of Technology
MOWM	March on Washington Movement
NAACP	National Association for the Advancement of Colored People
NCSW	National Conference of Social Work
NHS	National Health Service
NIRA	National Industrial Recovery Act
NLPCW	National League for the Protection of Colored Women
NLRA	National Labor Relations Act
NLUCAN	National League on Urban Conditions Among Negroes
NNRI	Near North Redevelopment Initiative
NRA	National Recovery Administration
NUL	National Urban League

NYA	National Youth Administration
NYSES	New York State Employment Services
NYUL	New York Urban League
OPM	Office of Price Management
OWI	Office of War Information
SLC	Stockyard Labor Council
SWOC	Steel Workers Organizing Committee
TERA	Temporary Emergency Relief Administration
UNIA	Universal Negro Improvement Association
USES	United States Employment Services
USHA	United States Housing Authority
WC	Workers' Councils
WMC	War Manpower Committee
WPA	Works Progress Administration (1935–38)
	Works Projects Administration (1939–43)

Introduction

The wisest among my race understand that the agitation of questions of social equality is the extremest folly, and that progress in the enjoyment of all the privileges that will come to us must be the result of severe and constant struggle rather than artificial forcing.—Booker T. Washington, 1895

Men have a right to demand that the members of a civilized community be civilized; that the fabric of human culture, so laboriously woven, be not wantonly ignorantly destroyed. Consequently a nation may rightly demand, even of a people it has consciously and intentionally wronged, not indeed complete civilization in thirty or one hundred years, but at least every effort and sacrifice possible on their part toward making themselves fit members of the community within a reasonable time.—W. E. B. DuBois, 1899

On September 18, 1895, Booker T. Washington cemented his status as the nation's most "responsible" black leader with an address before the Atlanta Cotton States and International Exposition outlining the proper role of blacks in the political economy of the New South. Less than a year before the United States Supreme Court handed down its ruling in *Plessy v. Ferguson*, the former slave–turned-principal of Alabama's Tuskegee Institute called upon members of his race to direct their attentions not to the rapid erosion of political and civil rights taking place throughout the south but to economic preparedness. Washington's speech, like his work at Tuskegee, proceeded from the view that neither blacks nor whites were ready for Afro-American equality. The freedmen and their descendants required time and guidance to equip themselves for the responsibilities of citizenship, while whites needed evidence of blacks' worthiness of inclusion in civil society.[1] Proffering a model of gradual racial progress predicated on self-help and the cultural evolution of Afro-Americans, the Wizard of Tuskegee's philosophy dovetailed with the economic aims and race ideology of southern business and political elites.[2] Indeed, as critics of the day noted, Washington's characterization of blacks as devoid of the intellectual tools necessary for modern civilization helped legitimate the return of Bourbon rule and Republican indifference to the plight of the Negro in the south.

While Washington's "Atlanta Exposition" laid plain a particularly constrained vision of racial progress, many of his contemporaries shared a related faith in the ability of social guidance and moral probity to elevate the race. Just four years after the Wizard of Tuskegee's Atlanta address, W. E. B. DuBois, Washington's chief antagonist at the turn of the century, issued his own call for stewardship of the race's less-advanced elements in *The Philadelphia Negro*. DuBois's landmark study of Philadelphia's Seventh Ward undercut the charge that blacks were universally debauched by illuminating cultural and economic distinctions among the city's Afro-Americans. Though DuBois conceded the existence of a "vicious element" as well as a general "moral laxity" among black belt denizens, in contrast to the city's white reformers the Berlin-trained sociologist rooted the sources of ghetto malaise in specific social, rather than biological, processes.[3] DuBois's research struck at the heart of racist justifications for inequality. Nevertheless, he viewed race relations through an evolutionary civilizationist frame similar to Washington's. DuBois believed that integration required that blacks embrace Victorian middle-class values such as thrift, temperance, monogamy, and industry. Identifying bourgeois cultural traits as the bedrock of modern civilization, he viewed acculturation as a means of both countering race prejudice and preparing Afro-Americans to be constructive citizens.[4] Thus even as DuBois attributed social problems afflicting Philadelphia's black belt to structural as well as cultural influences, like the Wizard of Tuskegee, he perceived the moral guidance of the masses as crucial to the race's advancement.

Washington's and DuBois's identification of acculturation and self-help as integral components of racial progress was indicative of a broad philosophical shift occurring in Afro-American politics in the aftermath of Reconstruction. Collective self-help, or racial uplift, had been a major facet of black liberation projects since the dawn of the nineteenth century. Antebellum uplift endeavors such as the abolitionist and common school movements evinced an egalitarianism rooted in natural-rights ideology and Christian humanism. By the late nineteenth century, however, the democratic impulses that had informed uplift were vitiated by a building racial conservatism that suffused national culture and politics. America's tightening embrace of Social Darwinian notions of civilization had an especially significant impact on black uplift ideology. Portraying racial and class inequality as inexorable products of natural order, Social Darwinism and, later, eugenics became the dominant lenses through which to view these issues through the Great Depression. Afro-American reformers imbibed contemporary race and class conservatism,

Wow!

leading many Progressive Era black leaders to base their claims to equality not on an inalienable right to liberty but on the race's capacity to evolve.[5] In so doing, uplift substituted culture for race as a condition of admission to civil society. Racial uplift would as a result of this shift encompass a range of complex class perspectives of group advancement that often revealed their own inegalitarianism.

Historiography Flaw

Since the 1980s, a growing body of scholarship has explored how the class identities of Afro-American Progressive Era activists shaped their visions of group advancement. Focusing largely on the stated goals and avowed perspectives of black reformers, much of the recent historiography on black uplift has claimed that the uniqueness of the black experience imbued Afro-American activists with class views that were necessarily distinct from those of their white counterparts. Historians Evelyn Brooks Higginbotham[6] and Stephanie Shaw,[7] for example, have each argued that whites' failure to acknowledge economic and cultural differences among Afro-Americans led middle-class black women to develop a sense of collective responsibility that generally muted the class tensions influencing other reform movements of the era. While these studies, as well as those by Glenda Gilmore, Paula Giddings, and Kevin Gaines,[8] have greatly enhanced our understanding of how black reformers viewed themselves, their focus on activists' aims apart from close examination of their actual programs has led many to gloss over the class fissures dotting the landscape of black self-help. Presuming a necessary consonance between the asserted goals and deeds of middle-class Afro-American reformers, uplift historiography frequently takes for granted that racial uplift was comparatively free of the biases pervading contemporaneous reform movements.

Thesis

This book attempts to make sense of the class perspectives shaping racial uplift through an examination of the ideology and policies of the National, New York, and Chicago Urban Leagues between 1910 and 1950. By viewing the League's reform ideology in the light cast by its actual programs, this study ultimately seeks to render a more complex account of both the class implications of black uplift and the nature of the Urban League's work than has been offered to date. Though I am critical of the League, my intent is not to impugn the motives of the countless men and women involved with the Urban League movement. Indeed, the writings and publications of prominent League staffers such as Charles S. Johnson, George E. Haynes, T. Arnold Hill, and Lester Granger leave little doubt that Urban Leaguers, like other black reformers, understood themselves to be committed to a broad vision of collective advancement. The issue addressed here, then, is not the sincerity of Urban Leaguers' commitment to racial progress. Rather, the book's focus is intended to explore how particular class concerns and ideological influences shaped the League's vision of group advancement and the consequences of its endeavors. Examining the Urban League's work in housing, community development, job placement, vocational guidance, and union organizing, this project attempts to determine how the League defined the problems confronting black workers and tenants; the methods Urban Leaguers recommended for treating these ills; and, of course, which Afro-Americans were to benefit from League policy and why. The study also situates the League's activities within the broader ideological and social currents of its day, exploring the impact of migration, the Depression and the New Deal, World War II, and postwar downturns on the League's policies and philosophy.[9]

I have chosen to focus on the uplift programs of the Urban Leagues of New York and Chicago in particular largely because of the challenges confronting these organizations. Charged with the responsibility of meeting the needs of the nation's largest urban black communities, the New York and Chicago affiliates were forced to contend with massive migrant populations, discriminatory housing and labor markets, and a number of militant and radical political movements. The League's work in Chicago and New York also bore the distinct imprint of influential institutions, including philanthropic foundations, industrial and commercial business interests, and even universities. Though many of the difficulties confronted by the New York Urban League (NYUL) and Chicago Urban League (CUL) were typical to League affiliates, the branches themselves maintained important roles within the Urban League movement. Both the New York and National Leagues would, at different times, take responsibility for black Manhattan as well as the surrounding boroughs, ensuring personnel and methodological ties between the two. The Chicago League likewise trained a number of noteworthy National Urban League (NUL) staffers. Moreover, several individuals serving with each of these groups were prominent academics, including Charles S. Johnson, E. Franklin Frazier, and Ira De Augustine Reid. Influenced by social unrest, philanthropic and business interests, and even intellectuals, the National, New York, and Chicago Urban Leagues offer valuable insights into the social and ideological forces undergirding the uplift projects of middle-class black reformers.

The origin and meaning of the Urban League's philosophy and approach have been subjects of serious scholarly debate. Since the 1970s, two distinct schools of thought have emerged regarding the influences shaping the League's work. In one camp, historian Nancy Weiss argues that the NUL's emphasis on self-help places the organization in the conservative tradition of Booker T. Washington.[10] In the other, historian Jesse T. Moore contends that the

NAACP vs Tuskegee

League's social-work focus stressed structural rather than behavioral remedies for inequality, leading the group to adopt an approach that owed more to the bourgeois militancy advanced by W. E. B DuBois's National Association for the Advancement of Colored People (NAACP) than the Tuskegee Institute.[11] While each author has contributed substantially to both Urban League and civil rights historiography, their stark assessments of the League obscure many of the complex issues shaping Afro-Americans' reform endeavors.[12] Indeed, Weiss's and Moore's claims ultimately rest on characterizations of Washington and DuBois that wave aside the thorny nature of the their respective uplift strategies.[13] As a result, these authors' attempts to define the Urban League's philosophy as either conservative or militant lead each to sidestep proximate philosophical influences over the group and by extension some of the more important implications of its programs.

This study advances the view that the Urban League's uplift vision, from its inception through the Second World War, was shaped by theories of assimilation pioneered by the famed Chicago School of Sociology. Presuming the inherent plasticity of disparate peoples, Chicago School models of assimilation offered powerful antidotes to eugenicists' allegations regarding the innate deficiencies of blacks and other groups. Rather than leading Leaguers to focus on structural remedies for discrimination, the League's embrace of social science theory caused it to devote particular attention to the relationship between Afro-Americans' behavior and racial and economic inequality. In practice, this approach revealed sharply skewed class assumptions about migrants and poor Afro-Americans generally.

The Urban League's identification of social science theory as a tool for racial uplift grew organically from its mission. Established in 1910 by black sociologist George E. Haynes, the League was a social-work organization. Responding to the rising tide of migrants inundating New York and other northern cities, the Urban League's primary aim was "to promote and to do constructive and preventive social work for improving the social and economic conditions of Negroes in urban centers."[14] To this end, the NUL and its locals not only performed field studies to assess the quality of black life but also used their research to guide their own uplift program. Though the Urban League expanded the scope of its activities during the New Deal and Second World War, its work centered on two related self-help strategies. First, the League attempted to prepare Afro-Americans for life in the industrial city. It offered blacks moral and vocational training intended to enhance their efficiency and attentiveness in both workplace and community. It would also assist migrants and longtime residents in locating appropriate housing, employment, and city services. Second, the Urban League encouraged employers, unions, and landlords to open jobs and housing to blacks. Leaguers hoped that this two-pronged approach would not only expand available employment and housing but over time bridge physical and psychological divisions between the races.

The League's emphasis on self-help undoubtedly reflected the paucity of options available to blacks in the early twentieth century. Its bare-bones practicality notwithstanding, the group's efforts to adjust Afro-Americans to urban life were likewise illustrative of its embrace of Chicago School theories of assimilation. As a social-work organization, the NUL and its Chicago and New York branches were staffed largely by trained sociologists and social workers. Versed in social science theories and methods, Leaguers incorporated sociological concepts into their assessments of black life. Two models of assimilation, ethnic cycle and social disorganization and reorganization, played especially important roles in the group's uplift strategy between the 1910s and 1940s. A facet of interaction cycle theory, ethnic cycle examined the social dynamics shaping relations between subordinate and dominant groups.[15] Social disorganization and reorganization, on the other hand, focused on the forces shaping the values and attitudes of communities and individuals, devoting particular attention to the impact of migration and urbanization on the institutional strength of ethnic groups.[16] Since both models traced the racial and ethnic tensions of the day to environmental rather than biological influences, they would naturally hold some appeal to Urban Leaguers. In the context of black migration, ethnic cycle and social disorganization and reorganization provided comparatively optimistic lenses through which to view the problems confronting urban blacks. But while these models struck crisp blows to racist assumptions about Afro-Americans and other groups, the implementation of programs influenced by Chicago School sociology frequently led Leaguers to emphasize the needs of the so-called Negro better classes at the expense of poor Afro-Americans.

The class perspectives shaping the League's uplift approach found clear expression in the housing and employment programs of the National, Chicago, and New York Leagues. Consistent with ethnic cycle theory, the League's work in these areas hinged on the group's ability to create harmonious interactions between blacks and whites. Indeed, the Urban League's attempts to open access to both better occupations and better housing were predicated on Afro-Americans' ability to demonstrate that they could be efficient workers, responsible tenants, and virtuous citizens. This approach led the League to identify the "better classes" of blacks—defined as such by their embrace of middle-class values as well as their economic standing—as the vanguard of collective uplift. As a result, not only did the League's housing and employment programs emphasize the importance of finding homes and jobs for the so-called talented tenth, but its efforts to elevate the material conditions of blacks in Chicago and New York frequently included projects intended to insulate middle-class Afro-Americans from their benighted brethren.

The Urban League's perception of the Afro-American lower classes—comprised largely of migrants and poor blacks generally—as disorganized likewise reflected black elites' class concerns. Whites' tendency to judge the race as a whole by the deficiencies of unacculturated Afro-Americans prompted Leaguers to pursue remedial as well as punitive programs directed toward so-called maladjusted blacks. League policies vis-à-vis migrants and poor Afro-Americans thus oscillated between attempts to reorganize their communal institutions in accordance with the dictates of the industrial city and efforts to assist employers and landlords in weeding out those who failed to make the grade. Accepting the social and economic order of the industrial city, the Urban League set out to ensure mutually beneficial contact between the races. This approach ultimately required the organization to discipline black workers and separate the deserving from the undeserving poor.

Since the League set out to elevate the material condition of Afro-Americans, the group's uplift projects were nothing if not dynamic. Indeed, League affiliates generally tailored their particular housing and employment programs to the moment. Locals, moreover, had a fair amount of latitude to shape their own policies. My discussion of the Urban League's work is therefore structured around specific ideological and material concerns.

Chapter 1 examines the Urban League's origins and the philosophical influences shaping its project. In addition to exploring the circumstances leading to the creation of the NUL and its branches, this chapter draws connections between the League and the Chicago School of Sociology. While the discussion illustrates personnel links between the Chicago School and the National, New York, and Chicago Urban Leagues, the chapter's primary aim is to establish the appeal and relevance of Chicago School models of assimilation to Urban Leaguers.

From there the project's focus shifts to the League's housing, employment, and union activities. Because the New Deal and World War II altered certain aspects of the Urban League's approach, the book's analysis of the organization's goals and projects consists of two sections that take the New Deal as the dividing point. Thus Chapters 2 through 4 look at the League's work between 1910 and 1932, while Chapters 5, 6, and 7 focus on the period from 1933 to 1950. I have chosen to conclude the study in 1950 with the Urban League's Pilot Placement Program, initiated by the National and New York Urban Leagues between 1947 and 1948 and the Chicago League in 1950.[17]

Chapter 2 examines the League's housing and community development programs from the group's inception to the New Deal. This chapter explores the implications of the Urban League's identification of maladjustment as a major source of housing and neighborhood decay. The chapter also considers the tensions stemming from the League's efforts to secure better housing for black tenants, devoting particular attention to the difficulty the Urban League experienced meeting the needs of both benefactors and beneficiaries.

Chapter 3 focuses on the employment, job placement, and training programs of the Urban Leagues of Chicago and New York. It demonstrates that the League's emphasis on workplace competence as an engine of economic uplift frequently led it to propose and even manage programs that were of greater benefit to employers than employees. It also contends that Leaguers viewed vocational training as a means of both enhancing Afro-Americans' human capital and providing constructive outlets for restless minds.

Chapter 4 considers the multiple factors undergirding the League's interest in organized labor in the years before the New Deal. Though many Leaguers viewed participation in the union movement as a vehicle for improving blacks' economic status, they also perceived unionization as a means of combating social disorganization while easing racial tensions. Afro-American involvement in mainstream labor unions, Leaguers hoped, would provide alternatives to radical politics and create mutual empathy between the races.

Chapters 5 through 7 examine the impact of the New Deal, World War II, and the postwar downturn on League programs. Since perpetually high rates of black joblessness ensured that Urban Leaguers in this period were far more invested in employment issues than they were in housing, this section of the book begins with a look at the social-work group's job placement, vocational training, and union policies between 1933 and 1950. My account of the League's employment efforts devotes special attention to the influence of the interventionist state and global war over the Urban League's work in this regard. Chapter 5, therefore, focuses on the Urban League's jobs and union initiatives throughout the era of the New Deal, while Chapter 6 explores these efforts during World War II and its immediate aftermath. Chapter 7 wraps up this section with an analysis of the impact of the burgeoning welfare state on the Urban League's housing and neighborhood projects.

Between the 1930s and 1940s, League policy shifted significantly not only as the group's officials embraced federal intervention in the nation's economy but also as many adopted a greater political militancy. Leaguers would also devote more attention to structural sources of inequality. Nevertheless, the Urban League's housing, employment, and union activities continued to be shaped by many of the same class biases influencing its activities in the earlier period. Leaguers remained invested in efforts to mitigate the deleterious effects of social disorganization in order to ensure harmonious interaction between the races. As a result, League housing policy, which emphasized the importance of integration as well as public housing and thereby marked a major shift, continued to stress the need to insulate the better classes of Afro-Americans from unacculturated blacks. The Urban League's employment activities in this period likewise stressed the importance of elevating the status of the better classes. Indeed, the expansion of the welfare state actually allowed the League to devote even greater attention to making job placements for the talented tenth. Leaguers, moreover, maintained their perception of unionization and job training programs as vehicles through which to combat social disorganization.

1. The Ideological Origins of the Urban League

Interracial Goodwill Through Social Service.—CUL, 1928

[handwritten: UL More U of C sociology than Tuskegee.]

This chapter examines the issues surrounding the Urban League's creation as well as the background of key personnel in order to draw out the ideological forces shaping the League's approach. While some have traced the Urban League's philosophical lineage to Booker T. Washington, this chapter contends that the League's uplift project owed more to models of assimilation advanced by sociologists such as W. I. Thomas and Robert Park than the Wizard of Tuskegee.[1] Applying concepts such as social disorganization and reorganization, ethnic cycle, and urban ecology to the Negro problem, Leaguers devoted particular attention to the relationship between blacks' behavior and racial and economic inequality. As a result, the Urban League's work would come to reflect many of the biases associated with Progressive Era social science theory.

■ On October 16, 1911, the city of New York witnessed the birth of the National Urban League. Among the League's primary concerns was Gotham's growing community of black migrants. In the decade preceding the NUL's creation, New York City's black population increased by roughly 50 percent, consisting of nearly 92,000 individuals by 1910. Following a trend that continued unabated until the Great Depression, southern migrants accounted for the bulk of this growth. As Gotham's Afro-American population expanded, so too did the problems associated with the city's black belts. Between 1900 and 1910, racial tensions flared regularly in New York. Indeed, the decade was marked by state legislators' efforts to implement Jim Crow laws, two race riots, and an increase in allegations of crime and immorality among Afro-Americans. Longtime black residents as well as some whites blamed the swelling southern migrant population for the apparent decline in both race relations and the social health of Negro New York. As historian Gilbert Osofsky has noted, northern blacks generally attributed "the spread of black race antipathy" to migrants' ignorance of northern life.[2]

In response to the growing tumult in New York, a number of black and white reformers banded together to address the problems confronting and allegedly created by black migrants. Though the League would eventually play a major role in such endeavors, prior to 1911 its activities were carried out by three separate organizations: the National League for the Protection of Colored Women (NLPCW), the Committee for Improving Industrial Conditions of Negroes in New York (CIICN), and the Committee on Urban Conditions Among Negroes (CUCAN). The Urban League and its parent organizations shared the view that rural migrants bore much of the blame for recent social upheavals. But while Afro-American leaders such as Booker T. Washington discouraged black migration, arguing that the south was the Negro's natural home, the League and its predecessors attempted to redress issues such as crime, delinquency, unemployment, overcrowded housing, and even race riots by facilitating black migrants' adjustment to the city. In practical terms these activities consisted largely of projects intended to provide migrants both moral guidance and assistance in acquiring decent homes and jobs. The Urban League, along with the NLPCW, the CIICN, and the CUCAN, thus embraced a common faith in the ability of reform endeavors to ease the social decay accompanying migration.

The NLPCW was the first of the League's parent organizations to appear in Gotham. Officially established in 1906, the NLPCW's founder, Frances A. Kellor, actually initiated its basic program one year earlier as director of the Inter-Municipal Committee on Household Research (IMCHR) of New York and Philadelphia. The principal goal of both the IMCHR and the NLPCW was to facilitate southern black women's adjustment to the northern cities by directing migrant women to respectable housing and employment. To this end, the NLPCW concentrated on two basic areas of service. First, it discouraged southern girls from migrating to the north unless they had either definite work opportunities or specialized skills. Second, it offered those who had already migrated assistance in finding respectable employment and housing.[3]

Ultimately, the NLPCW endeavored to remedy the sources of crime and immorality that Kellor had identified as outgrowths of migration. Chief among the organization's objectives was the elimination of causes of prostitution.[4] Kellor, a trained social worker, rejected biological explanations for the wanton behavior said to afflict New York's black belts. Instead, she attributed the growing sex trade within the city's ghetto communities to migrant women's vulnerability and ignorance of urban life. Traveling alone, migrant women were often cut off from institutions such as family and church. As a result, they were both deprived of community resources and freed of important behavioral checks.[5] By directing migrant women to reputable employers and boardinghouses that might look after them, the NLPCW hoped to provide women with a social grounding that could insulate them from unsavory influences.[6] Such efforts, Kellor's organization believed, might not only save migrant women from lives characterized by improbity and degradation but also soothe race relations by eliminating a major source of racial animosity.

Black + Tans source of Race Animosity

The CIICN and the CUCAN engaged in related campaigns against the causes of personal demoralization. Established in spring 1906, the CIICN was founded by William H. Bulkley, one of New York City's most influential black educators.[7] Like Kellor's group, Bulkley's committee focused on two tasks. It assisted blacks in acquiring useful skills while simultaneously negotiating with potential employers to open new occupations to Afro-Americans. The committee's overarching aim was to demonstrate the versatility and efficiency of black workers. In so doing, the CIICN hoped to mitigate employer prejudice, thereby expanding the opportunities available to Afro-American workers. This is not to suggest that Bulkley believed that workplace efficiency was a panacea. In fact, the CIICN's program presumed that vigorous efforts were needed to persuade employers to hire blacks. Nevertheless, Bulkley wanted to ensure that Afro-Americans were well poised to seize opportunities when they presented themselves.[8]

The committee's emphasis on vocational guidance reflected a common fear that race prejudice fueled criminal and immoral conduct among Afro-Americans. In 1906, Bulkley asserted that the CIICN's efforts were motivated by humanitarian concerns as well as a self-interested desire to reduce the causes of maladjustment within the city's ghetto communities. Racism, he argued, made it all but impossible for New York's black migrants to "find wholesome housing conditions or helpful vocations." Bulkley went on to warn that lack of opportunity would "stifle laudable aspirations, provoke discouragement and invite all the evils that an idle brain can conceive."[9] Bulkley, therefore, identified training as a means of both improving blacks' economic prospects and providing constructive outlets for restless minds.[10]

The activities of George E. Haynes's CUCAN overlapped the CIICN's. A former member of Bulkley's group, Haynes created the CUCAN in May 1910 after a failed attempt to reform the CIICN. Like Kellor and Bulkley, Haynes proceeded from the view that Afro-American migration held the potential to erode blacks' status in the north.[11] Haynes was especially concerned that maladjustment, that is black migrants' ignorance of urban life, had compounded the difficulties Afro-Americans encountered as a result of race discrimination. In his doctoral thesis at Columbia University, for example, Haynes observed that black crime rates in the north increased at pace with the growth of a city's migrant population. While he believed that discrimination in both the workplace and the judicial system were partly to blame, Haynes implied that the cultural traits possessed by black newcomers contributed to this problem. Crime rates, he declared, declined "as the Negro becomes adjusted to the urban environment."[12] Maladjustment, according to Haynes, likewise undermined blacks' employment prospects. The combination of inadequate training and excessive mobility among migrant workers led to inefficiency at the job, resulting in high levels of joblessness and poverty.[13] Although Haynes concluded that workplace competence alone could not remedy the problem of black unemployment, he believed that job efficiency was one of the few means at blacks' disposal of combating employment discrimination.[14]

While Haynes's organization shared the NLPCW and CIICN's commitment to improving black New Yorkers' housing and employment prospects, the CUCAN's approach differed significantly from its predecessors. As a social-work organization, the CUCAN's uplift project relied heavily on social science methods and training. Haynes's organization thus emphasized the importance of field research, placing particular importance on the compilation of data pertaining to blacks' living and working conditions in order to target its efforts. The CUCAN also encouraged Afro-Americans to pursue studies in social work and the social sciences in an attempt "to prepare them for leadership in urban centers."[15]

Haynes was a central figure in the creation of the National Urban League. In order to enhance the CUCAN's efficiency, Haynes sought cooperation with other social service organizations. Due perhaps to Haynes's decision to expand upon the work of existing associations, the CUCAN's membership overlapped the NLPCW's and the CIICN's. In fact, Frances Kellor and William H. Bulkley were among the first to join the CUCAN. Sharing both their base of support and membership, the CUCAN, the NLPCW, and the CIICN discussed consolidating their activities as early as April 1911. By October, the three organizations merged to form the National League on Urban Conditions Among Negroes (NLUCAN), the NUL's moniker until 1916.[16]

Like its predecessors, the National Urban League set out to redress the sources of social decay precipitated by migration. The association therefore incorporated all of the activities of its parent organizations. Though the Urban League was unquestionably the product of three groups, Haynes's CUCAN exerted the greatest influence over the agency. In fact, the League's program extended directly from the activities of the CUCAN, a contention that is affirmed by the fact that the National Urban League itself has long identified the creation of the CUCAN in 1910 as its birth. Haynes's committee and the National Urban League shared both a common leadership and focus.[17] Haynes served as the League's executive secretary from 1911 until his formal resignation in 1918. Under his leadership the Urban League's program centered on social work, placing particular emphasis on training. In its first annual report, for example, the NLUCAN listed among its chief objectives the promotion of "constructive and preventive social work," the training and utilization of black social workers, and the design and implementation of field research in cities. These activities were ultimately intended to assist the League in improving "the social and economic conditions of Negroes in urban centers."[18]

Haynes identified the training of social workers as an indispensable component of the Urban League's work. During his tenure, the League initiated a fellowship program, providing financial support to black college students majoring in the social sciences, and began efforts to create a social-work training center in Nashville, Tennessee. League fellows took up course work at Fisk University in Tennessee and at Columbia University's New York School of Philanthropy. Haynes was personally responsible for supervising the fieldwork of Urban League Fellows at Fisk, and he played an important, though less direct, part in its operation at Columbia. The "New York School of Philanthropy provided grants for two League Fellows, accredited their field work and arranged enrollment and study privileges at Columbia University." Urban League Fellows affiliated with the New York School of Philanthropy were supervised by either Haynes or his deputy, Eugene Kinckle Jones.[19]

The League's emphasis on social-work training did not preclude efforts to cooperate with Booker T. Washington. Indeed, the centrality of education in Haynes and the League's uplift vision led the agency to court the Wizard of Tuskegee. As head of the CUCAN, Haynes corresponded regularly with Washington in order to obtain his official endorsement. The National League likewise extended several invitations to him to join the organization. Though Washington initially declined the League's overtures, he nonetheless acknowledged the NUL's importance by formally endorsing its program in April 1914. At the start of the new year, Washington finally accepted a place on the Urban League's board. His tenure with the League was cut short, however, by his death in November 1915. Serving as a board member for less than one year, Washington likely exerted little direct influence over the League's basic approach.[20] Social work thus remained at the core of NUL's activities in its formative years.

To be sure, Haynes was more invested in training black social workers than most Leaguers. Indeed, Haynes spent much of his tenure with the NUL pursuing this goal as an instructor at Fisk University. In addition to supervising Urban League fellows, Haynes taught graduate and undergraduate courses in social work, sociology, and economics at Fisk. His overarching objective was to transform the university into a model center for training blacks in social science methods and theories, which other institutions might "emulate and draw experience from."[21] While yielding some rewards, Haynes's efforts to create a training center in Nashville eventually placed him at odds with the National Urban League's executive board. As black migrant populations surged across the north following the outbreak of the First World War, the NUL's executive board decided that the creation of local branches was of greater necessity than Haynes's social-work center. Believing his activities at Fisk distracted him from more pressing issues, the board demoted Haynes to a "consultant" in 1917 and then forced him to resign the next year.[22]

Haynes's replacement, Eugene K. Jones, shifted the League's focus to more tangible matters such as housing and employment. But while the League devoted less attention to training black social workers after Haynes's departure, it did not give up these activities altogether. Rather, it actually expanded its fellowship program after abandoning Haynes's training center concept. Hiring a full-time recruiter of black college youth in 1919, the NUL launched a campaign to encourage Afro-American students to pursue studies in social work and the social sciences. Alexander L. Jackson, the League's recruiter, engaged in a related effort to widen the Urban League's fellowship program. Meeting with college administrators and faculty, Jackson set out to extend the program beyond Columbia. By the conclusion of the 1920s, Jackson and the League had secured openings for League fellows in graduate programs at Simmons College, the University of Pennsylvania, the University of Pittsburgh, the Carnegie Institute of Technology, Bryn Mawr, Mount Holyoke, Ohio State, New York University, and the University of Chicago. Due in no small part to Jackson's efforts, "the actual number of League fellows expanded" during the 1930s "to as many as six in one year, plus an unrecorded number of 'broken' Fellows—that is, college students doing their field work under local League direction."[23]

The Urban League also stepped up its presence in professional social-work associations. From its inception, it was actively involved with the National Conference of Social Work (NCSW), the major association for professional social workers at the time. In 1911 George E. Haynes became the first NUL official to speak before the NCSW, originally called the National Conference of Charities and Correction. Between 1913 and 1917, Haynes and the League either hosted or organized a number of sessions and panels sponsored by the NCSW. The topics proposed by the League ranged from health issues affecting Afro-Americans to the effects of "home and school" on black children. Following Haynes's departure, Urban Leaguers attained even more significant roles within the social-work conference. In 1924, for example, the NCSW elected Eugene K. Jones to its executive board. That same year, Urban Lea-guers Jesse O. Thomas and John T. Clark "were elected to NCSW committees." The League's active involvement in professional social-work organizations continued unabated through the 1950s. In fact, Lester Granger, the NUL's third full-time executive secretary (1940–61), was elected president of the NCSW midway through his tenure with the League.[24]

The Urban League's methods further evinced the importance of social work and the social sciences to the agency's uplift project. The housing and jobs programs of the NUL and its Chicago and New York branches relied heavily on field studies. From the organization's inception, the NUL and its locals performed numerous surveys of ghetto residents and employers. Urban League fellows, as well as the official directors of the League's Departments of Research, Housing, and Industrial Relations, were often responsible for carrying out these projects. From their inceptions, the National Urban League and its Chicago and New York branches crafted studies designed to explore employment patterns, housing conditions, and the social health of black neighborhoods, including rates of crime and juvenile delinquency. As Haynes had envisioned, the NUL and its locals conceived such inquiries as a means of both dismantling the barriers Afro-Americans encountered in housing and labor markets and soothing race relations. Following the Chicago and Harlem riots, for example, the CUL and the NYUL participated in mayoral commissions investigating the causes and consequences of the conflagrations that had flared in their respective cities. The NUL was likewise involved in similar projects during the Depression and World War II.

Haynes's departure thus did little to diminish the role of social scientists and social science method in the League's uplift program. Social work remained at the core of the League's activities. Consequently, most officials of the Urban League's upper echelon were either professional social workers or sociologists. The Urban League's fellowship program helped ensure that the NUL and its locals were able to maintain competent social workers on staff. In fact, a number of the organization's officers had been League fellows. James H. Hubert, the executive secretary of the New York Urban League from 1919 to 1943, and Howard Gould, the Chicago Urban League's secretary of industrial relations from 1934 to 1945, were among the more prominent League fellows.[25]

In addition to social workers, sociologists played crucial roles in the Urban League movement, holding many key positions within the organization. In fact, the NUL's first two executive directors held advanced degrees in sociology. George E. Haynes studied sociology at the University of Chicago and Columbia University, earning a doctorate from Columbia's New York School of Philanthropy, the university's School of Social Work, in 1910.[26] Eugene K. Jones, the NUL's executive secretary from 1918 to 1936, possessed a master's degree in sociology and economics from Cornell University.[27]

Other high-ranking National Urban League officials possessed similarly impressive sociological credentials. T. Arnold Hill, director of the NUL's Department of Industrial Relations (1925–35), undertook one year of graduate work in sociology and economics at New York University.[28] Charles S. Johnson, the NUL's secretary of research (1921–28), pursued a doctorate in sociology at the University of Chicago (1917–19), where he developed a close intellectual relationship with sociologist Robert Park. While military service during the First World War, along with other personal and professional commitments, ultimately prevented Johnson from completing the degree, he became one of the most influential black social scientists of the first half of the twentieth century.[29] Ira De Augustine Reid, who eventually succeeded Johnson as head of the National Urban League's Department of Research, also held advanced degrees in sociology. Like Haynes, Reid studied sociology at both the University of Chicago and Columbia University. After receiving a master's degree from the University of Pittsburgh, Reid went on to earn a Ph.D. in sociology from Columbia.[30]

The New York and Chicago Urban Leagues likewise employed a number of prominent sociologists. Many of these individuals were intimately connected to the NUL. Prior to the official creation of the New York League in late 1919,[31] the National Urban League took on the problems confronting black Manhattan. Haynes and Jones were therefore initially responsible for the League's activities in New York. On the heels of the formal creation of the NYUL, Ira Reid served as the New York branch's secretary of industrial relations from 1924 until 1928.[32] Beginning his career with the NUL in 1914 as Eugene K. Jones's protégé, T. Arnold Hill played a major role in the creation of the Chicago Urban League. After the CUL was formally established in 1916, Hill became the branch's first executive secretary, holding the post until his return to the national organization in 1925.[33] Charles S. Johnson likewise cut his teeth with the Urban League movement through his affiliation with the League's Chicago branch. Before heading the NUL's Department of Research, Johnson held the same position with the Chicago Urban League between 1917 and 1921.[34]

The Chicago Urban League attracted a particularly impressive group of scholars, a number of whom were affiliated with the University of Chicago. Two of the Chicago League's founders, for example, held faculty positions at this prestigious university. Sophonisba P. Breckinridge, professor of social work and political science, and Robert Park, Distinguished Professor of Sociology, were actively involved in the creation of the Chicago branch. Park held multiple positions with the CUL, serving as both its first president and its unofficial secretary of research from 1917 to 1919.[35] Park's influence over the Chicago branch exceeded his tenure with the organization, as he encouraged a number of his black graduate students to seek employment with the CUL. In fact, all the Chicago League's research secretaries from 1917 through the Depression had pursued doctorates in sociology at the University of Chicago. Among them were Charles S. Johnson, E. Franklin Frazier, and Earl Moses.[36]

The prevalence of sociologists within the Urban League was indicative of the close ties between sociology and social work in the early twentieth century. Prior to the 1920s, few universities made distinctions between the two fields. The University of Chicago, for example, only formally separated its schools of sociology and social work in 1920.[37] The intimacy between the disciplines inevitably led sociology to exert significant sway over social work. In the years before the parting of fields, many notable sociologists, including Chicago's Albion Small, worked closely with reformers and social workers.[38] While the split between the two disciplines meant that social workers were more likely than sociologists to lead civic crusades, it did not bring about an end to sociology's influence over its academic stepchild. In fact, sociology would provide a theoretical lens through which social workers viewed the worlds of race and poverty well into the twentieth century.[39]

The Chicago School of Sociology played a crucial role in shaping the discipline and by extension the Urban League's social-work program. Beyond the personal connections that League officials such as Haynes, Reid, Johnson, Frazier, Moses, and Park had to the University of Chicago, Chicago sociology was *the* dominant force in the discipline from the turn of the century through the Great Depression. The university's influence stemmed from the pioneering work of its faculty as well as its ties to key sources of funding. Chicago sociologists such as W. I. Thomas, Robert Park, and Earnest Burgess developed theories of assimilation and urban social relations that are still in use today. The school's influence over the discipline was further enhanced, according to historian Alice O'Connor, by its ties to philanthropists. Supported heavily by the Rockefeller Fund in the 1920s, the Chicago School employed researchers and graduate student fieldworkers in numbers unparalleled by other sociology departments. It was therefore well equipped to reproduce its intellectual DNA through the prolific production of research and Ph.D.s.[40]

The University of Chicago's dominance over sociology all but ensured its influence over the Urban League's uplift vision. As a social-work organization, the League would naturally draw upon sociological research and theories. The thrust of Chicago sociology was especially important in determining the school's intellectual sway over the Urban League. Much of the research produced by Chicago during its heyday, from the late 1910s through the Depression, focused on ethnic assimilation and urbanization. Coming of age in a period marred by race riots, nativism, and eugenics, the Chicago School offered a "reassuring framework for understanding ethnic conflict as an inevitable part of urban growth and modernization."[41] Chicago sociologists thus rejected the kinds of biological explanations for social unrest and inequality advanced by eugenicists, focusing instead on culture. The Chicago School, therefore, attributed the social problems associated with immigration and even black migration—crime, poverty, etc.—to rural peoples' failure to adjust to urban life. This perspective held particular sway with Leaguers, as it both presumed the plasticity of all peoples and offered universal models of assimilation and integration.

The Urban League's program reflected the influence of three major concepts derived from Chicago sociology: social disorganization and reorganization, ethnic cycle, and urban ecology. Each posits a model of human progress that explores the consequences of interactions between disparate peoples at different stages of social development. As alluded to above, research produced by the Chicago School in the first third of the twentieth century emphasized group and individual responses to the so-called social process, the transition from primary to secondary social relations. Primary group contacts, also known as gemeinschaft, refer to a form of social organization characteristic of "primitive" or rural communities. These units of human interaction were allegedly organized on a nonrational basis, meaning that individuals were bound together largely because of tradition or custom. Secondary group contacts, or gesellschaft, were observed in modern commercial societies. Shaped by market forces, social relations within these groups were rational and impersonal; individuals made pragmatic choices in response to rapidly changing conditions. Chicago sociology thus advanced models of assimilation and human progress that revolved on a rural-urban axis.[42]

Ultimately, Chicago sociologists such as W. I. Thomas and Robert E. Park believed that the transition from gemeinschaft to gesellschaft held the potential to liberate the human spirit. Establishing social order through personal obligation and custom, primary groups lacked flexibility, which stifled individuality and creativity. Secondary groups, by contrast, offered a plethora of outlets for individual talents and tastes because of their economic and demographic heterogeneity. While individuals in secondary groups maintained some communal obligation, they attained far greater latitude for self-expression. The advantages of secondary social contacts notwithstanding, the Chicago School attributed the increase during the early twentieth century in what they would call personal demoralization—social problems such as juvenile delinquency, crime, prostitution, etc.—to the transition from primary group interactions to secondary group interactions.[43] Social disorganization and reorganization, ethnic cycle, and urban ecology theories offered comparatively optimistic frames in which to understand and redress the internal problems experienced by groups undergoing this transition, tracing the issues fueling tensions within as well as between groups to specific environmental inputs.

Social disorganization and reorganization theory was Chicago sociology's conceptual foundation. The Chicago School generally defined social disorganization, a concept pioneered by W. I. Thomas, as a decrease in the influence of existing "social rules" of behavior on members of a particular group. In an organized society, established conventions, attitudes, and values—the "social rules"—restrained individual desires. Disorganized societies were thus characterized by the lack of effective social rules to curb aberrant behavior among individuals. As mentioned above, Chicago sociology identified demographic shifts, especially those involving rural populations, as the major source of social disorganization.[44] In his landmark The Polish Peasant, for example, Thomas attributed the prevalence of antisocial behavior among Polish immigrants to their transition from gemeinschaft to gesellschaft. Describing Polish communities as primary groups, Thomas argued that immigration introduced Polish peasants to attitudes associated with secondary societies, leading them to question the relevance of traditional institutional mechanisms of social control, such as family and church. Consequently, old primary group institutions became incapable of offering outlets for healthy expression of individual desires in America, resulting in high levels of personal demoralization among immigrant populations.[45]

Thomas and the Chicago School proffered optimistic assessments of America's growing immigrant populations. Identifying the collapse of institutional life, rather than heredity, as the cause of the social malaise afflicting immigrant communities, Thomas argued that the newcomers could be adjusted to American cities through the process he called reorganization. Reorganization entailed establishing new institutional outlets designed to bridge the gap between primary and secondary group interactions. With the assistance of "social technicians," or social workers, immigrants would create "closed social groups," voluntarist organizations such as immigrant cooperatives, in order to mediate tensions between the individual and the community. These new ethnic-American institutions afforded immigrants viable outlets for the basic human desire for new experiences, recognition, power, and security, thereby fostering new social controls tailored to ethnic-American

life. Perhaps as importantly, since newcomers and natives were to work together in this model, Thomas believed the two would engage in a cultural
exchange. Learning to appreciate each other's heritage, natives and strangers
would eventually create a new culture while soothing relations between
the two.[46]

Ethnic cycle and urban ecology echoed the major themes explored by
Thomas. Indeed, both models incorporated Thomas's theories of social disorganization and reorganization. Rather than simply following the conceptual
trail blazed by Thomas, however, proponents of ethnic cycle and urban ecology set out to refine his work. Drawing upon concepts pioneered in botany
and biology, ethnic cycle and urban ecology described assimilation as a process of ecological succession in which groups were either assimilated or expelled in a metabolic fashion. Devotees of both models ultimately attempted
to construct universal processes of assimilation that applied to both racial and
ethnic groups. This is not to suggest that all Chicago sociologists viewed race
and ethnicity as posing equal challenges to assimilation in the American
context. But because Chicago sociology proceeded from the view that race
and ethnicity were social constructs, the school's disciples generally applied
the same conceptual frames and remedies to the adjustment of blacks and
white ethnics.[47]

While social disorganization and reorganization theory focused largely on
internal problems within immigrant groups, ethnic cycle devoted particular
attention to the tensions arising between groups following initial contact.
Tracing the evolution of group contacts through several stages, Robert Park
and other proponents of the ethnic cycle model argued that interactions
between disparate peoples moved through an inexorable sequence of stages
from initial contact through competition, conflict, accommodation, and assimilation. As with Thomas's model of reorganization, ethnic cycle perceived
steady interaction between peoples as essential to assimilation. This was so
partly because the tumult following initial contacts was not simply a reaction
to competition for material goods but also a visceral response to the introduction of individuals and cultures that were simply alien. Proponents of the
ethnic cycle model thus claimed that familiarity would over time eliminate
animosities between peoples and eventually foster mutual empathy. Accommodation set the stage for assimilation by stabilizing group interactions. As a
result, groups participated in an organic cultural exchange that infused elements of each culture into one. An assimilated society therefore consisted of,
at minimum, distinct groups that tolerated if not appreciated each other's
differences.[48]

Though Robert Park eventually reconsidered ethnic cycle's applicability to

Afro-Americans, prior to 1937 he believed that interaction theory offered a clear window onto southern race relations. In "Racial Assimilation in Secondary Groups," published in 1914, Park argued that the origins of contemporary southern race relations dated back to the south's transition from primary to secondary group contacts following the Civil War. Transforming slaves into free labor, emancipation broke the bonds of mutual obligation that had characterized antebellum race relations. Forced to compete for land and employment, blacks migrated in search of opportunity. Due to the combination of the growing physical distance between the races and cultural lag, conflict soon followed. Black-white relations stabilized, according to Park, only when the two struck an accommodation in the form of segregation. While Park did not perceive segregation as a permanent solution to the Negro problem, he did believe that Jim Crow provided blacks space to strengthen their own culture and institutions. Park thus assumed that as blacks progressed artistically and intellectually, visceral prejudices would eventually whither, allowing Afro-Americans to assimilate into mainstream society.[49]

Not all disciples of ethnic cycle theory perceived assimilation in such mechanistic terms. Many of the Chicago School's black graduates, including E. Franklin Frazier and Charles S. Johnson of the Chicago and National Urban Leagues, argued that the racial competition Afro-Americans encountered was of far greater magnitude than that experienced by white ethnics. Rejecting the claim that assimilation was a fait accompli, these and other scholar-activists—including Ira De Augustine Reid, T. Arnold Hill, and Lester Granger—proceeded from the view that social scientists and reform associations would have to engineer satisfying interactions between blacks and whites to breach the barriers dividing them.[50] By 1937, even Robert Park conceded that ethnic cycle did not necessarily conclude in assimilation but that both caste and permanent separation could be the end result. Such modifications notwithstanding, Chicago sociologists continued to identify interaction between different ethnic communities as necessary, though perhaps insufficient, to achieving assimilation. Urban ecologists maintained a similar view.[51]

Taking America's great metropolises as the apotheosis of secondary contacts, Chicago sociologists treated cities as their principal laboratory. Urban ecology profoundly influenced researchers' perceptions of both social disorganization and the operation of the ethnic cycle within the city. Likewise pioneered by Park, urban ecology described the city as a functioning organism in which an ecological process of competition, specialization, and segregation determined the distribution and character of urban populations. Shaped by the inevitable tides of the market, cities were comprised of concentric zones loosely consisting of a central business district at the core, followed by slums,

[handwritten margin note: Chicago Black Sociologist recognize they are not same as ethnicity]

E. Franklin Frazier (Photographs and Prints Division, Schomburg Center for Research in Black Culture, The New York Public Library, Astor, Lenox and Tilden Foundations)

then apartment house areas, and finally a homeownership zone at the outer edge. Believing that residents were either assimilated or expelled in a meta-bolic fashion by their immediate environments, urban ecologists claimed that each zone was characterized by distinct cultural traits. The commercial func-tion of the innermost zones fueled excessive mobility among their residents, resulting in increased rates of disorganization and demoralization. The set-tled nature of the outermost zones, by contrast, fostered stable institutional life, ensuring robust social controls. The challenge for urban ecologists was to bridge the cultural divide between zones. By establishing a sense of mutual purpose among urban denizens, ecologists hoped to counteract disorganization while simultaneously reducing competition and conflict between communities.[52]

E. Franklin Frazier's *The Negro Family in Chicago,* written during Frazier's tenure with the Chicago Urban League, offers one of the most well known applications of urban ecology to black assimilation. Dividing the city's black belt into seven zones, corresponding to the distribution of the city's other ethnic groups, Frazier observed that demoralization and disorganization among Afro-Americans gradually declined as one moved outward through successive zones. Frazier attributed the contrast in rates of personal demoralization between zones to corresponding disparities in family formation. Though troubled by the situation in the inner zones, Frazier argued that the cultural division between communities was an organic product of the "civilizational process." Inner zone residents tended to maintain loose family structures of the sort prevalent during slavery. These "natural families," as he called them, were maladjusted to urban life, resulting in demoralization. Outer zone residents, by contrast, generally formed "institutional families." Based on legal marriage and property ownership, these family units were fully capable of enforcing communal norms. For Frazier, the difference in family structures between zones was indicative of blacks' adaptability. Outer zone residents, for example, had successfully reorganized their institutions in accordance with modern society.[53] Though inner zone residents had yet to do so, Frazier hoped that participation in the labor movement might provide the institutional apparatus necessary to assist them in adjusting to the industrial city.

Although Frazier traced institutional weakness among inner zone residents to the peculiar nature of Afro-Americans' transition from gemeinschaft to gesellschaft, he was clear that racism greatly complicated the challenges confronting black assimilation. Specifically, race discrimination held the potential to stifle the reorganization of black institutional life. Competition, he argued, would eliminate those Afro-Americans failing to reorganize on a "more intelligent and more efficient" basis. Efficiency was, therefore, the key to the race's progress in that it held the potential to increase blacks' participation in communal life, thereby facilitating the establishment of viable outlets for personal expression and social control. Frazier hinted at concern, however, that racism could nullify the effects of efficiency.[54] While he did not explore the implications here, they are nonetheless clear. If unchecked, social disorganization could imperil Afro-Americans' advancement.

The Chicago School's models of assimilation posed important counterpoints to both nativism and scientific racism. Social disorganization and reorganization, ethnic cycle, and urban ecology presumed that nurture trumped nature. Racial and ethnic group assimilation were therefore largely a matter of adjusting individuals' attitudes and group values. Still, Chicago sociology's focus on behavior had clear limitations. Though the Chicago School's vision hinged on community action, its principal aim was to "smooth the process of assimilation rather than to challenge existing social arrangements."[55] In fact, Chicago sociology's equation of industrial capitalism with rationality led it to actually downplay the impact of structural sources of inequality. For the Chicago School, crime and poverty were the consequence of institutional decay; ethnic ghettos were simply part of a natural process of succession; and conflict between groups would whither on its own as the groups became more comfortable with each other. Since social unrest was merely a stage in a cycle of adjustment that would resolve organically, the Chicago School generally viewed state intervention with circumspection, perceiving it as a potential retardant to group assimilation. Sociologists such as Thomas and Park believed that any efforts to redress social disorganization should be undertaken by voluntarist organizations intimately connected to the afflicted communities. Thus the Chicago School's models identified self-help as essential to collective progress.

The Urban League's uplift activities in the fields of housing and employment drew directly from Chicago sociology and therefore emphasized the importance of reorganizing black institutions. Like the Chicago School, the Urban League perceived black migrants' transition from gemeinschaft to gesellschaft as a major source of social disorganization. Believing that increased rates of personal demoralization undermined blacks' integration into mainstream American society by fueling social disorganization and, by extension, racial antagonism, Leaguers viewed the acculturation of Afro-Americans as essential to bringing about the elimination of racial barriers in housing and employment. The League therefore attempted to provide new institutional centers for blacks in the industrial city to establish viable social controls. To this end, the Urban League also worked closely with employers and landlords, assisting them in weeding out individuals who had failed either to adjust to the expectations of industrial capital or to embrace middle-class domestic relations. This approach ultimately led the League to devote disproportionate attention to the needs of the so-called better classes of Afro-Americans.

2. Community Development and Housing, 1910–1932

[A] family of sound Christian character finds itself living across the narrow long, dark hall from a family which is obnoxious, if not vicious. Cheek by jowl with the deacon lives the dope fiend.—Roscoe C. Bruce, 1931

Within fifteen years of the outbreak of the First World War, the black communities of New York City and Chicago grew to become the largest in the nation. Although New York's Afro-American population actually declined throughout much of the nineteenth century, it set out on a path of steady growth just after the Civil War.[1] As with other "ethnic" groups, the increase in the city's Afro-American population was due chiefly to migration. Between 1870 and 1920, the percentage of Afro-Americans living in the city who were born in the state declined from 74 percent to just 31 percent. During the Great War, New York City's Afro-American migrant population exploded. Between 1910 and 1920, Gotham's black community increased by more than 66 percent (from 91,709 to 152,467 people). Over the next ten years, black New York grew by 115 percent, to 327,706 people. Less than 25 percent of the city's black residents in 1930 were born in New York State.[2]

Prior to the Great Migration, Gotham's blacks lived in a number of scattered enclaves. During the 1910s, however, residential discrimination combined with New York's ever increasing Afro-American population to create a fairly distinct black belt located in the city's largest borough.[3] By the end of World War I, radical demographic changes were taking place in Manhattan. As the borough's white population declined by 18 percent during the 1920s, its black population grew by 106 percent. As a result, the borough contained a disproportionately large share of the city's Afro-Americans.[4] Residential segregation, moreover, confined much of black Manhattan to Harlem, which by 1930 contained roughly 75 percent (nearly 190,000 individuals) of the borough's Afro-American population.[5]

Thus in the space of just a few decades, New York had become home to one of the nation's largest black ghettos.

Chicago's black population underwent demographic changes similar to those taking place in New York. Afro-Americans lived in the Windy City from its inception. Chicago's first permanent resident was a black trader named Jean Baptiste Du Sable who established a post in the area in 1779. Although Chicago did not develop until some time after Du Sable relocated, blacks were among the town's original residents when it was incorporated in 1833. Until the migration, however, the number of Afro-Americans in the city remained relatively small. In 1910, blacks comprised just 2 percent of Chicago's population. By 1920 their numbers would more than double, and by 1930 blacks would represent almost 7 percent of Chicago's population.[6]

From the beginning, the majority of Chicago's blacks lived in the South Side. Because black Chicagoans were clustered in small colonies in proximity to, but clearly separate from, the "white residential districts where many of them worked as domestics," these communities were comparatively diffuse through most of the nineteenth century. During the 1890s, however, a distinct black enclave began to take shape on the South Side due largely to the influx of thousands of southern black migrants. By 1900, several of the old Negro colonies had merged, forming a "long narrow Black Belt on the South Side" where the majority of Chicago's Afro-Americans resided.[7] As the Windy City's Afro-American population grew, the black belt's population density soared. Although the city's 30,000 blacks comprised just under 2 percent of Chicago's total population in 1900, "over half of the city's black population lived in three contiguous South Side wards which, taken together, were 16 percent black."[8] By 1910, Chicago's black community had grown to about 44,000, with the bulk of Afro-Americans living in three adjoining wards that were now 20 percent black.[9] By 1920, nearly 36 percent of all black Chicagoans lived in census tracts more than 75 percent black. Ten years later, two out of three of Chicago's 233,000 Afro-Americans lived in census tracts that were at least 90 percent black.[10]

Blacks in New York and Chicago were generally forced to live in these cities' worst neighborhoods. The black belts of New York and Chicago were beset by crime, vice, and poverty. Furthermore, ghetto homes were usually rundown and in dire need of repair. Adding insult to injury, Afro-American tenants were frequently compelled to pay exorbitant rents for overcrowded units that either were unattractive or lacked amenities.

Urban Leaguers attributed blacks' concentration in "unsavory" ghetto communities to two factors. Racial discrimination posed the greatest obstacle to neighborhood integration. Leaguers believed that a pernicious mix of prejudice and ignorance prevented whites from distinguishing between respectable and dissolute blacks, thus leading many whites to exclude Afro-Americans from their communities through acts of violence and/or restrictive covenants. Whites' failure to make such distinctions ultimately meant that the mere presence of blacks, irrespective of their cultural attributes, undermined property values, further fueling racial antagonism. Prejudice on the part of white landlords, real estate developers, and bankers complicated matters even further. Leaguers argued that the dearth of comfortable and attractive accommodations stemmed partly from landlords' ignorance of the profit potential of attractive modern housing in ghetto communities. White property owners and real estate developers thus were unlikely to consider building new and wholesome accommodations for respectable Afro-Americans and apt to allow black belt properties to slide into disrepair.

The second cause of the poor condition of ghetto neighborhoods, according to the League, was the behavior of black residents themselves. Although the communities in which Afro-Americans resided were often in decay long before their arrival, black newcomers' peasant outlook—their alleged unawareness of proper conduct and indifference to the upkeep of their properties—added to neighborhood deterioration. Moreover, the poor wages blacks commanded and the dearth of adequate recreational facilities in their communities resulted in higher rates of crime and delinquency, which further undermined living conditions in black neighborhoods.

With its eye on alleviating the unwholesome conditions plaguing ghetto communities, the Urban League attempted to elevate the character of ghetto neighborhoods through two strategies. First, it offered assistance in reorganizing the lives of black tenants and their children through the provision of wholesome influences and direct guidance. Not only would this approach equip Afro-Americans with the cultural tools necessary to survive in the city, but the improved behavior of Afro-Americans would strike a powerful blow to racist stereotypes. Second, the Urban League worked directly with landlords and real estate developers to improve the quality of housing in ghetto communities. Although the League's desire to improve neighborhood conditions along these lines was not unreasonable, such endeavors ultimately reflected the class concerns shaping the League's ideology as well as the practical limitations of its particular brand of uplift.

Community Development

In an effort to fully appreciate Afro-American New Yorkers' living conditions and the quality of their neighborhoods, the National League for Urban Conditions Among Negroes (NLUCAN)[11] performed a house-to-house survey of Harlem in 1913. Although the study's objectives were limited, it revealed that the population density of New York City's black belt was increasing at an alarming pace. The League determined that 49,555 blacks lived in about 1,100 houses in a mere twenty-three-block area. Given that more than 60,000 Afro-Americans lived in all of Harlem only three years earlier, these figures indicated that black New York was highly concentrated. The concentration of New York's Afro-American population impressed upon Leaguers the importance of devoting greater attention both to blacks' housing needs and to the character of their neighborhoods. Thus shortly after the League concluded its survey, it created the Housing Bureau of New York.[12]

The NLUCAN identified its housing bureau as a "Registration Bureau of Tenants." As such, it would continue to provide systematic studies of community life in order to help achieve its overarching goal of improving the moral and physical conditions of Harlem's tenements. The housing bureau hoped to enhance the quality of ghetto life through a four-pronged approach that would serve as the foundation of the League's housing work for years to come. First, it certified houses that were both "physically clean and wholesome" and "tenanted by respectable people." Second, it served as an advocate for tenants, reporting legal infractions and health code violations to owners and/or the appropriate city agencies. Third, it hoped to aid "in developing moral conscience on the part of Negro citizens of New York" to induce "tenants to refuse absolutely to tolerate carelessness and indifference in the management and control of houses advertised for rental to respectable tenants." Fourth, it educated black tenants in the "practical knowledge of the sanitation and upkeep of properties they occupy."[13]

Like most Urban League programs, the housing bureau viewed research and the collection of data as a major facet of its work. Thus over the next few years, the bureau expanded its efforts to acquire accurate information on living conditions in Harlem. Its research soon revealed that black New York was in the midst of a housing crisis. Between 1914 and 1915, the housing bureau surveyed "1,002 families in 726 apartments and 443 houses in Harlem between 131st and 142nd streets." The bureau also found that black Harlemites had an average annual income of just $791, but paid $281 a year—36 percent of their wages—toward rent. By contrast, the NLUCAN discovered that on average German Jews in a comparable, neighboring district, paid only $207 a year for slightly better housing. Because German Jews, like whites generally, tended to have higher annual incomes than blacks, rent accounted for a much lower proportion of their wages.[14]

Though black New Yorkers' inability to secure comfortable homes at reasonable rates would lead the Urban League to seek assistance from landlords and real estate agents, the desperate conditions endemic to urban black enclaves also led Leaguers to pursue efforts to alter the character of ghetto residents through the organization of tenants and the provision of wholesome influences. Urban Leaguers were especially concerned that the difficulties Afro-Americans had acquiring decent accommodations adversely influenced the composition of ghetto neighborhoods. The prevalence of lodgers among the city's blacks posed a particularly significant problem to community cohesion, according to Leaguers. George E. Haynes's Committee for Urban Conditions Among Negroes (CUCAN), for example, noted in 1910 that the exorbitant rents charged to black tenants forced many Afro-Americans to take in boarders. As a consequence, the CUCAN's report asserted, "respectable Negro neighborhoods find themselves unable so far to keep out persons of doubtful or immoral character."[15]

Sharing these concerns, the NLUCAN's housing bureau identified the "indiscriminate mixing of reputable and disreputable persons in tenement houses" as a major component of its efforts to improve life in Harlem. The League therefore set out to try to strengthen the moral integrity of ghetto neighborhoods. In the bureau's first six months it not only investigated the quality of homes in which many Afro-Americans lived, but it also "was responsible for having a number of 'undesirables' dispossessed," the majority of them prostitutes. The bureau further assisted blacks in need of apartments in finding wholesome homes run by responsible landlords.[16]

To be sure, most renters likely appreciated the NLUCAN's efforts to evict sex workers and other tenants engaged in illicit pursuits. Nevertheless, activities of this sort were tied to a vision of collective advancement that required the League either to contain to particular locations blacks who reinforced negative perceptions of the race or to pursue steps to reorganize their lives. In the realm of housing, each of these approaches had clear class implications.

For Haynes, the close proximity in which respectable and disreputable Afro-Americans lived in segregated neighborhoods represented a threat to blacks' assimilation into the larger society. While fully acknowledging that racial discrimination was a palpable check on blacks' aspirations, Haynes held that moral fortitude and competence greatly mitigated the pernicious affects of racism. Self-confidence, he argued, played an essential role in determining the accomplishments of those Afro-Americans who managed to achieve success in the face of seemingly insurmountable prejudice. Blacks who believed themselves equal to whites, Haynes contended, were more likely to perform proficiently at their jobs and in many cases to acquire skills and education. Haynes's formulation all but conflated middle-class status with moral integrity, as he implied that by their nature, the better classes were more self-secure. Personal resolve of this sort, he alleged, was most evident among the class of black entrepreneurs, the most significant of whom were West Indian.[17]

Though self-confidence was hardly a panacea, Haynes believed that the relative success of West Indians—who emigrated from countries where race discrimination did not limit their horizons—was illustrative of the power of skill and personal fortitude to conquer race prejudice. Since blacks' resolve formed the foundation of their ability to demonstrate their equal human status, proper moral influences were essential to their progress as a race. The poor conditions of New York's black neighborhoods, however, threatened to undermine the moral integrity of such residents, as they could not escape the unwholesome influence of disorganized and discouraged Afro-Americans. Because Haynes alleged that working conditions in the south undermined blacks' work ethic, the influx of southern migrants in the 1910s imbued the issue of neighborhood disorganization with special importance.[18]

For the League, the moral integrity of black communities held profound implications for race relations and the advancement of Afro-Americans. Urban Leaguers and other middle-class blacks feared that the strain on employment and housing engendered by the migration worked together with the maladjustment of Afro-American newcomers to heighten racial tensions. Since racial animosity limited the employment and housing opportunities available to blacks, the progress of the race was in great jeopardy. The recent histories of New York and Chicago appeared to validate this view.

In the decade prior to the creation of the NLUCAN, New York experienced two race riots. The first was in 1900, in the West Forties, while the second occurred in 1905 in Columbus Hill.[19] Chicago's history was much more violent. As the Windy City's black migrant population grew in the 1910s, so too did white hostility. During the migration, mobs drove out countless black families who dared to move into "white neighborhoods" and even some who had lived in such communities for many years in peace. Some white rabble-rousers even used bombs to drive out their black neighbors.[20] By the summer of 1919, racial animosities heightened by Chicago's tight housing and labor markets finally culminated in one of the nation's bloodiest race riots. The conflict erupted on July 27 after a group of whites killed a black child who inadvertently swam across the invisible color line separating the black and white swimming areas at Lake Michigan. In just a few hours following the murder, Afro-Americans and whites took up arms in rebellion throughout the city. The violence continued for more than a week, and when the rioting finally concluded, the Chicago Commission on Race Relations conservatively

George E. Haynes (General Research & Reference Division, Schomburg Center for Research in Black Culture, The New York Public Library, Astor, Lenox and Tilden Foundations)

Conservative Estimates from Commission.

estimated that the riots had claimed 38 lives, injured approximately 537, and rendered more than 1,000 homeless and destitute.[21]

Popular assessments of the disturbances in both New York and Chicago were consistent with the view that the maladjustment of black migrants added to racial hostilities. Immediately following the riot of 1905, the *New York Sun*—known for its "anti-Negro" sentiment—asserted that the chief cause of the uproar was the prevalence of vice among the black newcomers. Blacks allegedly disrupted the lives of hardworking whites, consequently stoking the flames of white hostility.[22]

Even before the 1919 riot, Chicago's white press lambasted black migrants for their alleged predisposition to crime and vice. In fact, the CCRR reported that over half of the articles on race printed by Chicago's three major daily newspapers—the *Tribune*, the *Daily News*, and the *Herald Examiner*—derided blacks or focused on violence, crime, and vice. After the riot, all of these papers printed articles attributing the conflagration in Chicago to dissolution and depravity among Afro-Americans.[23]

Worse yet, the perception of Afro-Americans as a homogeneous and morally suspect group appeared to be partly responsible for limiting the amount of housing available to blacks. Blacks attempting to move out of overcrowded ghetto communities into white neighborhoods were often targets of assault in cities such as Chicago. The CCRR—which relied heavily on data collected by the CUL and its secretary of research, Charles S. Johnson—found that the many bombings and other acts of violence visited upon a number of the city's neighborhoods prior to the riot were partially rooted in white homeowners' fears that the presence of blacks would reduce property values. Such concerns were not merely dispassionate and pragmatic assessments of the reality of real estate investment; they were indicative of whites' racial prejudices. A number of whites interviewed by the commission alleged that the unsavory conditions endemic to previously stable neighborhoods in Chicago's growing black belt were the result of the Negro "invasion" of South Side. As the *Property Owners' Journal* asserted: "There is nothing in the make-up of a Negro, physically or mentally, which should induce anyone to welcome him as a neighbor. The best of them are insanitary [*sic*], insurance companies class them as poor risks, ruin alone follows in their path."[24]

The NYUL found that white homeowners and renters in New York articulated similar apprehensions about blacks. In a survey performed in the mid-1920s, the New York Urban League reported that most whites polled stated they opposed the introduction of blacks into their communities because they identified Afro-American tenants with crime and low housing standards. Consequently, whites utilized a variety of techniques to exclude Afro-Americans from their neighborhoods.[25]

Though the Urban League believed that whites' perceptions of blacks were filtered through the warped lens of racism, Leaguers shared the view that black newcomers were not well suited to urban life. Unlike most whites, however, Leaguers presumed that nurture not nature was responsible for the prevalence of unwholesome activities such as vice and crime in black neighborhoods. Believing the migration and the poor quality of home life in ghetto communities were chiefly responsible for such problems, the Urban League offered a variety of forms of guidance to newcomers.

Declaring the Windy City's housing situation urgent, the Chicago Urban League spent the better part of its first year of operation investigating the black belt's housing. The majority of the more than 400 apartments the League inspected between 1916 and 1917 were in disrepair. The CUL therefore assisted a number of residents of run-down units in finding wholesome accommodations.[26] In its 1926–27 activity year, the Chicago branch even opened an emergency lodging house with the assistance of Alderman Louis B. Anderson of the Second Ward. Although the Chicago Urban League urged city officials to prevent occupancy of physically unfit housing, little appears to have come of such efforts.[27] The League, therefore, relied largely on voluntarist solutions to blacks' housing problems.

Partly to dispel racist sentiments among whites, the Chicago branch, like the National and New York Leagues, offered blacks printed instructions outlining proper comportment in the city. The local and National Leagues, often in concert with the black press, provided migrants with lists of "Do's and Don'ts." In addition to suggesting that newcomers "not loaf" and that they "get a job at once," a handbill printed by the CUL urged them "not to live in crowded rooms," asserting that others "can be obtained."[28] It also suggested that migrants not "carry on loud conversations in street cars and public places." A more involved list of "Do's and Don'ts" distributed by both the NUL and the CUL implored migrants to "bring about a *new order of living*" in the communities in which they lived. It impressed upon them the need for neatness in their "personal appearance on the street or when sitting in front doorways." The poster also encouraged migrants to "prevent the defacement of property by children and adults."[29]

The Chicago Urban League continued such activities through the 1920s. Identifying itself as an information clearinghouse, it hoped to improve the black belt's housing by educating tenants and their children and coordinating activities with other uplift organizations.[30] In its 1922–23 activity year the Chicago League, aided by black clubwomen, distributed some 10,000 cards offering advice to the city's newcomers. These handbills emphasized "the necessity of being orderly citizens, efficient working-men and good housekeepers." The clubwomen further offered "verbal advice as to the things [newcomers] should do and know," and they provided residents with a "card of admonition with the name and address of the Urban League." The CUL also attempted to encourage "civic betterment" by teaching black Chicagoans habits of thrift, cleanliness, health, and good behavior.[31]

Publications and "educational" work of this sort were as much indicative of black newcomers' ignorance of urban ways as they were of black middle-class apprehensions about them. Many Afro-American longtime residents shared the view that improper behavior among migrants fueled racial animosity. As historian James Grossman notes, prior to the riots, a member of one of Chicago's oldest black families declared her concerns about the ramifications of the influx of uncouth migrants. "They look terrible," she asserted. "They sit down on the street car beside white people and I am sure there is going to be trouble." After the 1919 riot, tensions between native blacks and migrants increased. The Chicago *Defender* even went so far as to assert, erroneously, that "there was absolutely no friction until the advent of a handful of undesirables who 'felt their oats' and cut loose upon the slightest provocation." Ironically, such perceptions were rooted in an unrealistic faith in the ability of respectable behavior to dispel racial stereotypes. They also demonstrated Afro-Americans' awareness that whites made no distinctions among blacks, regardless of class and/or accomplishment.[32]

The messages in such printed matter further illustrated the League's occasional callousness to poor blacks, and migrants in particular. For example, in directing Afro-Americans not to rent overcrowded apartment units because others could be obtained, the CUL placed an unreasonable burden on the shoulders of poor blacks. Nearly from the Chicago Urban League's inception, the black belt lacked a sufficient number of units to house its residents. In fact, when the rest of the city had a housing surplus in 1917, the black belt experienced a severe shortage. The return of the doughboys exacerbated an already abysmal situation. By the summer of 1919, the number of Chicago families in need of housing exceeded available units by 50,000. Residential segregation, followed by a citywide housing shortage, left black Chicagoans little choice but to accept whatever apartments they could find.[33]

Printed guidelines, however, could not fully address the issues the League believed were the root of the problems confronting ghetto communities. Urban Leaguers such as George E. Haynes, Ira De Augustine Reid, and Charles S. Johnson believed that the migration eroded communal norms and the traditional institutions establishing social controls. Johnson, for example, argued that while the church had been an important agent of acculturation in the south, low wages, unemployment, commercialized entertainment, and deteriorating neighborhoods undermined the church's sway in the urban north.[34] Although Haynes held a more optimistic assessment of the church's significance for urban blacks, he nonetheless urged black clergymen to expand the scope of their work by engaging in activities akin to social work. Shortly after Haynes resigned from his position as the NLUCAN's executive secretary, he called upon Afro-American churches in Harlem to survey neighborhoods and to offer a kind of guidance to newcomers that paralleled the work of the Urban League. The League's efforts to improve the conditions of black neighborhoods by elevating their residents' character were therefore directed toward reorganizing black newcomers' lives through the creation of new institutions uniquely suited to urban life.[35]

The development of new social controls was a major part of the Urban League's efforts to elevate the standards of black neighborhoods. The provision of organized activities was essential to this task. Viewing cooperation between landlords and tenants as indispensable to neighborhood improvement, the League hoped to train Afro-American renters and their children to keep up their own communities. From the Urban League's perspective, the active participation of black neighbors in their own uplift was necessary both to demonstrate blacks' worthiness of inclusion and to counteract the damage inflicted on black institutions by the migration.

One of the greatest threats to the social health of Afro-American communities in this period was the rise in black delinquency and criminality. Though the actual reports of the NYUL's and CUL's housing work reveal little about the extent of their programs to curb this trend, the research efforts of Chicago League staffers offer a useful window onto the Urban League's views on delinquency as well as other sources of personal demoralization and social disorganization. Of particular importance is the research of Earl R. Moses, who succeeded E. Franklin Frazier as the Chicago branch's secretary of research. Like Frazier, Moses worked for the CUL while pursuing his doctorate in sociology at the University of Chicago. Although Moses' dissertation focuses chiefly on black youth misconduct, his research reveals the ideological underpinnings of the Urban League's efforts to combat disorganization through collective action.[36]

Believing that "bad housing equaled juvenile delinquency," the CUL identified youth misconduct as a major concern. According to Earl Moses, delinquency and criminality among blacks in Chicago increased at an inordinate pace following the migration, rising faster than blacks' share of the general population. While the percentage of Afro-Americans in Chicago tripled between 1900 and 1930, increasing from 1.8 percent to 6.9 percent of the general population, the proportion of black male delinquents in this period grew by six times. Between 1900 and 1906, blacks comprised only 3.5 percent of the total number of male delinquents brought before Cook County Juvenile Court. This number grew to 6.6 percent between 1917 and 1923, and in 1920 black males and females comprised more than 12 percent of the total number of Chicago's delinquents. By 1929, 22.2 percent of young men brought before the Juvenile Court of Cook County were black, comprising 4.3 percent of Chicago's black male population between the ages of ten and sixteen.[37] One year later, Afro-Americans accounted for more than 21 percent of the city's male and female delinquents.

As with delinquency, black adult criminality rose significantly after the migration. Even before World War I, blacks were overrepresented among those arrested for crimes in the Windy City. In 1900, Afro-Americans accounted for 7.8 percent of arrests in Chicago. By 1930, nearly 22 percent of men and more than 50 percent of women arrested were black. While misdemeanors accounted for a significant number of arrests, felony offenses comprised a disturbing percentage of the crimes with which blacks were charged.[38] In fact, for the years 1913, 1920, and 1930, black men accounted for, respectively, 8.6 percent, 13.3 percent, and 21.1 percent of felony arrests in Chicago. For the same years, black women comprised 17.9 percent, 17.4 percent, and 28.6 percent of felony arrests, respectively. Felony conviction rates were even higher for Afro-American men and women. Of felony convictions for the years 1913, 1920, and 1930, black men accounted for 9 percent, 17.9 percent, and 29.4 percent, respectively. Over this same period, black women comprised 14.1 percent, 16.9 percent, and 19.8 percent of felony convictions. Arrest and conviction rates for murder were also higher for Afro-Americans than for whites.[39]

Moses believed that several factors contributed to the high rates of delinquency and crime among Afro-Americans. In the tradition of the Chicago School, he rooted delinquency in the ecological features of neighborhoods. Youthful misconduct and criminality, he claimed, were perpetuated by two means. Delinquency was either "indigenous," arising from the unique conditions of the communities in which it was observed, or "transplanted" through migration. In the case of Chicago, Moses believed that most delinquent behavior was indigenous in origin.[40] The dearth of either sufficient or satisfying employment opportunities was, of course, a major factor influencing delinquency and crime among black youth. In fact, Moses found that economic exploitation of southern migrants by unscrupulous employers contributed significantly to the demoralization of Afro-American newcomers, pushing many into petty crime.[41] During the 1910s and 1920s the League noted the influence of economic issues on the integrity of ghetto communities and thus framed many of its employment and job training programs with this concern in mind. According to Moses and other Leaguers, housing and family life was no less important to the social health of young people and their neighborhoods.[42]

Consistent with the view that "indigenous patterns are most frequently acquired in a community situation," Moses argued that "the abnormally high increase in juvenile delinquency among Negroes . . . [was] due largely to the settling of Negro migrant families in areas of deterioration and disorganization."[43] Racial discrimination forced Afro-American newcomers to live in Chicago's worst neighborhoods. Segregation and whites' belief that blacks were "a homogeneous mass, devoid of differences," Moses asserted, placed Afro-American migrants in "areas of deterioration [in which] delinquency, crime, vice, poverty, and other pathological conditions abound and run unchecked." Though other migrant groups, including white ethnic immigrants, had begun their stays in the Windy City in such communities, segregation prevented Afro-Americans' escape. Moses observed that even the more economically advanced Afro-Americans were confined to such depressed urban enclaves. Thus, in spite of the fact that black Chicagoans were constantly on the move in search of better housing, racial discrimination confined Afro-Americans of all classes to unsavory areas.[44]

Like Johnson and Reid, Moses believed the migration and the realities of urban life eroded social institutions fundamental to the maintenance of social order. The instability of ghetto households bore much of the responsibility for the prevalence of social pathologies in black communities. The dearth of black homemakers and Afro-Americans' residential mobility were of particular concern to Urban Leaguers. The low wages black men commanded required Afro-American women to seek gainful employment at higher rates than white women, thus reducing black mothers' presence in the home. According to Moses, "The absence from the home of both parents leaves the child largely to his own devices, or in the care of more or less half-interested relatives or friends." "Consequently," Moses declared, "the process of emancipation from parental control is hastened," thereby increasing the sway of unwholesome outside influences over children and young adults.[45]

Similarly, Moses claimed that Afro-Americans' extreme mobility hindered the formation of cohesive community interests, enervating a valuable check on individual conduct. The prying eyes of neighbors helped to reinforce conventional social and moral standards by shaming those who deviated from communal norms. "Community mores," Moses asserted, "challenge any radical variation from conventional community behavior, and non-observance of community standards," reducing "individual prestige." However, by maintaining residences for short periods of time, perhaps a year or less, black families were less likely to become subject to community sanctions. From this perspective, ghetto neighborhoods' comparative lack of social controls reduced inhibition among black youth and even adults, thereby increasing their participation in illicit activities.[46]

According to Moses, the instability of ghetto life appeared to alienate black youth. He noted that older children, in particular, were developing a "hopeless sense of despair about the future" and a pronounced feeling of futility about "going straight." Poor housing and job insecurity exposed young black men and women to unsavory environments and undermined their ability to secure financial independence. Moses concluded that many black youths coming before the Cook County Boys' Court had "become so demoralized as to seek constant companionship in vicious situations," including theft, vandalism, and "sex orgies." These young men, Moses claimed, were developing a need for constant stimulation and a corresponding inability to defer immediate gratification. Furthermore, Moses alleged that the "lack of economic resources, feeling of inferiority, or a host of other situations" causes many of these unattached boys to "withdraw from institutional facilities."[47]

Believing proper social influences were essential to shaping the behavior of black newcomers, Urban Leaguers were greatly concerned about the withdrawal of Afro-Americans from communal institutions. Like its job training and union activities, the League's efforts to improve neighborhood conditions were intended to impart order to the lives of black folk by providing constructive outlets for the restless minds of ghetto residents. Quoting the Chicago Commission on Race Relations, a 1923 article in *Opportunity* argued that supervised activities were urgently needed to assist in the acculturation of Afro-American newcomers. "Recreation centers for adult and juvenile Negroes," the article asserted, "should be planned and provided as soon as possible in areas where the process of racial adjustment is far from complete." The author argued that wholesome recreation—including parks, playgrounds, libraries, short course work, and museums—might even curb delinquency among blacks. "Play," the piece declared, "is a more powerful competitor than vice."[48]

Moses and the CUL shared this view. Indeed, Moses argued that one of the most significant obstacles to shoring up the moral integrity of Chicago's black belt was a lack of "facilities."[49] Since Moses believed that community life shaped the character of ghetto children, "play group or gang associations" and other organized outlets for young people were crucial to promoting proper conduct among youth. Moses found, however, that black Chicago lacked sufficient salubrious influences for young people.[50] Quoting the chief probation officer of Cook County, Moses argued that a lack of facilities and institutions, particularly for girls, contributed significantly to the large number of juvenile delinquents among the city's Afro-American population.[51]

Moses and the Chicago League's concerns about delinquency and ghetto disorganization were echoed by the New York League. Reporting findings for 1925, the NYUL claimed that while blacks comprised only 4 percent of the city's population, they accounted for 8 percent of New York's criminal court cases. More startling was that criminality and misconduct appeared to have taken hold of black children, who were overrepresented among New York's juvenile delinquents. Although the League could take some solace in the fact that most of the offenses with which Afro-American young people were charged were minor, black children were nonetheless overrepresented among cases relating to personal conduct and morality. In fact, Afro-American young people comprised a disproportionately large number of those charged with disorderly conduct; furthermore, no less than 85 percent of black girl delinquents were deemed "ungovernable and wayward" or charged with desertion.[52]

While the New York Urban League argued that "retardation" was to blame for a small percentage of black delinquency, the chief source of youth misconduct, the NYUL claimed, was Afro-Americans' maladjustment to urban life. Like Moses, the New York League argued that the lack of parental control stemming from the prevalence of working mothers and the dearth of opportunities for supervised recreation were largely to blame for the city's high rate of juvenile delinquency. Compounding the problem of youth misconduct was that black children passed through the criminal justice system at an excessive rate. Although only a small percentage of New York's black juvenile delinquents were actually convicted, a significant number were institutionalized. In fact, of the 543 black children arraigned as delinquents in 1925, 107, or 20 percent, were committed to institutions. The remaining 436 were placed on parole. For Leaguers, the prevalence of black youthful offenders stood both to reinforce negative stereotypes about Afro-Americans and to further alienate youth who had already been damaged.[53]

Ultimately, the view that urban life threatened the moral health of city dwellers pushed the Urban League to devote special efforts to develop organized outlets for parents and their children. The League's concerns about juvenile delinquency led it to pursue a variety of strategies on the part of troubled youth. In its 1911–12 activity year, the NLUCAN handled a number of cases involving girls that it claimed were "on the verge of becoming delinquents." The League "counseled and advised" these young women and their parents or guardians, presumably providing guidance on child rearing, household upkeep, and employment opportunities. The NLUCAN also helped to remove many troubled girls "from their unwholesome environment" to more uplifting settings, making "special efforts . . . to secure homes for such girls in suburban towns."[54] The National League continued to engage in home placement activities through the mid-1910s.

Direct intervention such as home placement was, of course, a last resort. The NLUCAN and local Leagues relied more heavily on the provision of wholesome recreation and other organized activities. To counteract social disorganization, the League offered outlets for children outside of the city. In fact, in its 1911–12 activity year, the NLUCAN secured accommodations for "591 colored mothers and children in fresh-air day parties." It also managed to send 142 boys from New York to camp in Verona, New Jersey, an increase of 36 over the previous year. The NLUCAN continued to use the Verona camp for its "Fresh Air Work" for a number of years, sending 136 boys there in its 1912–13 activity year and 104 boys between 1913 and 1915.[55]

More important were the League's endeavors to provide outlets for black newcomers within city limits to counter the effects of social disorganization. In addition to directing recent arrivals and their offspring to friends and wholesome households, the NLUCAN inspected pool and dance halls to ensure that both offered only legal entertainment. In the mid-1910s, the NLUCAN also launched what turned out to be an unsuccessful campaign to acquire playground space in Harlem. The failure to secure more recreational facilities for Harlem was a great disappointment to the League, which observed that the two playgrounds New York's Afro-American children had access to provided important outlets for "youthful vigor."[56] The New York and Chicago Urban Leagues pursued similar efforts. In the mid-1920s, the CUL worked closely with city officials to find a site for a small park in the black belt. According to the city's park commissioner, however, the Chicago League's efforts failed because of some unspecified political reasons.[57]

The League also organized black children and their parents into associations such as neighborhood unions and boys and girls clubs. These activities were intended to counter both whites' prejudices about blacks and the alienation Leaguers believed was at the root of ghetto social pathologies. One of the most significant of these organizations for young people was the Juvenile Park Protective League in Harlem (JPPL). The JPPL recruited 626 schoolboys, who cooperated "with all of the city departments in trying to make the city better and cleaner." The boys reported on "obstructed fire escapes, unlighted hallways, illegal sale of liquor and cigarettes to minors, littering on streets and other infractions of city ordinances." In order to impress upon the boys that good citizenship had its rewards, the League conferred "badges of meritorious service" to those who were especially enthusiastic. In keeping with ethnic cycle theory, the Urban League thus channeled the raw energy of black boys into socially constructive avenues in an effort to "reduce the friction" between the races.[58]

Similarly, by enhancing residents' commitment to their homes and communities, neighborhood unions provided constructive outlets for adults to improve community life. The NLUCAN assisted in the establishment of neighborhood unions throughout the 1910s. Though the records reveal little about the activities of such organizations in New York, and nothing on Chicago, a piece in *Opportunity* provides some insight into the purpose and activities of such associations. The article discusses a neighborhood union in Atlanta in the mid-1920s that offered assistance to black residents consistent with the League's work. Ultimately, the union hoped to strengthen ties between residents and to ensure that safety and high household standards were maintained within the community. Encouraging residents to participate in programs that would meet the unique needs of their community, the union organized classes in home economics, such as sewing, cooking, home nursing, and handicraft. The neighborhood union also campaigned to establish wholesome recreation for young people.[59]

Like the Urban League's printed guidelines, programs designed to adjust migrants through the reorganization of their lives reflected the tensions between middle-class and poor blacks. Believing that racism could be mitigated by good behavior, Leaguers designed programs intended to combat social disorganization through the implementation of new social controls. Many poor blacks undoubtedly benefited from programs and activities such as the camp in Verona, day parties, the Juvenile Park Protective League, and neighborhood unions. However, the good intentions of these works were infused with the so-called better classes' concerns and apprehensions about migrants and poor Afro-Americans in general.

Projects of this sort were intended both to improve the quality of life in ghetto communities and to help open up the housing options available to blacks. Though the Urban League understood that proper behavior could not by itself eliminate residential discrimination, the elevation of behavioral standards in black neighborhoods was nonetheless an important precondition to improving blacks' housing options. From this perspective, the perception of blacks as debauched spendthrifts who were slow to pay rent and demonstrated little regard for the upkeep of property provided material justification for white hostility and helped to limit the housing stock available to Afro-Americans. Furthermore, the Urban League believed that poor maintenance and dissolute tenants in Afro-American neighborhoods discouraged white property owners and real estate developers from providing decent housing for ghetto residents. Immoral conduct and apathy about maintenance of property undermined blacks' material and social advancement, requiring the Urban League to acculturate and, on rare occasions, contain those who jeopardized progress in its effort to improve black communities.

Housing

The Urban League did not ignore the role of landlords in the dire conditions of black neighborhoods. In fact, the National and New York Urban Leagues spent much of the 1910s and 1920s encouraging developers and property owners to provide decent housing for ghetto residents. The fruits of such labors, however, would remain far beyond the reach of most Afro-Americans. Ultimately, the Urban League's endeavors to provide respectable housing for hardworking Afro-Americans were of greatest advantage to both landlords and the "better classes" of blacks. The Urban League's work in this field reflects the class contradictions inherent both to its own approach and to racial self-help generally.

In addition to organizing tenants and children to alleviate some of the problems confronting ghetto neighborhoods, the National Urban League tried to enlist the assistance of landlords. As the housing bureau's mission statement suggests, the Urban League viewed cooperation between landlords and tenants as essential to improving the condition of ghetto housing. To combat overcrowding and the so-called lodger evil in the 1910s, for example, the League's housing bureau called for "inducing responsible real estate companies to take over" a number of apartment houses, "modify them for small families, [and] manage and rent them for reasonable fees with the goal of eliminating undesirable tenants." Both to curb exploitation of tenants and to increase their morale, the League also promoted the use of black superintendents, rent collectors, and real estate agents, who were to serve essentially as race relations managers. In addition, the League compiled a list of respectable accommodations for single men and women, thereby separating the attached from the unattached.[60]

As significantly, the Urban League of New York tried to encourage new construction in Harlem to increase the number of decent, affordable apartments available to blacks. From its earliest years, the Urban League believed new construction would play a major part in improving New York's housing. As executive secretary of the National Urban League, Eugene K. Jones courted entrepreneurs to construct housing in Harlem. Although little is known about the League's early attempts to attract investment in Harlem's real estate, there is some evidence indicating that such attempts reflected the League's class orientation.

Ironically, Jones's endeavors "to induce responsible real estate companies to take over" were at odds with the League's objective of providing Afro-Americans with affordable housing. At the start of his tenure as executive secretary, Jones called for using social workers' housing research to direct potential investors to Harlem. Jones's efforts were well intentioned; however, he ultimately promoted the exploitation of black tenants. According to Jones, "the vacancies in the Harlem district are from two to five percent," a rate that was apparently "much smaller than . . . other parts of the city." Since, on average, Harlem's rents were "much higher than in other parts of the city," he argued that investing in this district would be a "wise" and lucrative decision. While Jones qualified his remarks by asserting that he did not condone the fact that blacks were charged exorbitant rents, he went on to state that high rents proved that this "would be a safe investment" that was to the mutual benefit of both tenants and property owners.[61]

Although Jones declared in the 1910s that the League had achieved a measure of success in attracting responsible real estate investors to Harlem, no records exist of the results of these early efforts. It is therefore not possible to evaluate whether the fruits of the League's work to attract investment in Harlem's housing in this period were of disproportionate benefit to entrepreneurs and the better classes of Afro-Americans, as Jones's efforts might imply. The New York Urban League's housing work in the 1920s, however, does shed some light on this issue.[62] During the 1920s, the League enlisted the services of philanthropist John D. Rockefeller Jr. to improve Harlem's housing conditions. Rockefeller's Dunbar Apartment Complex offers a useful window onto the class implications of the Urban League's housing policies and the difficulty confronting the black self-help organization.

The basic housing issues the League identified in the 1910s continued to plague Gotham over the next decade. By the 1920s, however, Leaguers believed that the situation had become desperate. Perhaps the most pressing problem was that New York City's Afro-American community grew faster than available housing. Between 1910 and 1920, the city's black population grew from 91,709 to about 160,000. By 1927 the New York Urban League estimated that black New York had grown by some 140,000 residents to exceed 300,000. Construction of housing had increased significantly during the same period, keeping pace with the city's overall growth. In fact, the NYUL reported that the number of units available to tenants between September 1920 and September 1925 grew from 1,320,000 suites to 1,588,000. Yet, according to the Urban League, the increase in existing units was of little consequence to most black New Yorkers. While the number of new apartments had increased by 20 percent, New York's Afro-American population had grown by more than 25 percent. Worse yet, because of the location of construction and discrimination in housing, blacks had access to few of these new homes. The NYUL claimed that of the 268,000 units built between 1920 and 1925, "less than 12 of the total number of houses constructed were available for the colored population of Harlem."[63]

Not surprisingly, most of the housing that was available to Afro-Americans was of poor quality. In its 1927 report "2,400 Negro families in Harlem," the NYUL noted that 48 percent of the 2,326 respondents indicated that their housing was "poor," "bad," or "Needed Cleaning." The most common complaints among those reporting dissatisfaction were that their rentals were either "overrun with rats" and roaches, in need of repairs to physical plant—including walls, ceilings, roofs, and floors—or lacked sufficient heating and ventilation. The fact that many apartments had no heat or electricity was particularly problematic for both Leaguers and, of course, tenants. Although the New York League was pleased to find that 80 percent of respondents lived in heated apartments, the realization that 20 percent lived in "coldwater flats" was of some concern. In addition to the fact that more than half of these "coldwater" apartments, 251 flats, had no baths, they all relied on individual stove units for heating rather than a central system such as steam. Worse yet, the New York Urban League found that in a cruel irony many landlords would not permit tenants to use their stoves, encouraging them instead to install gas heaters. Tenants usually had to incur the expense of amenities such as gas or electricity, either directly by paying for installation themselves or indirectly by agreeing to pay higher rents upon provision of new facilities and services.[64]

Adding insult to injury, Harlem's rents continued to be higher than the city's average. More than a decade after the League first compared the rents paid by black and white tenants, the NYUL found that landlords still charged Afro-Americans more than whites for less appealing accommodations. On average, black Harlemites paid between seven and ten dollars more per month for three-, four-, and five-room units, the most popular size apartments.[65] Because Afro-Americans earned less than whites, rent continued to account for a higher share of blacks' wages. To maintain a comfortable existence, the New York Urban League claimed, tenants should pay no more than 20 percent of their wages for rent. Yet in 1927, the NYUL found that rent accounted for no less than 20 percent of the wages of 95 percent of families surveyed. More startling was the fact that for nearly half the families sampled, rent accounted for more than 40 percent of their wages.[66]

Urban Leaguers believed the shortage of decent housing at affordable rates profoundly affected the social character of black neighborhoods. The scarcity of inexpensive rentals reduced the length of tenancy of a large percentage of black New Yorkers who were constantly on the move in search of better housing.[67] Leaguers held that excessive mobility reduced tenants' stake in the upkeep of their apartments, imbuing them with a sense of apathy. The terms of rental arrangements were partially responsible for Afro-American tenants' heightened mobility. The New York branch observed that most black families rented on a month-to-month basis instead of yearlong leases. Harlem's plethora of potential renters offered landlords little incentive to provide even hot water, let alone formal contracts offering mutually beneficial terms.[68]

The dearth of adequate housing was also largely to blame for overcrowding in the ghetto. The New York League defined overcrowding as the point at which the number of residents exceeded the number of rooms by half. According to this definition, the League declared that roughly 10 percent of Harlem's households were overcrowded in 1927. Sadly, many of those living in homes that were not technically overcrowded were not much better off. In about 62 percent of apartments sampled, the number of rooms was greater than or equal to the number of household members.[69] In as many as 28 percent of apartments, however, the number of residents was almost double the number of rooms.[70]

As they had in the 1910s, Leaguers continued to claim that irresponsible landlords contributed significantly to the problem of apartment house overcrowding. The New York Urban League argued that the practice of subdividing single-family homes into multifamily units both added to residential congestion and undermined neighborhood upkeep. In fact, in 1927, the NYUL declared that the houses that had become deteriorated in Harlem were largely "Second-hand houses."[71] Remodeling of this sort often adversely affected tenants' privacy. For example, many Harlemites lived in units called "railroad" apartments, wherein several rooms were "directly connected, usually running the length of the building." The problem of maintaining one's personal space occurred when landlords subdivided four- and five-room railroad apartments into two separate units. The new smaller apartments often shared one sink, which placed the two families into intimate contact with one another. Many other apartments provided only one bath that was to be shared by several families occupying different units.[72]

For Urban Leaguers, overcrowding and the resulting lack of privacy made a bad situation worse. Leaguers believed that arrangements requiring multiple residents to share one bathroom, for instance, were not only inconvenient for tenants but also harmful to family life. Housing congestion of this sort reduced residents' ability to choose with whom they came into contact. Parents and their children were thus at greater risk of exposure to morally suspect individuals. Moreover, the League held that cramped and/or unsavory accommodations bred indifference among tenants, undermining their interest in their building's maintenance.

Although renters of small apartments comprised a sizable number of the overcrowded, even those renting large units often lived in congested homes. Standard definitions of overcrowding did not consider room size, which would have undoubtedly affected the amount of usable space tenants had at their disposal. Moreover, most tenants with large apartments had large families whose members often surpassed the number of available rooms. Among renters of large flats, however, lodgers were the most common and alarming cause of overcrowding.[73]

A lodger was usually defined as a household resident who was not a close blood relative.[74] Tenants generally took in boarders to assist them in paying Harlem's high rents. In fact, the NYUL found that lodgers were most common in large apartments, units of seven or more rooms, which were usually the most expensive homes. Lodgers were commonplace in Harlem's residential life. As early as 1913, the League observed that a large number of black New Yorkers were boarders. In fact, the NLUCAN housing bureau's 1913–14 report revealed the unsettling discovery that roughly 62 percent of apartments surveyed in New York City housed lodgers. Indeed the League estimated that roughly 42 percent of all adults in Harlem were boarders. Lodgers continued to comprise a large share of Harlem's population through the 1920s. Of the 12,601 Harlemites the NYUL surveyed in 1927, 3,314—or about 25 percent—were lodgers.[75]

The "lodger-evil" had long been a source of concern for Urban Leaguers. While the NYUL attributed much of the deterioration of Harlem's housing to landlords' indifference, it identified lodgers as an additional source of household disorder. Its apprehensions about lodgers were no different from its concerns about other sources of overcrowding. As "unattached" young men and women, Leaguers believed that lodgers lacked sufficient stake in the upkeep of property. They thus contributed to the deterioration of Harlem's tenements by failing to assist in the general maintenance of their residences. Lodgers, moreover, threatened the privacy and moral integrity of the family.[76] According to James H. Hubert, executive secretary of the New York Urban League, "family morale is broken down through the taking in lodgers."[77] Because boarders actually shared renters' homes, the threat lodgers presented was in many ways more serious than that posed by other forms of overcrowding.

Like Eugene K. Jones before him, James H. Hubert hoped to improve housing conditions in Harlem by attracting investors who understood black New York's unique needs. The desperate shortage of decent homes suitable for the "small wage earner" following the Great War imbued the construction of new units with great significance for the New York League. Hubert spent much of the early 1920s aggressively courting a variety of potential investors, and his efforts were finally rewarded by the middle of 1926. That summer, philanthropist John D. Rockefeller Jr. purchased an entire block in north Harlem to be devoted to the construction of a model tenement for blacks. Rockefeller added three more blocks to his project a few months later, and by February 1928 Harlem's Dunbar Apartment complex was open for occupancy.[78]

The New York Urban League greeted Rockefeller's housing complex with much anticipation. The League believed that the model apartments, named for Afro-American poet Paul Laurence Dunbar, offered Harlemites an unprecedented opportunity to acquire decent modern homes. As important, the objectives of the Dunbar Apartments were consistent with the Urban League's philosophy for improving Afro-Americans' housing conditions. Much like its employment and labor programs, the League's housing plan identified cooperation, in this case between tenants and owners, as essential to elevating conditions among blacks. The New York League, for example, declared its intention "to bring together the many divergent interests represented by tenants, owners, landlords, [and] both primary and secondary mortgages." The education of these "divergent interests," the NYUL asserted, was "necessary before housing standards can be materially improved."[79] Rockefeller's approach to housing mirrored the League's, as he too hoped to foster mutually beneficial arrangements between tenants and landlords that demonstrated the profit system's ability to promote self-reliance and social health among Afro-Americans.

In his dual effort to teach Afro-Americans the value of self-sufficiency and the need for personal investment in their homes, John D. Rockefeller Jr. designed the Dunbar Apartments as a cooperative. Cooperatives appealed to advocates of social reform because they allegedly fostered a mutually beneficial relationship between tenants and landlords that provided both parties greater security than rentals. In addition to offering the stability of leases, Rockefeller's cooperatives gave tenants a financial interest in their residences. As the *Dunbar News* declared, "Every dollar the tenant-subscriber pays into the cooperative increases his stake in the venture, impelling him to remain in his apartment home, if humanly possible, until the very end of his subscription agreement." Increased retention of tenants would help to decrease the rates of delinquency and criminality, improve the maintenance and upkeep of property, and increase landlord's profits by reducing the number of empty units. Cooperatives also provided members a measure of financial protection, in that the equity—or savings—a tenant accumulated could be used toward monthly fees if he/she were to become unemployed.[80] The *Dunbar News* argued that such an arrangement benefited both the residents, who were partially insulated from eviction, and their landlord, who was all but assured the timely collection of rent receipts.[81] Rockefeller's cooperative plan further reinforced black self-sufficiency by setting terms by which residents would eventually pay for the very buildings in which they lived. In fact, according to Dunbar's managing director, Roscoe Conkling Bruce, the cooperative's rates and fees were set so that tenants would "liquidate the principal within 22 years."[82]

The Dunbar Apartments were undeniably a major improvement over most of the existing housing in Harlem. The buildings were generally praised for their beauty and functionality, and were honored with the American Institute of Architecture's first prize in 1927. The apartments came standard with an array of amenities that were absent from most tenements in Harlem. For example, each building possessed its own boiler, providing renters with low-pressure steam heat. Apartment units also came with electricity, hot water, washtubs, gas ranges, refrigerators, and dumbwaiters. In addition, the complex provided childcare facilities, including a nursery for children up to five years old and recreational equipment such as slides, seesaws, sand boxes, and "gymnasium apparatus."[83]

Perhaps what was most significant about the Dunbar Apartments was that they were intended to provide modern comforts at an affordable rate. As construction on Dunbar approached completion, the New York Urban League complained that only "the more economically substantial" members of the race could afford Harlem's better apartments. By contrast, the Dunbar Apartments were designed to provide "the small wage earner a comfortable home at a moderate rental."[84] With such objectives in mind, black New Yorkers jumped at the chance to live in Dunbar. Even before the apartments opened, the New York Urban League was inundated with applications. In the fall of 1926, the NYUL received more than 5,000 applications for the complex's 511 units.[85] By May 11, 1928, less than six months after the first tenants moved in, all of the buildings' suites were sold.

More than an apartment complex, Dunbar was an experiment in racial uplift. From the ground up, the Dunbar Apartments were designed to combat the problems Leaguers and other reformers associated with ghetto housing. The brainchild of award-winning architect Andrew J. Thomas, Dunbar's layout emphasized the remedial effects of greenery. Thomas was influenced by the British Garden City movement, which sought to counter urban ills through the creation of planned communities that incorporated elements of village life such as town greens and public recreation. Thomas, who wanted to design a community that was both aesthetically pleasing and socially salutary, thus devoted half of the entire site to gardens, setting the complex's six independent buildings around a large rectangular green. The extensive gardens not only added to Dunbar's beauty but also offered vital outlets for the residents' children. Planners included a playground located at the center of the garden, which, along with the apartment's youth clubhouse, was to provide wholesome recreation for young people. While these features were undoubtedly meant to reduce noise within the complex, they were also explicitly designed to combat sources of criminality and misconduct among children.

As Roscoe Conkling Bruce asserted, there were no "better safeguards against juvenile delinquency" than provision of supervised play.[86]

The grounds were not the only facet of Dunbar's design and operation devoted to the uplift of its residents. Rockefeller and Bruce shared the Urban League's view that many of the difficulties Harlem's renters experienced stemmed from the poor maintenance and management of their apartments. Absentee landlords who were concerned only with profits, constant rent increases, and disreputable rent collectors and janitors all served to frustrate black New Yorkers' efforts to acquire decent homes. To avoid exploitation at the hands of management, the Dunbar Apartment management employed a large staff that included a full-time manager and on-site maintenance personnel. Moreover, in line with the NYUL's suggestion for improving the function and maintenance of Harlem's tenements, Dunbar's staff was largely black. Although it is not clear whether the Urban League had a direct hand in this decision, Leaguers had urged landlords for some time to employ Afro-American superintendents and janitors in order to reduce friction between owners and tenants. The Urban League argued that harmonious relations between landlords and renters was essential to the proper upkeep of buildings; management personnel that appeared to be uninterested or even hostile toward Afro-Americans would reduce tenants' personal stake in their buildings and their upkeep. The decision to employ black workers was thus consistent with Dunbar's owners' general objectives to imbue tenants with a sense of pride and a personal stake in their property.[87]

The layout of apartments was further intended to promote the social health of Dunbar's subscribers, and they were clearly designed with the perceived size and needs of the average Harlem family. To avoid overcrowding, Dunbar's designers offered relatively few large apartments—units with six and seven rooms. In fact, the complex's average unit had only three and a half rooms, with the half room serving as a dining bay.[88] Four- and five-room apartments were also available and in high demand. The modest size of Dunbar's units was intended to reduce the need to take in lodgers to meet the high rents associated with larger apartments. Since boarders were generally excluded from the building, moderate-sized units were essential to satisfying Harlem's housing needs. Dunbar therefore provided accommodations in line with the perceived needs of the average Harlem family.

Dunbar management also addressed the character of tenants and their neighbors. Like the NYUL, Bruce argued that segregation and exploitation forced many Afro-Americans to live in overcrowded and "sordid apartment houses." Echoing the views articulated more than a decade earlier by George E. Haynes, Dunbar's manager expressed concern about the mingling of disparate classes of Afro-Americans brought about by the indifference of landlords. Most landlords in Harlem, Bruce declared, employed "practically no selection or classification of tenants." Since landlords were interested only in "who can and will pay the rent," frequently "a family of sound Christian character finds itself living across the narrow long, dark hall from a family which is obnoxious, if not vicious. Cheek by jowl with the deacon lives the dope fiend." To avoid such problems, Dunbar's leases barred lodgers, outlined strict rules regarding parties and loud music, and retained authority to evict residents for immoral conduct. Moreover, prospective tenants submitted to a rigorous interview process in which reviewers gauged the character of applicants—with the assistance of three references—as well as their ability to pay.[89]

Tenants appear to have been largely appreciative of the buildings' design and operation. Certainly the flood of applicants the project received was a testament to Dunbar's relative advantage over most tenements in Harlem. Although Bruce reported that many subscribers were initially dissatisfied with the strict provisions regarding noise—specifically the playing of loud music—and the units' small rooms, most, he claimed, quickly embraced the advantages the apartments offered. Dunbar's management believed that residents' feelings about their homes were best reflected in their attitudes, which were described as generally "positive." In fact, management praised tenants for their commitment to the maintenance and upkeep of their buildings.[90]

It is not surprising that residents would have held the Rockefeller project in high regard. Dunbar offered subscribers the ability not only to become homeowners but also to live in a clean, safe environment, ideally suited to family life. But while the Dunbar Apartments provided many Afro-Americans wonderful homes, the complex's operation, and its selection of tenants in particular, ultimately reveals the tendency of the League's brand of uplift to design or promote programs that were of disproportionate benefit to capital and the so-called "better classes" of blacks.

Unfortunately, the records do not reveal the qualities that the NYUL, which assisted in the tenant review process, and Dunbar's management believed characterized an ideal applicant. Therefore, with the exception of extreme cases—such as convicted or suspected prostitutes, drug dealers and addicts, racketeers, etc.—it is not clear what sort of behavior might bar one from residence in the cooperative. This means it is impossible to determine whether the personality traits, habits, and political affiliations Dunbar and the League believed were most desirable were indicative of middle-class bias. What is readily apparent, however, is that a tenant's "ability to pay" was a major factor in determining admission. While choosing tenants who could more easily afford the complex's units was a sound business practice, this greatly limited the

Dunbar Apartments' ability to provide housing for the average black New Yorker.

Although the New York Urban League and Dunbar's management initially praised the apartments as a major advance for the "small wage earner," most Harlemites could not afford to live there. Ironically, the cooperative structure, which was intended to foster mutual understanding between tenants and their landlord by providing both greater economic security, was the first financial barrier to admission. Dunbar's cooperative rate required residents to buy "common stock of the corporation equivalent in value to the apartment" they hoped to purchase. The stock, or down payment, was a flat rate of $50 per room. Since Dunbar's apartment units ranged from three to seven rooms, tenants paid between $150 and $350 just to buy into the apartment building.[91] During the 1920s and 1930s, this would have been a heavy burden for most black New Yorkers. In a 1927 survey, the New York Urban League found the average Harlemite earned only about $96 a month, or $1,160 a year. In a survey conducted just one year later, the NYUL found that the average wage of a head of household in Harlem had decreased to just $85 a month, or $1,032 per year.[92] Dunbar's down payment schedule thus represented between 13 and 30 percent of the more generous 1927 estimate of the average Harlemite's annual wages. Not even taking into account the monthly fees that would follow the down payment, it is likely that the stock purchase itself would have kept most Harlemites out of the buildings. Aware of this problem, management did offer subscribers the option to finance down payments over their first year of residence. However, this arrangement still required that tenants put down a minimum of $100, while the balance would be factored into their monthly fees over just one year.[93]

More discouraging than the price of Dunbar's stock was the fact that the complex's rents were significantly higher than the average for Harlem tenements. The average apartment in Dunbar cost $14.50 per room per month, though rents actually ranged between $11.50 and $17.50, depending on a unit's location within the buildings. The monthly rents Dunbar's residents paid for three-, four-, and five-room apartments, the most popular size units, thus averaged $43.50, $58.00, and $72.50, respectively.[94] In contrast, three-, four-, and five-room apartments throughout Harlem averaged only $36.28, $41.79, and $51.12, respectively.[95] Even the cheapest apartments in Dunbar tended to be more expensive than the average across Harlem. While Dunbar's most reasonable three-room apartment was only $34.50 a month, about $2.00 less than Harlem's average, one could pay as much as $52.50 (70 percent higher than black New York's average) for a comparable apartment in a different part of the building. More importantly, Dunbar's least expensive four-

and five-room apartments were $46.00 and $57.50, respectively, several dollars more than Harlem's average.

The Dunbar Apartments' high cost meant that, financially, most residents were significantly better off than the average Harlemite. In fact, many of Dunbar's residents were employed in the more sought after occupations for blacks. A sample of more than 300 of Dunbar's occupants revealed that only 3 percent of them worked as unskilled laborers, while 30 percent worked as clerks, 16 percent worked as porters (including Pullman porters), 7 percent worked as chauffeurs, a combined 8 percent worked as post office letter carriers and teachers, and 3 percent worked as apartment superintendents. The earnings of Dunbar's tenants were consistent with the relative status of their occupations. In a 1931 article, Roscoe Conkling Bruce said that the monthly wages of Dunbar residents ranged from $122 to $177. The median wage of the apartments' subscribers was $148 a month, more than $50 greater than the NYUL's 1927 estimate of the average monthly wage earned by black New Yorkers in general. This meant that fully half of Dunbar's residents earned between $1,776 and $2,124 a year, or from $616 to $964 (53–83 percent) more than Harlem's average worker. Even Dunbar's poorest resident earned over $300 (about 25 percent) more annually than the average Harlemite.[96]

Dunbar's inability to provide housing for the small wage earner was illustrative of both the limitations of the Urban League's practice of basing claims for black inclusion on challenges to racist stereotypes and the class implications of its approach to interracial compromise. Ultimately, the Dunbar Apartments served as a demonstration project for the profitability of ghetto housing. The Urban League had long attempted to attract real estate development to Harlem by promoting the potential returns of such endeavors. As discussed previously, Eugene K. Jones had even tried to entice investment in housing for black New York in the 1910s by advertising the inflated profits engendered by segregation. Maintaining its commitment to establishing common ground between black workers and white capital, the Urban League hoped that the success of the Dunbar Apartments would attract additional real estate development to the area.

From the earliest stages of Dunbar's development, the New York Urban League argued that Rockefeller's project held the promise of improving the general condition of housing available to Afro-Americans throughout the city and even the country. "Providing a maximum of sunlight and air," the NYUL asserted in 1926, the Dunbar Apartments were "a great step . . . toward improving the standards of housing for the large Negro population of New York City, which will have a direct effect on Negro housing in cites throughout America and on the consideration given the Negro population in social reform."[97] An article in *Opportunity* echoed these sentiments three years later, arguing that Dunbar's "greatest value is in the influence it must ultimately have on the movement of capital in neighborhoods largely occupied by Negroes." Although the League acknowledged the apartment's success would probably attract entrepreneurs with less altruistic motives than Rockefeller's, it argued that a profitable Dunbar would provide investors with empirical evidence establishing the practicality of constructing modern homes for Afro-Americans.[98] The League thus hoped that the profit motive could be used to achieve the social end of constructing decent modern homes for blacks.

Given the desperate condition of Harlem's housing in the 1920s, the Urban League's position was understandable. Nevertheless, the repercussions of the venture's failure were serious. For the NYUL, the apartment's solvency affected not just Rockefeller but the condition of Harlem's housing for years to come. The importance of ensuring a population of tenants who, at the very least, could be counted upon to meet their financial obligations in a consistent and timely fashion cannot be overstated. If Dunbar experienced high turnover due to lease violations or tenants' inability to pay rent, the buildings' promise would remain unfulfilled. In fact, the apartment's management took this issue seriously enough that it boasted publicly that fewer than 2 percent of subscribers either were "dispossessed" or left due to "financial embarrassment" between December 24, 1927, and December 1, 1928.[99] But because Dunbar did not allow tenants to take in lodgers in its first few years, the financial obligations the Dunbar Apartments presented would have automatically eliminated Harlem's least privileged members from consideration for residency.

This is not to suggest that Dunbar's management was completely insensitive to tenants' economic straits. In fact, during the Depression, the complex lowered its rates to attract new subscribers. Moreover, the Dunbar Apartments offered unemployed tenants both job training and placement.[100] In the end, however, management's efforts to create a socially salubrious environment had to give way to market concerns. Prior to the Dunbar Apartments' rate reductions, for example, the complex loosened its restrictions regarding the cohabitation of nonfamily members. Indeed, by August of 1931, *Dunbar News* had even begun advertising the advantages of "joint residency" of its larger apartments—units with six and seven rooms. Dunbar had originally frowned upon such arrangements, identifying lodgers as a threat to the upkeep and social health of the complex.[101] In spite of its initial objection to boarders, however, the complex's need for profit undermined its own social reform agenda.

Within a few years of Dunbar's opening, the Urban League was forced to acknowledge that the apartments were beyond the financial means of most Harlemites. In spite of this problem, however, Leaguers continued to assert publicly that the apartments were a boon to even those who could not afford them. According to the New York League, the mere presence of these modern apartments in Harlem would improve the condition of existing units by inspiring tenants to refuse absolutely to tolerate mismanagement, filth, and a dearth of amenities. Competition with Dunbar and the corresponding elevation of Afro-Americans' expectations would thus help to improve black housing. Yet when one considers that Dunbar contained only 511 units, and beyond the majority of blacks' means, it is unlikely that Rockefeller's apartments would have provided more than a lucky few the option to refuse any sort of housing. The NYUL continued to claim that Dunbar's existence benefited all of Harlem as late as 1931, which is especially surprising given the rising eviction rates in Harlem during the Depression. At a time when Afro-Americans were organizing active protests against the large number of evictions in New York City, such assertions would have seemed especially naive and even offensive to many black New Yorkers.

■ The Urban League's housing work in this period reflects the organization's general optimism about the prospects of the future. The League's projects in this field were ultimately predicated on the notion that the proper behavior of black tenants and their children could mitigate the pernicious consequences of racial prejudice. The League, therefore, set out to improve the living conditions in ghetto communities by, first, assisting Afro-American newcomers in adjusting to their environments and, second, working directly with landlords and real estate agents to improve the quality of ghetto housing. In treating demonstrations of black respectability as essential to the race's uplift, the Urban League's housing projects reflected both middle-class Afro-Americans' and white landlords' circumspection about poor blacks.

Because the League's philosophy was predicated on the notion that nurture not nature was essential to the progress of Afro-Americans, the housing situation in both New York and Chicago took on particular urgency. Taking the position that demonstrations of black worthiness would do much to undermine racist stereotypes, the plasticity of black migrants was as much a liability as it was an asset. Since the large urban black populations springing up across the north were plagued by poverty, crime, vice, and disease, Leaguers were concerned that the introduction of thousands of malleable black newcomers to such environments might adversely affect Afro-Americans' adjustment to urban life. Residential segregation also held the potential to damage those hardworking and morally grounded blacks who were native to such cities by exposing them to unsavory influences. To ensure the race's advancement, the League thus had to protect Afro-Americans from their most vulnerable brethren.

Although the Urban League's efforts to elevate the standards of black renters relied more heavily on shaping tenants' behavior than on containing or eliminating them from their homes, the League's neighborhood work nonetheless reflected its anxieties about poor blacks, and migrants in particular. The Urban League's work in this regard ultimately revolved around efforts to establish social controls over the poor. To be sure, such endeavors were frequently benign. They were, nonetheless, indicative of the perceived threat to order posed by ghetto disorganization.

The Dunbar Apartments also reflected the class limits of the League's uplift approach. Like the League's community work, the apartments were intended to provide a socially salutary environment. To achieve this end, the project was designed not only to eliminate undesirable tenants but also to positively shape the character of its residents. By providing tenants with safe, clean housing, designers intended to instill residents with a sense of pride that was essential to the development of responsible renters. In the end, however, the Dunbar Apartments' efforts to improve Afro-American tenants' personal investment in their residences undermined its ability to meet the housing needs of the "small wage earner."

As was the case with the Urban League's job placement and labor programs, the compromises Leaguers worked out between Afro-American workers and capital in the realm of housing were often more advantageous to capital and the better-off blacks. In designing the Dunbar Apartments as a cooperative, Rockefeller provided many Afro-Americans a much sought after opportunity to own property. It also improved the stability of his investment, since tenants could use their equity toward fees during lean times. Though a mutually beneficial relationship at the surface, this arrangement was ultimately of greater benefit to the "better classes" of blacks, and perhaps to Mr. Rockefeller himself, than the average Harlemite.

Furthermore, the League's faith in the ability of the apartments to improve the general housing conditions in Harlem also reflected the limits of the group's philosophy. Leaguers believed that Dunbar would eventually improve the general quality of ghetto housing. First, Dunbar's success could inspire additional investment in Afro-American communities. If Rockefeller's venture proved profitable, other entrepreneurs might be inspired to construct good, affordable housing for black tenants. Second, the League contended that the mere existence of the Dunbar Apartments, providing clean and affordable housing complete with modern amenities, would encourage black renters to refuse to accept substandard accommodations. In the end, however, these assumptions were naive. Because of blacks' meager wages, the profit system was ultimately incapable of providing affordable housing for them. Consequently, only Harlem's better classes could afford these apartments.

3. Vocational Training, Employment, and Job Placements, 1910–1932

IF YOU DO WELL YOU WILL SERVE NOT ONLY YOURSELF BUT THE ENTIRE RACE.—Chicago Urban League, 1918

From its inception in 1910, the National League on Urban Conditions Among Negroes' vocational activities in New York attempted to impress upon Afro-Americans the opportunities afforded by vocational guidance and training. The League hoped to improve blacks' employment options by equipping them to work in more secure occupations, particularly in skilled trades. To ensure the proficient performance of the workers it assisted, the League used vocational guidance to direct applicants to the occupations that best suited their talents. In its first year of operation the NLUCAN's Committee for Improving Industrial Conditions of Negroes in New York (CIICN) posted openings for skilled mechanics, verified the references of prospective employees, and secured employment for workers meeting standards set by the League. By 1912 the League's Vocational Exchange opened a joint office with its housing bureau, providing references and serving as a clearinghouse for employment information. The CIICN also performed in-depth interviews of applicants, so that it might find jobs for "efficient and reliable workers."[1]

Industrial arts training naturally played a significant role in the League's vision of blacks' economic uplift. In addition to assisting in job searches for reliable workers, the League directed the less proficient to vocational and technical schools. By 1913 the NLUCAN extended its vocational work to schoolchildren, creating a guidance program for high school students that preached the value of the industrial arts.[2] That same year the League expanded its educational work with adults. In its efforts to improve the employment prospects of Afro-American men and women, the NLUCAN hired speakers and distributed literature urging Harlemites to enroll in public night school courses.[3]

Job placements were an important aspect of the NLUCAN's industrial work as such efforts were wed to its vocational activities. Since training was intended to improve Afro-Americans' employment opportunities, the League was compelled to assist blacks in finding jobs. The League therefore cultivated relationships with local businesses and worked in concert with private and public employment agencies. Yet in spite of the NLUCAN's many contacts, its placement efforts were not immediately rewarded. Although in its 1913–14 activity year the Urban League extended the scope of its job searches to a twenty-mile radius from New York City, it found work for only 181 of 800 black job seekers. The next year the League found jobs for just 308 of 1,557 applicants. During the NLUCAN's 1915–16 activity year, however, Afro-Americans' economic fortunes took a turn for the better. The League was able to place more than 1,300 workers in New York City, in a year when only 774 applied to the NLUCAN for assistance.[4]

Ironically, the League's inability to find jobs for a significant number of applicants actually strengthened its commitment to industrial arts training. In response to the economic downturn of 1914, the National League was instrumental in establishing five classes in household arts that served sixty-two young black women. That same year, in cooperation with the mayor's Unemployment Committee, the NLUCAN operated a workshop promoting skills and efficiency for nearly 800 idle workers.[5]

Ultimately the League's attachment to industrial arts training was rooted in its belief that demonstrations of Afro-Americans' competence in the workplace could mitigate or even eliminate race prejudice's impact on hiring decisions. Naturally, as a black uplift organization staffed largely by Afro-Americans, the basic assumption undergirding the League's philosophy was that the differences between blacks and whites were only skin deep. Leaguers believed that both black unemployment and poor job performance were the result not of innate racial differences but of some combination of environmental and economic factors. Presuming that capitalists were driven largely by their desire to increase productivity and profits, the League assumed that the efficient performance of black labor would eclipse employer race prejudice. Therefore, in certifying workers as "good industrial risks" and directing the less proficient to vocational training courses, the NLUCAN hoped to increase blacks' employment opportunities by convincing employers of Afro-American labor's malleability and productive potential.

The NLUCAN had some experiences with employers that supported the view that job proficiency would allow blacks to establish a foothold in certain industries and occupations. In 1915, for example, the National League capitalized on a springtime labor shortage in New England by supplying the

Connecticut Leaf Tobacco Association with "permanent Negro labor from New York City and [the] vicinity, and temporary harvest hands from Negro colleges and agricultural schools of the south." The League sent nearly 700 workers to the Hartford area, more than 200 of whom remained. By the end of the summer the Connecticut Leaf Tobacco company was so satisfied with the young men's performance that it anticipated utilizing the League's services the next year. The company asserted that the young men's "efficient and conscientious" work "won the approval of both the planters . . . and the members of the different communities which they have lived." This confirmed the League's assumption that job proficiency was essential to blacks' advancement in the workplace. The desire to assist Afro-Americans in adjusting to industrial dictates, combined with the fear that their poor performance on the job might reaffirm race prejudice led the National and local Leagues to identify vocational guidance as a crucial component of economic uplift.[6]

The League's decision to treat vocational guidance as a means of dispelling the belief in the innate inferiority of black labor was not without merit. Employers often justified the exclusion of black workers from industry on the grounds that Afro-Americans were less efficient than whites. Although much of the labor force segmentation experienced by blacks in the 1910s and 1920s was racially motivated, it was also true that migrants frequently possessed neither the training nor the experience needed to gain access to skilled occupations in the north. As many of the more recent social histories of the Great Migration have demonstrated, former farm hands often lacked industrial work habits, leading quite a few employers to charge that Afro-American workers were inattentive and prone to tardiness and absenteeism. Likewise, a large number of southern black professionals and skilled craftsmen were unable to pursue their chosen vocations in the north because of inadequate preparation.

But while the League's commitment to industrial arts training as a means of economic advancement was not unreasonable, in practice it reflected the organization's class biases and the inherent inability of vocational training to improve the lives of the poorest of the poor. The Urban League's decision to hinge blacks' economic advancement on the "respectable" job performance and behavior of Afro-American labor frequently had negative implications for the very people it purported to assist. This problem had already begun to manifest in the League's earliest vocational endeavors. In September of 1917, for example, the National Urban League utilized the services of the New York Police Department to assist its vocational training programs. In anticipation of the War Department's "work or fight" order, the League requested "the Police Department to assign two colored policemen to . . . [its] Harlem office to corral idle young men who were hanging around poolrooms and clubs and to send them to positions found for them through the League's employment service." The NUL continued this campaign for a period of ten weeks, which, it declared, "helped to clear the streets of Harlem of ruffians and dissolute women."[7]

Although the records do not divulge how the young men picked up by the police felt about their encounters with the NYPD and the League's vocational training sessions, it is unlikely they were appreciative. More importantly, this incident reveals that the League's vocational endeavors were infused with a desire to maintain social order. Leaguers ultimately perceived idle and unproductive workers as threats to the race's advancement. Bearing the imprint of ethnic cycle theory, the League's vocational and job placement work presumed that mutually satisfying interactions between employers and black workers to be an essential element of economic uplift. Leaguers thus feared that deviations from either employers' expectations or predominant values would sabotage economic progress. As a result, the vocational and job placement efforts proposed or managed by the Leagues of Chicago and New York frequently required the punishment or exclusion of workers who might undermine blacks' gains in industry.

Each local offers different insights into the tensions and constraints inherent to the League's vocational self-help programs. Chicago provides perspective on the League's work with industry, especially in regard to its advisory role to employers. More to the point, the Chicago Urban League demonstrates the difficulty the branch had in balancing the needs of employers with those of employees, forcing it to define the needs of workers in a way that disproportionately benefited employers. New York, on the other hand, offers a window into the League's vocational training endeavors and its interest in treating these programs as a form of industrial and civic socialization.[8] At the same time, the League's interest in industrial arts work had an intragroup class skew, as the New York branch was more interested in providing direct assistance to the better-trained workers.[9]

At the turn of the century, the majority of gainfully employed blacks in New York City worked as domestic and personal service workers. Prior to World War I, domestic and personal service work were the only fields in which Afro-Americans had gained a firm footing. Fully 70 percent of gainfully employed black men were engaged in these occupations as late as 1890. Over the next ten years the number of black men employed as domestic workers increased by 109 percent, compared with just 45 percent for white ethnics. Domestic and personal service work were even more important for black women; nearly

90 percent of them were employed in these fields in 1905.[10] By 1910, however, black men would begin to make significant gains in other fields.

While the proportion of black women employed as domestic and personal service workers increased in the decade after the turn of the century, by 1910 the number of black males employed in these occupations declined to about 50 percent. As domestic work became more important for black women during this period, the number of black men employed in industry increased from 7 percent to 14 percent. Between 1910 and 1920, the employment opportunities available to black New Yorkers increased even more significantly. In the space of a decade the proportion of Afro-American men employed in manufacturing and mechanical industries grew to 21 percent, while the number of black men employed as service workers dropped to 35 percent. More than 8 percent of gainfully employed Afro-American men worked as clerks, and another 7.9 percent worked as foremen or skilled workers.[11]

The economic advances made by Chicago's black residents were even more impressive than those made by their New York counterparts. In the years preceding the Great Migration, black Chicagoans were similarly underrepresented among the city's industrial employees. In 1900, nearly 65 percent of Chicago's Afro-American men and more than 80 percent of the city's Afro-American women were employed as domestics and personal servants. Only about 8 percent of working black men and fewer than 12 percent of black women were engaged in manufacturing. By 1910 the basic pattern remained the same as nearly half of gainfully employed black men worked as porters, servants, waiters, and janitors while more than 60 percent of the city's Afro-American women were employed as either domestic servants or laundresses. The First World War, however, bolstered Afro-Americans' employment prospects in the Windy City, as blacks were hired as laborers in a number of industries that had all but excluded them just a few years earlier.[12]

Between 1910 and 1920 the percentage of black male workers employed in Chicago's domestic and personal service trades fell from 51 percent to only 28 percent. At the same time, the percentage of black unskilled and semiskilled workers employed in manufacturing increased five- and tenfold, respectively, as Afro-Americans more than doubled their share of manufacturing jobs and tripled their representation in trade.[13] Most of the advancements in trade and manufacturing were made in the meatpacking and steel industries. By 1918, between ten and twelve thousand blacks worked in Chicago-area packinghouses. The number of Afro-Americans employed in the city's steel and iron industries increased from 220 in 1910 to 4,313 a decade later.[14] By 1920 blacks were employed in manufacturing and trade in Chicago at rates roughly equivalent to their proportion of the city's general population.[15] In only ten years factory work had replaced domestic and personal service as the most significant source of employment for black Chicagoans.[16]

But while World War I and the corresponding reduction of European immigration to the United States had greatly improved the opportunities available to Afro-Americans, their employment prospects were far from ideal. Blacks made few gains in skilled occupations and thus remained at the bottom of the employment ladder. In 1920 two-thirds of New York's gainfully employed Afro-Americans labored as unskilled workers. Although the city's black male workers made significant gains in industry, their concentration in unskilled positions left them with little income and highly susceptible to layoffs. Moreover, black women made far fewer advances in employment than their male counterparts and continued to depend largely on service work.[17]

Conditions in Chicago were no better. In 1910, blacks comprised roughly 2 percent of all of Chicago's manual laborers, about 20 percent of all domestic workers, and only .07 percent of white-collar workers. By 1920, they accounted for 6 percent of manual laborers, nearly a third of domestic workers, and just 1 percent of white-collar workers. More than half of the black men employed in Chicago-area manufacturing worked as unskilled laborers. Moreover, the gains Afro-American men made in trade were due primarily to their penetration of the stockyards, where they likewise tended to work as unskilled labor. Even in the transportation industry blacks were generally relegated to unskilled jobs in service or labor.[18]

The CUL's reports reveal less about its vocational training programs than the New York Urban League's do about theirs. The Chicago branch's records nonetheless offer useful insight into its efforts to improve working conditions in industry as well as the means by which it attempted to increase black productivity. Although its overarching aim was to improve Afro-Americans' economic condition by opening access to jobs that had previously been denied to them, the Chicago League believed that the education of both employers and their workers was essential to the task at hand. The League's industrial education program thus consisted of three major components. It promoted the use of black labor through the collection and dissemination of "facts" illustrating black workers' efficiency. It attempted to ensure the continued use of black labor through programs intended to reinforce Afro-Americans' competence in the workplace. And, as I discuss in Chapter 4, it advised black workers as to the practicality of unionization.

In order to gauge areas of both progress and continued discrimination, the Chicago League performed a number of surveys and investigations of the city's industrial and nonindustrial employers. The objective of these inquiries was to ascertain the general satisfaction with black labor and to compare Afro-Americans' proficiency with that of whites. Ultimately, the CUL treated its examinations of blacks' on-the-job experiences as a means of enhancing its own efficiency, since such data enabled the League to target its efforts to the most urgent tasks. As importantly, the Chicago branch intended to use its findings to demonstrate to employers the conditions that optimized black workers' productive capacities.

In the most detailed of such studies the League made a number of discoveries that offered grounds for optimism about Afro-Americans' prospects for the future while drawing attention to areas in desperate need of improvement. In a survey published in the Chicago Commission on Race Relations Report *The Negro in Chicago*, the CUL polled more than 100 area employers. In questioning businesses on Afro-Americans' efficiency, reliability, regularity, and rates of turnover, the League found that Chicago-area employers were generally satisfied with black labor. In fact, in all but one of the above categories of workplace achievement, the majority of employers interviewed indicated that blacks and whites performed equally well on the job. Still, the findings revealed one major problem. More often than not, employers asserted that turnover was greater among Afro-Americans than whites.[19] In response to these charges, the League looked to black workers.

Upon interviewing employees, the League found that no fewer than 10 percent of Afro-Americans in three different industries complained that their opportunities for advancement had been circumscribed by racist foremen. In comparing the data, the League observed at least a partial correlation between poor treatment from supervisors and blacks' higher attrition rate. The CUL concluded that Afro-Americans' inability to move up the occupational ladder engendered a sense of apathy that undermined their commitment to their jobs. Blacks' greater turnover, 70 percent as compared with just 14 percent for whites at one plant, was directly attributed to boredom and their lack of hope for improvement of status.[20]

By the 1920s the CUL devoted particular attention to the potential ramifications of workplace despair and ennui. In fact, the League's interest in combating this phenomenon was expressed plainly in its efforts to engineer mutually satisfactory relationships between employers and Afro-American workers. Like the New York and National Leagues, the Chicago organization was concerned that the race's progress might be hindered by the poor performance of inefficient and maladjusted individuals. In its 1920 report the CUL asserted that since black workers were "unused to the requirements of Northern industry, unaccustomed to going long distances to work, not knowing how to compute wages on the piece-work basis and skeptical of the attitude of their fellow white workers," it was essential that they receive "instruction, admonition and direction, lest their individual defects should be regarded as racial or constitutional failures." To prevent the conflation of individual shortcomings with racial characteristics, the League preached "the gospel of punctuality, regularity, and general efficiency" directly to black workers through vocational classes, lecture series, and even handbills.[21]

Because the League presumed that the poor performance of black workers stemmed from a combination of Afro-Americans' ignorance of industrial imperatives and employers' lack of understanding, it set out to foster mutual empathy in the workplace. The CUL thus attempted to bridge the gap between the expectations of employers and those of employees and achieve satisfactory workplace performance "by advising employers as to the best ways of using [Afro-Americans'] services, by interpreting to superintendents, foremen and bosses [black workers'] points of view, by insisting upon efficiency and proper conduct on the part of our workers, and by advising preparation for occupations which we anticipate finding for them from time to time."[22] But while the Chicago League attributed the problems many Afro-Americans had in "making the grade" in industry to a system that engendered misunderstanding on the part of employers and their workers, its emphasis on the potential threat inefficient blacks posed to collective progress often led it to propose and even manage programs that punished and/or contained those who failed to meet employers' standards. Perhaps the clearest example of this tendency is found in the CUL's work in the employment offices of some of the Windy City's industries.

In the 1920s the CUL managed to obtain direct influence over the hiring practices of several Chicago-area firms. League social workers were employed in the personnel departments of a number of employers and provided guidance to companies such as International Harvester, Deering Twine Works, McCormick, and Nachmann. In acquiring positions within such firms, the League was able to perform plant-specific surveys that ultimately allowed it to customize its efforts to improve both worker performance and employee-employer satisfaction. As would be expected, the CUL set out to increase black workers' productivity by improving working conditions and encouraging greater efficiency among Afro-American employees. Leaguers lectured foremen on the most effective techniques to handle black labor; they called for changes in wage scales; they worked to increase Afro-Americans' opportunities for advancement within the plant; and they provided guidelines that clearly defined workplace requirements and expectations for Afro-American workers.[23]

The outcomes of these efforts varied. In some instances the CUL was able to take direct action against abusive employers and supervisors who took advantage of black migrants' ignorance and vulnerability. To improve the work environment of one company, for example, the CUL successfully lobbied for the termination of a foreman who had explicitly stated his intentions to drive out Afro-American workers.[24] In a case where company executives complained that black women's productivity remained unsatisfactory even after a reasonable apprenticeship, the League's investigation concluded that employees failing to produce as much as whites complained of "sweatshop tactics." Although the records divulge little information about the conditions at that particular plant, in many such instances the CUL, in cooperation with the Women's Trade Union League, called for a minimum living wage.[25] But while the League's labor policies indicate an undeniable commitment to racial fair play, its efforts to combat prejudice through demonstrations of black workers' competence nonetheless had unfortunate implications when implemented at "the firm." Perhaps the best example of this is found in the pages of *Opportunity*.

In "Making Over Poor Workers," Urban Leaguer Helen Sayre described her efforts to bring the "practical operations [of] the League's plan of industrial adjustment of Negro labor" to Chicago's Nachmann Company. Nachmann employed several hundred black women in the production of automobile seat cushions; however, problems with Afro-American workers' output caused the company to raise the "very critical question" of whether to continue employing blacks.[26] After interviewing the plant's black employees, Ms. Sayre, who worked in Nachmann's Welfare Department, concluded that the continued use of Afro-American laborers required the adjustment of their attitudes: "The most important task, it seemed, was that of developing in the worker's mind her personal responsibility to become a regular and efficient employee and of showing her the requirements and standards of satisfactory service." Because workers were paid piece-rates, Sayre argued that improved efficiency would naturally result in increased wages. Reasoning that better pay would lead workers to be more interested in their personal productivity, Sayre urged the company to post the wage scales and the daily production rates of the plant's employees. Moreover, Sayre called for establishing a clear system of rules that would allow for the swift termination of the indifferent worker. The continued use of Afro-Americans, therefore, required that the League try to increase the worker's commitment to her employer while assisting the company in excluding those blacks who did not comply with its standards.[27]

Sayre's tautological identification of the attitudes of black workers as the source of discord and low productivity within the company legitimized Nachmann's mode of operation. She assumed that while employees may not have been interested in their work because of low wages, they received low wages because they were "indifferent." Thus the onus for improving conditions within the company rested squarely on the shoulders of the workers who needed first to prove their worth.

Nachmann was not an isolated case. The CUL's 1920 annual report noted that three firms with which the League maintained relationships threatened to fire black workers for inefficiency, particularly in the form of tardiness and irregular attendance. As with Nachmann, the Chicago League carefully selected replacements for the offenders, which the CUL claimed ultimately led the companies to retain their black workers. The Chicago group also frequently recommended that employers improve black workers' productivity through the use of piece-rate rather than daily or hourly wage scales. The CUL's acceptance of piecework at Nachmann and other plants and its recommendations to use it to increase efficiency, hold striking implications given workers' sentiments about such pay schemes.[28]

Piece-rates grew out of a range of industrial experiments developed in the late nineteenth century, including the cooperative movement and profit sharing, designed to improve workers' output by increasing their stake in production. In response to the ubiquitous labor unrest of the Gilded Age and Progressive Era, farsighted employers hoped to use such reforms to infuse the moral purpose of work that had characterized preindustrial notions of labor with the cold efficiency of industrial production. Yet while piecework's exponents lauded it for its supposed ability to transform workers from "wage servants into laborers free to set their own pace and their own rewards," as historian Daniel T. Rodgers points out, the primary impetus behind capitalists' desire to use this device was their belief that it sped up production. Ultimately, piecework represented employers' attempt to induce labor to embrace speedup, that is, increasing output without an increase in pay. Utilizing the expertise of either freelance or staff efficiency consultants, firms set production quotas corresponding to a sliding wage scale that offered greater payment to more productive employees. Ambitious workers who managed to exceed production norms and thus significantly increase their own wages soon found, however, that their gains were ephemeral, since manufacturers almost without exception cut pay rates when general output levels rose. As a consequence, workers experienced with piece-rates often resisted the system's pitfalls through collective slowdowns, unionization, and even sabotage.[29]

Although there is no way to determine exactly how black employees laboring under League-sanctioned piece-rates felt about these arrangements, there is some indirect evidence indicating Afro-American workers' displeasure. Nachmann's problems adjusting its employees to piecework were not unique. The Chicago League concluded that the difficulties one local lampshade company encountered finding skilled workers to operate power machines, stemmed in part from the "low rates paid for piece work." Because rates were so low that only "experienced and rapid workers [could] earn more than $18.00 or $20.00 per week," the plant generally attracted applicants of inferior quality. Unfortunately, the records do not divulge the CUL's response to this dilemma, though in light of its proposals to Nachmann, the League may have simply urged the lampshade company to adjust its piece-rates.[30] Nevertheless, it is clear that, even according to the Chicago League's own assessment, "experienced" workers were no less than apprehensive about working for the company's piece-wages. Considering workers' general sentiments about piece-rates, it is quite probable that they were aware of the intrinsic limitations of this wage arrangement.

In spite of the difficulties in adjusting workers to this wage system, piecework would have appealed to Urban Leaguers employed in the personnel departments of Chicago-area plants for two related reasons. First, as employees of firms such as Nachmann, company welfare workers were responsible for implementing strategies designed to maximize production while reducing labor costs. Although Leaguers employed in such capacities were not blindly committed to any one approach, they were on staff to ensure black workers' productivity. Piecework's pay scales, at least when introduced, gave employees incentive to work more diligently and efficiently while simultaneously meeting employers' demands for greater output and reduced labor costs. The League's embrace of piecework was in keeping with both the group's efforts to integrate the workplace through demonstrations of Afro-American labor's proficiency and its hope to foster a "harmony of interests" between employers and employees. Yet far from composing a mellifluous symphony of shared concerns, piecework's tendency toward speedup and downward revision of wages suggests that the melody and meter of this arrangement were orchestrated first and foremost for the needs of employers.

The second source of appeal is piecework's dependence on input from a burgeoning class of personnel managers. Piece-rates were determined by efficiency experts and fine-tuned by staff social workers employed in the newly established welfare departments of Progressive Era firms. The constant revision of rates provided a steady supply of work for personnel staff that justified the existence of the growing managerial bureaucracies created to support this exploitative wage system. While welfare office staffers surely did not view themselves as mere midwives of bureaucracy, as social workers employed to mediate class conflict they would have embraced the expansion of an employment structure predicated on the management of economic antagonism. At the same time, these bureaus provided one of the few professional outlets for

black social workers and other college-trained Afro-Americans; and as significantly, some of these firms provided the Chicago League with valuable funding. Thus Leaguers' ability to improve black workers' productive capacities
could serve as an employment and financial boon to black workers, Leaguers,
and the CUL itself. This is not to insinuate that Leaguers' efforts to engineer
mutually beneficial relationships between employers and their workers was
anything but sincere; however, it is likely that the CUL's connection to employers influenced how it defined these shared interests.

The League's emphasis on Afro-American workers' efficiency took on
greater importance through the 1920s because of the Chicago branch's diminishing ability to make job placements. During the First World War, the Chicago League played a significant role in finding employment for large numbers
of black workers. According to the Chicago Commission on Race Relations,
the League placed more than 14,000 Afro-Americans in Chicago-area plants in
1919 alone.[31] This trend continued through the first half of 1920, when the
Chicago League took credit for placing no fewer than 15,000 of the 25,000
people seeking employment. But while the CUL made an impressive number of
job placements during and immediately following World War I, the wartime
labor shortages that facilitated the League's ability to find employment for
Afro-Americans ended with the return of the doughboys.[32]

Throughout the 1920s, the CUL was unable to find employment for most
black job seekers visiting its placement office. The change in the occupational
prospects for Afro-Americans occurred abruptly. In its report for 1920 the CUL
complained that while the year began with an unprecedented demand for
unskilled and semiskilled labor, it closed with widespread unemployment.
Between November 1922 and October 1923, the Chicago League received
13,300 placement orders from prospective employers; it found jobs, however,
for only 11,644 workers out of a total applicant pool of 29,722. By the conclusion of the 1925–26 activity year the CUL received only 3,515 orders from
employers. For the 1926–27 activity year the total number of orders placed by
employers dropped to just 2,462, and the League found work for fewer than
half of its 5,820 new job applicants.[33] By the Depression the CUL's job placement work grew even more discouraging. Between October 1, 1930, and
September 30, 1931, a year that was so bad for the Chicago League that it could
not even afford to publish an annual report, it was able to place only 850 of the
5,879 men and women who applied for work. The next year, the League placed
fewer than 500 of the nearly 6,000 prospective workers seeking assistance.[34]

The postwar downturn profoundly altered the scope of the CUL's employment activities, if not its basic approach. In the first year that annual reports
are available, the year ending October 1917, the League stated that its efforts

to create openings for blacks in jobs that had previously been closed to them was of paramount importance.[35] In response to the slackening demand for black labor, however, the League ceased its attempts to create new positions for Afro-Americans in October 1920. By 1923 the CUL acknowledged that it had been able to make few openings for black workers in factories and industries that did not already employ Afro-Americans, a trend that persisted throughout the decade.[36]

Not surprisingly, the quality of placements the League made declined in step with quantity. Although the Chicago branch was able to place some 2,000 young black women as clerks and typists in 1920—the most ever for this better type of employment—by the second half of the year the League would have no such luck. At the same time, the CUL claimed that even black workers' attitudes had begun to change in response to the worsening conditions. It noted that while early in the year Afro-American women eschewed domestic work in favor of factory jobs, by year's end conditions had grown so desperate that they clamored for even household work.[37]

The changing employment structure's impact on black workers' attitudes greatly troubled the League. The Chicago organization, like the New York and National Leagues, attributed discontent in the factory and at home to maladjustment engendered by the mismatch of skills Afro-Americans possessed and opportunities available to them. Consequently, in spite of the fact that the League officially ceased its efforts to make placements in the better types of work, its interest in these occupations persisted. The Chicago branch expressed concern that Afro-American factory workers rarely acquired jobs as foremen and advanced only as far as gang supervisor—a job entailing few responsibilities.[38] Two years later the CUL was elated by the acquisition of three managerial positions at the Standard Oil Gas Company, but it voiced the need for blacks to work efficiently. Though the League was able to assist very few applicants in finding white-collar and skilled industrial jobs both during and prior to the 1920s, its continued interest in blacks' ability to acquire "the better jobs" was inextricably tied to its efforts to combat disorganization.

Because of gaps in the CUL's records, it is difficult to assess the practical effect of its commitment to the notion that vocational guidance could both counter widespread unemployment and mitigate the effects of the corresponding social disorganization. Therefore, to gain some insight into this issue, it is necessary to turn to the job placement and vocational guidance campaigns of the New York Urban League. The NYUL's records are not themselves without gaps. Although the New York Urban League was founded in 1919, its records as a separate branch do not begin until the mid-1920s.

Nevertheless, the NYUL's existing records do provide some useful clues into its views on the acculturating effects of vocational training as well as the implications of its continued interest in finding employment for skilled blacks.

Of the job placements made by the New York Urban League's Department of Industrial Relations between January and June of 1925, 70 percent were in domestic and personal service while only 1 percent were clerical. The New York organization's failure to place a significant number of black office workers was particularly disappointing, given that it, like the Chicago League, hoped to create job openings in fields where blacks had made few inroads.[39] While never losing sight of the broader economic forces at play, the League ultimately attributed the weakness of its employment program to the quality of black job seekers. The NYUL contended that its ability to find jobs for efficient Afro-Americans was undermined by the "unfavorable criticism arising from the placement" of applicants who failed to meet employers' standards. This matter was of special concern to the NYUL as it focused on finding jobs for skilled blacks in part to offset the shabby treatment they received from public and private employment agencies.[40]

In order to improve its ability to secure jobs for conscientious and well-trained Afro-Americans, the NYUL eventually set more stringent job placement standards. It thus reorganized its employment program, requiring "satisfactory references from applicants"; refusing "to place applicants in low paid jobs with long hours"; and referring "applicants for common labor and personal and domestic service to the state [employment] office." Even after it reorganized its program, the New York organization viewed domestic placements as a drain on its resources, so in March of 1926 the League officially discontinued its "Domestic Placement Work," allowing it to devote its full attention "to securing the better types of positions which have been denied to Negro Workers." The change in the character of the New York League's employment work was immediate. By the conclusion of 1926 the League made 906 placements in industrial and clerical or public jobs but only 59 in domestic and personal service. One year later the NYUL found work for more than a thousand of the 3,791 workers registering with its employment department, none of whom were domestic laborers.[41]

Although the New York League emphasized placements in the "better occupations" to broaden Afro-Americans' employment prospects, this decision reflects the League's occasional callousness to the needs of lower-class Afro-Americans. While public agencies could theoretically handle placements in household work, there were only a few free employment bureaus in New York City in this period. Adding insult to injury, in spite of the League's opposition, the State Industrial Commission closed its Harlem branch in

1921, thus leaving only one free employment office in Manhattan. The office was located on 46th Street, well beyond convenient walking distance from Harlem, making it difficult for the poorest blacks to utilize its services.[42]

It appears as well that the League's indifference to domestic labor was inextricably tied to its negative perception of the workers generally employed in this field prior to the Depression. One of its justifications for cutting back and eventually eliminating domestic placements was that since "the trend" was moving "away from domestic service of any sort" it would be "difficult to keep an intelligent and industrious type of Negro interested in domestic service" without reorganizing it "on some systematic basis."[43] Rather than attempting to reform the field, however, the League discontinued its domestic placements altogether just one year later. Since household workers were the least industrious and intelligent constituents of the working class, went the League's logic, they were less deserving of its assistance.[44]

The League's relative indifference to these workers is made all the more apparent by the fact that its interest in domestic and personal service work was rekindled only with the onset of the Depression, when urban blacks of all levels of training were over-represented among the nation's unemployed. By 1929 the Urban League estimated that some 300,000 Afro-American industrial workers had been laid off nationwide. Throughout the Depression the black unemployment rate in Harlem was estimated to have been between one and a half and three times that of whites. Consequently, personal service and domestic work became even more important to blacks. In 1930, 55 percent of Harlem's employed population worked in these fields. By 1931, the Urban League estimated that approximately 80 percent of New York's gainfully employed black men worked as personal service and domestic workers.[45]

In response to the desperate conditions catalyzed by the Depression, the League revisited the potential benefits of domestic employment; thus, in 1931 the NUL created the National Committee on Employer-Employee Relationships in the Home. The National Committee's interest in domestic placements stemmed directly from the fact that even Afro-Americans with specialized training were now forced into this line of work. It declared that since "many persons thrown out of work in other fields have potential or hidden skills which often could be utilized within the home," household employment might be used as a "partial solution for unemployment in other industries." The committee was troubled, however, by the failure of many of those experiencing "technological unemployment" to seek jobs as domestics. Attributing this tendency to the stigma accompanying paid domestic labor, the League finally began to reorganize and improve the nature of this work. The National Committee therefore called for improving working conditions through "reorganization of many households on a more impersonal and businesslike basis" while reeducating individual workers "who through specializing in too narrow skills and living too cramped a life have become blocked in their development and are unable to adapt themselves to their present situation."[46]

At the same time, in a related program, the New York Urban League was attempting to improve the quality of paid housework. In 1931, the NYUL declared that because the "depression has increased the competition for all jobs," whites were now seeking positions in personal service and domestic work. In order to offset the loss of these jobs, the NYUL set up classes "where employed workers may improve their efficiency and the unemployed may use their *enforced leisure* in making themselves more efficient for future jobs." Using the Dunbar Apartments as an emergency center for industrial arts training, the League provided classes in cooking, cleaning, and decorating, as well as courses on management, maintenance, and supervision of buildings. In return for the cheap labor the students provided for the Harlem apartment complex, the League certified those who managed to complete its courses as "good industrial risks."[47]

Although the reorganization of paid housework was clearly an important task, the timing of this laudable endeavor is indicative of the League's fears that the Depression might lead to social disorganization among skilled and middle-class Afro-Americans. Surely the less skilled Afro-Americans who allegedly comprised the bulk of workers employed in these fields prior to the stock market crash would have also appreciated reforms to paid housework. From the League's perspective, however, such changes to the character of domestic labor were not as important prior to the Depression because there was less at stake. The reforms to domestic work in this period were designed to combat the maladjustment resulting from skilled, or "industrious" and "intelligent," blacks being forced into jobs that were not "stimulating." Job dissatisfaction could lead to poor workplace performance, which might undermine blacks' attractiveness to employers while laying the foundation for criminal activity, immoral behavior, and even militant political activism.

Training sessions were therefore often intended to provide constructive outlets for the energies of unemployed Afro-Americans from all class backgrounds. Because of the massive unemployment accompanying the Depression, "idleness" was a major concern to the League. T. Arnold Hill, director of the NUL's Department of Industrial Relations, for example, likened it to a contagious disease, whose "germs attack strong work habits and change industry to indolence, ambition to complacency, and independent existence to acceptance of charity." For Leaguers such as Hill, the only way to cure ghetto social malaise was to treat the Depression as a laboratory for vocational guid-

Ira D. Reid (Photographs and Prints Division, Schomburg Center for Research in Black Culture, The New York Public Library, Astor, Lenox and Tilden Foundations)

ance and training.[48] The New York and National Urban Leagues' vocational work should be understood in this light.

In referring to unemployment as "enforced leisure," for example, the NYUL divulged its fear of the percussions of the "improper" use of free time. As Ira Reid, former head of the New York League's Department of Industrial Relations, argued in a 1932 article on black criminality, Depression-era unemployment left "the individual in idleness—with time to contact chronic idlers, to seek any amusement and excitement to avoid ennui or thought of future consequences, if he does not find work." Because "bad social and leisure habits show[ed] a high frequency" in this period, he asserted, "social emulation, improvident expenditure of leisure, commercialized vice, [and] leisure-class dictates" further complicated matters by "provid[ing] a much more dangerous and sordid motive for crimes against property in particular than simple hunger." Reid was worried that drunkenness, emotionalism, and gang activity might flourish under such circumstances, which he believed would be of particular concern for "a weak or highly suggestible individual."[49] Though Reid made no specific recommendation to rectify matters in this piece, the New York League's effort to combat "enforced leisure" through vocational training clearly represented its attempt to provide constructive outlets for the unemployed that would ensure their civic virtue.[50]

The 1931 New York Urban League report that described its vocational training for domestics echoed Reid's concerns about Afro-American crime. The NYUL claimed that Afro-Americans' inability to gain rewarding employment and their failure to take the initiative to shore up their own economic status led to illicit and/or immoral behavior. "The snatching of purses from passing automobiles, rent parties, and taking in lodgers are regarded as occupations of dignity compared to some of the methods resorted to in the struggle to make ends meet," the League argued. Compounding the problem, the New York branch asserted, "despair over the failure to balance one's budget" frequently led to "lowliness, hardships and suffering of almost indescribable proportions." Ironically, while the New York League's discussion of black criminality acknowledged the difficulties black men with even specialized training had in finding employment commensurate to their talents, its only suggestions for improving their economic standing in this report were the domestic training classes offered at the Dunbar Apartments and other types of vocational guidance.[51]

The social implications that the loss of domestic work to whites would have for middle-class blacks was also a major issue for Leaguers. In the October 1929 edition of *Opportunity*, T. Arnold Hill expressed concern that middle-class Afro-Americans were becoming numb to the illegal activities taking place within their communities. While crime was an ancient phenomenon, he declared, the "wanton bargaining of it with more or less approval by the better classes of Negroes [was] new." In listing the sources of the appeal of illicit deeds, he pointed to consumer culture, the "laxity of law enforcement," and "rebellion against restricted personal liberties." Speculating that lack of opportunity may be the ultimate root of criminality, Hill believed the future was bleak, especially given blacks' increasing dependence on domestic work. He concluded that if Afro-Americans were "driven to commit crime" because of poor employment opportunities, "the number of legal violations, with indications that malefaction is spreading to *all strata of society*, suggests that if the

Negro is to transfer from domestic and personal service, as he is rapidly being forced to do, to purveyors of illegal goods, his field will be a large one."[52]

The League likewise appears to have viewed industrial arts training as a hedge against both militant and radical political activity. T. Arnold Hill declared in a generally positive assessment of the "don't buy where you can't work campaigns" in 1930 that picketing for better jobs was not a panacea. He asserted that before any meaningful change in occupational status were to occur, Afro-Americans needed to adjust their own attitudes since the success of protest efforts ultimately hinged on blacks' willingness to first take greater care in their work.[53] In a February 1932 article, "After the Depression—What?" Hill observed that while agitation for collectivization was becoming commonplace, capitalism was nevertheless the economic and political system to which Afro-Americans had to accommodate. Though Hill did believe that some degree of economic planning would be necessary to counteract cyclical and seasonal unemployment, he held at present that "the Negro youth must plan his career more wisely" to combat constantly increasing job competition. Hill thus recommended that "more study is required to select a suitable vocation and more application to master it than heretofore." He concluded that regardless of the economic system under which one labored, proficient performance was essential. "Even in Russia," he said, "efficiency pays more."[54]

The allure of vocational training had as much to do with the League's faith in the ability of workplace competence to mitigate, or even eliminate, race prejudice as it did with social control. The League often referred to Depression-era job losses as "technological unemployment," indicating that adequate training might insulate workers from "idleness." Although this belief may have afforded the League some solace in that it granted Afro-Americans a sense of control over events that were in reality beyond them, it led Leaguers to occasional victim blaming. T. Arnold Hill's unwavering commitment to the notion that Afro-Americans' efficiency and reliability would be greatly improved by carefully matching workers to the jobs that best suited their dispositions, expectations, and skill levels led him to blame blacks for their own hardships. Though he believed that Afro-Americans' circumscribed opportunities played a major role in instances of poor performance on the job, he contended—even during the first few years of the Depression—that Afro-Americans bore some responsibility for employers' negative perceptions.

Hill also believed that blacks had neglected to take the initiative in their own economic uplift. In an article published a few months before the stock market crash, Hill claimed that the source of the growth in black unemployment had little to do with racism. After noting that Afro-American workers no longer sought jobs commensurate to their abilities and were now simply "endeavoring to hold the line against" white workers' attempts at making inroads on black jobs, Hill proposed that "the motivating influence behind these changes is economic rather than racial." He believed that the matter could be rectified by developing a "plan for the Negro's occupational future." Arguing that the poor economy precluded any significant assistance from employers, Hill asserted that "industrial uncertainty makes it incumbent upon the Negro that he do certain things for himself." He concluded that since blacks lacked access to apprenticeship programs, they should pursue training in the mechanical arts in colleges and trade schools. Yet Hill's faith in the ability of skills and adequate training to eclipse race prejudice was fanatical and unrealistic. His piece closed with the charge that the depth of blacks' economic woes was partially due to Afro-Americans' failure to turn near-monopolies in certain occupations into entrepreneurial endeavors. If Afro-Americans had taken advantage of their experience as "cooks, barbers, caterers, domestic service [workers], laundresses, hackmen, mechanics, tenant farmers, moulders, street pavers, cobblers and longshoremen," Hill asserted, there might now be a significant number of black "drayage corporations, laundry establishments, building contractors, engineers, landowners, manufacturers," etc.[55]

■ The impact of Afro-Americans' job proficiency on the League's ability to place significant numbers of workers is not altogether clear. The history of the CUL demonstrates that while the efficiency of specific workers at individual plants may have had some effect on an employer's decision to hire or keep black workers, the driving force behind both the League's ability to find industrial employment for Afro-Americans and employers' willingness to keep them on was the shortage of white labor in the 1910s. More importantly, the histories of both the New York and Chicago Leagues indicate that the League's defensive commitment to workplace respectability and its limited abilities to positively effect the lives of black workers often led it to engineer punitive programs.

In choosing vocational programs as a means to combat prejudice, the League faced conflicting goals. Officially, its vocational programs were chiefly concerned with improving blacks' employment options. Because League locals could do so only as long as they were able to ensure black labor's productivity, however, the Chicago branch, for example, often pursued policies that required the acculturation or termination of workers who did not measure up. Furthermore, in order for the League to maintain relationships with employers that would allow it to find work for industrious and conscientious workers, it was forced to define ideal working conditions in a fashion that benefited employers disproportionately.

Similarly, since Leaguers believed that assimilation into mainstream society required that Afro-Americans accept predominant values and habits, the League needed to impart proper behavior to blacks. Vocational training was a major component of this program. The League viewed industrial arts as a means to enhance blacks' human capital as well as to assist in the acculturation of Afro-American workers to northern industrial and civil society. Because environmental factors were believed to have been the source of both inefficiency and social disorganization—including criminality, delinquency, and even political militancy—the League hoped to use vocational training not only to promote workplace proficiency but also to provide wholesome outlets for restless minds.

4. Labor Unions, Social Reorganization, and the Acculturation of Black Workers, 1910–1932

Isolation of Social Groups makes possible the development of Special and Uncorrected group opinions, beliefs, traditions, and antagonisms.
—Charles S. Johnson, associate executive secretary of the Chicago Commission on Race Relations, n.d.

Like its work in the fields of housing and job placement, the Urban League's interest in organized labor was consistent with a general desire to shape the behavior and attitudes of black workers. Although the Urban League left little doubt that it perceived unions as vehicles through which to improve Afro-American workers' wages, this chapter advances the view that Leaguers also conceived of the union movement as a means of reorganizing the lives of Afro-American workers while simultaneously promoting racial amity. In particular, many Urban Leaguers believed that Afro-Americans' involvement with unions could enhance job performance, reduce racial tensions, and fortify black workers' commitment to mainstream political institutions. Ultimately, these three principles influenced the League's desire to affiliate with the American Federation of Labor (AFL) and the union movement in general, and are thus essential to understanding both the Urban League's work with unions and its efforts to adjust black workers to urban life.

■ Within three years of its founding, the Urban League expressed interest in coordinating activities with the American Federation of Labor. In an appearance before the AFL's executive council in 1913, George E. Haynes, the League's executive secretary, declared the importance of educating blacks "in the correct ideas of the underlying principles of organized labor." First and foremost, Haynes believed that Afro-Americans needed to be disabused of the notion that labor unions were not interested in them. Aware of the discriminatory practices of many Federation locals and the difficulty inherent to interracial unionism, however, Haynes adopted a realistic if not conciliatory posture. Although he asserted the need for blacks to join white unions wherever possible, he was willing to accept the idea of separate black locals provided they were afforded "full privileges and rights of representation in the central councils and in the National convention." Haynes's willingness to tolerate Jim Crow unions under such circumstances was illustrative of the League's growing regard for organized labor.[1]

Despite the Urban League's avowed support for the union movement, the AFL refused to devote special attention to attracting "the Negro." Instead, AFL president Samuel Gompers asserted that black recruitment would not be distinguished from the Federation's general efforts to organize those unfamiliar with the benefits of collective bargaining. In itself, this attitude may not have seemed unreasonable. The AFL had for many years declared its desire to organize workers regardless of color. At its 1890 convention, the Federation recorded its opposition to racial bars in unions. Three years later, it reaffirmed this commitment by asserting the labor movement's belief in the principle of organizing workers regardless of creed, color, sex, nationality, or politics. In practice, however, the Federation's egalitarianism would prove to be little more than rhetoric. This was most clearly evinced by the AFL's 1902 constitution, which permitted the issuance of separate charters to all black unions, thus resulting in Afro-Americans' exclusion from all but impotent organizations.[2]

Although the Federation failed to create the necessary organizational apparatus to attract black labor, Haynes's meeting with the AFL did offer cause for optimism. Most significantly, the Federation council stated its desire to cooperate with the Urban League. Moreover, the AFL employed three black organizers between 1910 and 1914, and each of the its conventions between 1916 and 1919 endorsed the principle of organizing blacks. Ultimately, the Great Migration had forced the American Federation of Labor to devote at least some attention to the Negro question.[3]

By the late 1910s, the National Urban League's interest in black participation in the trade union movement manifested in official policy. At its 1918 "Negro in Industry" conference, the NUL explicitly encouraged blacks to affiliate with the AFL. One year later, the League declared its belief in both the "principle of collective bargaining" and "the theory of cooperation between capital and labor in the settlement of industrial disputes and in the management of industry." Echoing sentiments voiced by Haynes several years earlier, the League not only expressed its preference for interracial unionism, but it also recommended that blacks form separate organizations whenever appropriate. The NUL, moreover, responded to white labor's charges that blacks were a "scab race" by urging Afro-Americans to take jobs as strikebreakers only when the unions involved excluded them. Afro-Americans "should keep out of jobs offered in a struggle to deny labor a voice in the regulation of conditions under which it works," the NUL argued, asserting that blacks "should begin to think more and more in terms of labor-group movements, so as ultimately to reap the benefit of thinking in unison."[4]

The NUL's executive secretary, Eugene K. Jones, ultimately intended to reorganize the League's activities to emphasize the elevation of black industrial workers. Asserting that "the greatest problem that America has attempted to solve is the adjustment of labor in its relation to capital," Jones believed that the condition of Afro-American workers warranted special attention. In 1919, he urged the NUL's board of directors to create a position devoted to the study and improvement of the industrial conditions of Negroes. To achieve this end, Jones argued, the League's industrial endeavors should take place on multiple fronts. He called for efforts to change the psychology of both southern blacks and white workers, as well as for projects that would foster greater empathy between employers and employees. Perhaps most significantly, Jones called for using this position to increase black involvement in the trade union movement.[5]

By the mid-1920s the National Urban League's operational structure reflected its growing interest in the organization of black labor. In 1923 Eugene K. Jones solicited financial assistance from John D. Rockefeller Jr. in order to establish a separate Department of Industrial Relations. Jones believed the League's industrial department should be organized around three major tasks: standardizing and coordinating activities with local employment agencies; encouraging industrialists to employ blacks and to stimulate efficiency among Afro-American workers; and, finally, working directly with organized labor to support black involvement in the union movement. While Rockefeller was immediately receptive to the NUL's desire to devote special attention to the problems Afro-Americans faced in industry, he was less enthusiastic about Jones's call to stimulate black participation in labor unions. The philanthropist therefore agreed to provide financial support for the new department in 1924 only if the League eliminated the provision encouraging black unionism. Instead, Rockefeller urged the NUL to embark on what was in effect a more adventurous job placement program.[6]

Though the Urban League initially followed Rockefeller's directive, its Department of Industrial Relations, under T. Arnold Hill's leadership, reinstated its official support for organized labor in 1925. Hill had been a proponent of unionization during his tenure as executive secretary of the Chicago League. As director of the NUL's industrial relations department, Hill ignored Rockefeller's proscription and pushed the League to promote black unionism.[7] Indeed, in his second year as head of the industrial relations department, Hill launched an aggressive initiative that expanded the purview of the NUL's industrial work. In addition to the League's general efforts to improve Afro-Americans' employment opportunities, the department launched industrial campaigns in three cities; it put together a national survey on the status of black labor; it cooperated with the Workers' Education Bureau to improve black laborers' job preparation; and, most importantly, it worked with trade union organizations to increase black membership.[8]

T. Arnold Hill's decision to endorse black participation in the labor movement reflected a shift in the NUL's industrial activities. The League's willingness to risk offending one of its most important benefactors was illustrative of its deepening commitment to organized labor. Under Hill, in fact, the League's Department of Industrial Relations made trade unionism its chief priority, while industrial campaigns—vocational guidance, job preparation, etc.—became secondary issues.[9]

The NUL's increasing involvement with the trade union movement has a number of important implications. Historian Nancy Weiss has argued that the Urban League's work with the AFL was indicative less of a profound commitment to collective bargaining than of expediency. Skilled workers had greater job security and pay than unskilled laborers. For Weiss, trade unionism was but one of the League's endeavors to expand blacks' economic horizons. Because craft unions represented some of the largest and most important skilled occupations, Leaguers reasoned that black participation in the labor movement might offer access to new and better sources of employment. Weiss thus contends that the chief impetus behind the League's union drives in the 1910s and 1920s was its desire to treat participation in organized labor as a means of improving blacks' employment prospects.[10]

Although "expediency" undoubtedly accounts for much of the union movement's appeal to the League, two factors undermine this as a complete explanation. First, Leaguers were most interested in the AFL, and organized labor in general, at a point when the Federation appeared moribund. When the NUL made its initial serious overtures to the AFL during World War I, the great craft union was growing in national prominence. Wartime demand and the corresponding increase in profits allowed the AFL to secure nominal acceptance from government and business. Most impressively, Federation officials voiced workers' concerns through the National War Labor Board, affording them influence over labor disputes and work standards in a number of industries. The AFL's new legitimacy bolstered its membership, which accounted for more than three million of some five million union workers at war's end.

Yet because these gains hinged on the unique conditions of the war effort, they were ephemeral.[11]

Shortsighted leadership, welfare capitalism, company unions, and postwar labor surpluses all but precluded the Federation's continued success during the Roaring Twenties. Perhaps most importantly, capital's hostility toward organized labor immediately following the First World War led to the development of an aggressive antiunion campaign, known as the "American Plan," intended to roll back the advances labor made during the war. Manufacturers were especially antagonistic to the closed shop, which they attempted to abolish through repression and a propaganda machine that propagated the notion that unions were subversive and undemocratic.

In the end, the American Plan and welfare capitalism won. Between 1919 and 1922 some eight million workers went out on strike; although some of these efforts were successful, most were abysmal failures. Walkouts were suppressed across the land, and the federal government generally weighed in on the side of employers. The trade union movement was thus backed into a defensive strategy that merely sought to maintain the ground that it had won during World War I. Consequently, the number of strikes between 1920 and 1930 dropped sharply from a peak of about twelve per 100,000 nonagricultural workers to just under two. Union membership witnessed a corresponding decrease of about two million workers between 1919 and 1929.[12] The creation of the NUL's Department of Industrial Relations and the reorganization of its activities to encourage black unionism thus took place during the labor movement's nadir. Given the Federation's diminishing stature, it is unlikely that Leaguers would have been attracted to its brand of unionism simply for the sake of expediency.

The second factor undermining opportunism as the full explanation for the League's interest in the Federation is that the Urban League consistently called for major reform within the AFL. In addition to attempting to increase black representation among Federation unions, the NUL hoped to convince the AFL to revise its basic philosophy. Throughout the 1910s and 1920s, the League implored Samuel Gompers and his successor, William Green, to extend the AFL's scope beyond skilled craftsmen to include unskilled labor. In the 1920s, Urban Leaguers, pointing to the AFL's shrinking membership, argued that the Federation's pursuit of craft unionism was myopic, for the trend in industry was toward the de-skilling of labor. Therefore, they reasoned, organizing unskilled workers would prepare the AFL for the future.[13] Although the Urban League was clear that its interest in industrial unionism stemmed, at least in part, from the fact that the majority of black workers were employed as mere laborers, the effort and time needed to reorganize the Federation's work indicate a more complicated commitment to unionism than can be explained by mere expediency.

In addition to viewing participation in the trade union movement as a means of improving Afro-Americans' job opportunities, many Leaguers believed organized labor offered a potent means of adjusting the attitudes of black and white workers. As with vocational guidance, unionization, particularly affiliation with the American Federation of Labor, held the potential to equip Afro-Americans with the social checks and skills that individuals and the race needed to flourish in industrial society. The Urban League and the AFL shared the view that unions could improve job performance, reduce racial tensions, and provide practical outlets for workers stirred to radical political activism. The union movement thus provided the League another tool to aid its efforts to reorganize the unraveling social structure of black urban life.

The League first alluded to the socializing function of unions in its third year. In one of its earliest expressions of support for labor, it asserted that unions might, in some instances, improve blacks' job performance and character. In its 1912–13 activity year, the National League for Urban Conditions Among Negroes declared that the organization of workers in various occupations was one of its primary goals in the city of New York. Rather than reflecting an aggressive prolabor stance, however, the League's initial interest in unionization seems to have been grounded in concerns similar to those undergirding its vocational training endeavors. The NLUCAN claimed that organized labor benefited both employees and the general public, arguing that unionization "raised the standards of efficiency and reliability of workers, thus protecting the public from unscrupulous workers." The League's support for organizations representing the elevatormen and hallsmen in this period, therefore, placed at least as much emphasis on these unions' potential to raise the standards of the men who entered these vocations as it did the organizations' abilities "to render the conditions under which [their members] live more favorable."[14]

The Urban League's emphasis on unionism's acculturating properties may be partly attributable to the necessity of justifying its work with organized labor to its benefactors. In light of the NUL's experience with John D. Rockefeller Jr. just a decade later, fear of offending donors may have influenced its views on unions in this instance.[15] Nevertheless, the League's interest in the acculturating effects of unions was not simply an attempt to appease benefactors but rather a reflection of the reform impulses of its day.

The union movement's potential to enhance worker productivity and integrity was shared by both white reformers and the American Federation of

Labor. Among middle-class activists, social workers and settlement house residents were especially active in support of the union movement. Jane Addams, who was an original member of the Chicago Urban League, advocated unionism because she believed that collective bargaining could improve both working conditions and the integrity of workers.[16] Indeed, social workers and Progressive Era reformers frequently asserted that unions' emphasis on group action and education could improve workers' efficiency, sense of self, and use of free time.[17]

Organized labor expressed similar sentiments. As labor historian David Brody has argued, the Progressive Era "craft identity" contained a significant social component. Samuel Gompers held that unionization improved workers' standards and could even be utilized to enhance efficiency. Naturally the platforms of many Federation locals embodied these sentiments. Believing the "good reputation" of industrious craft workers was threatened by the bad habits of a few, the opening convention of the International Association of Machinists attempted to bring together craft workers of "honorable, industrious and sober habits." The constitution of the Brotherhood of Locomotive Engineers reflected a similar interest in the character of its members, as it compelled locals to expel any member who "conducted himself in a manner unbecoming to a man." Other craft unions also promoted the wholesome use of leisure time, which would enhance the personal growth of their members.[18]

Although it is unclear whether the League continued to view unions as a means of improving black productivity through the 1920s, the socializing effects of unionization remained a factor in Urban League policy. Its embrace of ethnic cycle theory would ultimately lead a number of prominent League staffers to perceive unionization as a means of promoting amicable race relations. One of the earliest examples of Leaguers' efforts to treat participation in the union movement as a means of improving race relations can be found in the work of the Chicago Urban League. The CUL was by no means an ardent proponent of unionism. In fact, its involvement with organized labor was characterized largely by circumspection and even antagonism. Nevertheless, some prominent CUL members expressed interest in using unions as a means of fostering interracial harmony. Its history, therefore, offers some insight into the complexity of the League's relationship with white labor, capital, and black workers.

Following the riots in the summer of 1919, the Chicago Urban League voiced concern regarding the ramifications of racial tensions on the job. The Chicago branch believed support from industry owners and foremen was essential to achieving harmonious race relations in the workplace. Vocational guidance and the establishment of personal relationships with employers were crucial components of this campaign. In the Chicago League's first few years, however, its leadership also flirted with the development of interracial job consciousness as a facet of this project. Indeed, shortly following his departure from the CUL, Charles S. Johnson would assert that the class status of the majority of Afro-Americans made alliances with employers less useful than harmonious relations with white workers.[19]

Though the clearest discussion of the connection between racial tensions and union and employment practices was articulated in the work of the Chicago Commission on Race Relations (CCRR), the commission's conclusions provide a window onto how some CUL staffers viewed this issue. The CCRR not only relied heavily on data compiled by the Chicago Urban League, but Charles S. Johnson organized the commission's reports on the sources of racial unrest within the city. In fact, Johnson took leave from his position as CUL's secretary of research to serve as the commission's associate executive secretary. As one of the report's two principal authors, Johnson played a crucial role in shaping the CCRR's findings. Though the commission conferred the title of executive secretary to Graham Romeyn Taylor, a white urban reformer and settlement house worker, Johnson, Taylor's widow acknowledged, "actually 'set up the study' and was by far the stronger researcher of the two men."[20] The importance of Johnson's influence is further illustrated by the continuities between his own analysis of ghetto unrest and the CCRR's. Indeed, a number of Johnson's essays called for combating the social disorganization plaguing ghetto communities through the creation of organized outlets for Afro-Americans, including union participation. Given the similarity in themes between Johnson's work and commission's, the latter's analysis offers important insights into the views of at least one prominent Urban Leaguer regarding unionization and uplift.[21]

Drawing from ethnic cycle theory, CUL staffers and other Chicago-area reformers argued that conflicts between Afro-Americans and whites were the result of misunderstandings brought about by the separation of the races. In a report drafted for the National Urban League regarding the Chicago riot of 1919, Johnson argued that "race riots between Negroes and whites" were essentially "acute symptoms of the atrophy of the structure supporting their relations with each other." Johnson ultimately believed that racism stemmed from ignorance and misunderstanding brought about by a lack of consistent interaction between blacks and whites. "Isolation of social groups," he asserted, "makes possible the development of special and uncorrected group opinions, beliefs, traditions and even antagonisms." Believing that racial conflicts were the result of Afro-Americans' and whites' separation from "ordinary occasions for contact," Johnson argued that racial amity could best be

Charles S. Johnson, circa 1938 (John Hope and Aurelia Elizabeth
Franklin Library, Fisk University)

achieved through a combination of "directed contacts and the full and frank
dissemination of information." Only by smashing "the barriers of physical and
spiritual isolation," he declared, would blacks and whites "come to recognize
each other as human beings and brothers."[22]

Although workplace matters were not the primary focus of Johnson's report to the NUL, the Chicago Commission on Race Relations drew similar
connections between racial amity and interracial contacts engendered by job
experiences and union affiliation. In a discussion of sources of racial tensions
within the city, the CCRR asserted that increased job competition might
heighten "the self-interest of white workers" and "cause them to resent the
presence of Negro workers." Remaining optimistic, the commission noted
that an integrated workforce would eventually reduce the significance and
prevalence of racial animosities. The commission asserted that shared job
experiences offered the potential to undermine racial stereotypes and demon-

strate blacks' humanity. "Through contact and association with Negroes during working hours," the CCRR argued, "white workers may come to look upon Negroes, not as members of a strange group with colored skin, but as individuals with the same feelings, hopes, and disappointments as other people."[23] However, since racism often kept black and white workers apart, both in their neighborhoods and at work, valuable opportunities to develop mutual empathy were lost.[24]

Leaguers such as Johnson and T. Arnold Hill understood that integrationism necessarily entailed disabusing white workers of their visceral prejudices. Unfortunately, this task was complicated by job discrimination and labor market segmentation. Treating blacks as a reserve army of labor, employers often used Afro-American hires to undercut the bargaining strength of white unionists, thus laying fertile ground for racial conflict within the workplace. Perhaps no two conventions played on white workers' prejudices more than the dual wage structure and employers' use of black strikebreakers. The League was especially concerned about the former, viewing the practice of hiring Afro-American workers at lower pay than whites as a major impediment to harmonious race relations. Firms often justified pay inequality on the grounds that white workers had greater experience, superior skills, and job seniority. Although the CUL conceded that poor training and job performance frequently undermined blacks' earnings, it believed that race prejudice was to blame as well.[25]

The Chicago Urban League could not determine the extent to which blacks were victimized by two-tiered wage scales; however, anecdotal evidence indicates the pervasiveness of pay inequality. A number of light-skinned blacks, for example, reported to the CUL that they had been mistaken for white and were hired for greater pay than other Afro-Americans employed in similar work at the same plants. The CUL was likewise inundated with complaints of sweatshop tactics in the needle trades, which were infamous for their refusals to pay "colored workers a wage equal to that of white[s]." On rare occasions, the CUL noted, dual wage structures could work to blacks' advantage. Indeed, in one unusual instance, a manager of an unnamed company informed the League "that the colored girls employed in their South Side Branch Office started at a wage in excess of that given to white girls for similar work in their main office."[26]

Occasional advantages notwithstanding, Leaguers ultimately believed that pay disparities were detrimental to both black and white workers. Depressed wages frustrated Afro-Americans' ability to establish stable home lives, forcing some into questionable activities that undermined the character and integrity of ghetto communities.[27] Racially differentiated wages, moreover, strained race relations. The practice of paying Afro-Americans less than pre-vailing rates exerted downward pressure on white workers' earnings since employers frequently used the threat of black replacement workers as lever-age in union negotiations, creating volatile rifts between black and white workers. In the wake of the 1919 race riot, the CUL had reason to be concerned about the tensions engendered by pay inequities. Citing the research of the Chicago Urban League, the CCRR asserted, "To the extent that Negro labor is being used to undermine wage standards, misunderstanding and race friction develop." Although the upheaval in Chicago was not directly inspired by concurrent labor disputes, workplace unrest had contributed to a number of riots across the country, including the recent conflagration in East St. Louis. Moreover, the history of labor turmoil in Chicago's meatpacking, steel, and railroad industries demonstrated the potential for racial strife in the Windy City's many industries. In order to reduce the chance of racial hostilities at work and at home, the League therefore called for equal pay for equal work.[28]

Interracial unions ultimately provided vehicles through which to achieve both parity in pay and peace. The Chicago Commission on Race Relations charged that Jim Crow unions were less capable of fostering these ends, since they were created under circumstances that undermined efforts to shore up race relations. Because separate Afro-American locals were generally orga-nized in response to blacks' exclusion from white organizations, they gener-ally engendered resentment and pitted Afro-American and white workers against each other. By contrast, the commission claimed, "wherever and whenever Negroes are admitted on an equal basis and given a square deal the feeling inside the union is nearly always harmonious."[29] Although the Chicago Urban League acknowledged that employers sometimes refused to hire black unionists at "white men's wages," union jobs were still less likely to be subject to pay disparities. Thus the CUL reported that "no complaint has come to our attention of inequality of wages in union shops employing white and colored workers."[30]

The Chicago League had some evidence that an integrated workforce could foster racial amity. The CCRR reported that there had been only one "serious case of violence in the Stockyards" during the 1919 riots. Fellowship between black and white workers appeared to have much to do with the peace within the packinghouse district. Stockyard employers informed the commission that far from expressing hostility, white yard workers were largely sympa-thetic to their black colleagues during the upheaval.[31] This was significant because the packinghouses were home to one of the most diverse labor forces in the city, and blacks were a major presence in the yards. Between 1909 and 1920 the percentage of Afro-American packinghouse workers in Chicago ballooned from just 3 percent to about 25 percent. By 1928, nearly 30 percent of Chicago's packinghouse workers were black.[32]

The findings likewise suggested that the union movement contributed to the relative peace in Chicago's slaughterhouse district. The CCRR noted that earlier in the century the stockyards were witness to intense racial and economic strife. In 1904, packinghouse employers used hundreds of Afro-Americans to break a major strike. Though the majority of strikebreakers were white, packinghouse owners flaunted the use of Afro-Americans, who were barred from the packinghouse union. According to the CCRR, this experience led the Amalgamated Meat Cutters and Butchers Union (AMC) to begin efforts, in 1917, to attract black workers. Black membership increased steadily over the next year and a half, and by 1919, Local 651, a black affiliate, claimed that 60 percent of Chicago's Afro-American packinghouse workers were unionized. Ultimately, the CCRR claimed, the union's endeavors to organize Afro-Americans had largely eliminated the antagonistic feelings that characterized the yards during the 1904 strike. Moreover, by connecting blacks' increasing presence within the AMC to a general sense of fellowship among workers, the commission implied that the union drive played a role in curbing mob violence during the riot.[33]

Interestingly, the Chicago Commission on Race Relations exaggerated both the extent to which the yards were spared from mob activity and the AMC's role in organizing black workers. In actuality, the packinghouse district had been the site of 41 percent of the clashes during the 1919 riot, as opposed to just a single assault.[34] Furthermore, while Local 651 was affiliated with the Amalgamated Meat Cutters union, the militant Stockyard Labor Council (SLC), of which the AMC was a reluctant member, initiated the drive to recruit Afro-American labor.[35] Nevertheless, the commission's allusion to organized labor's stabilizing influence on race relations had some basis in reality.

Beginning in 1917, the SLC undertook the daunting, but necessary, task of organizing Afro-American workers. The campaign was a modest success, and eventually led to the creation of two black locals, AMC Locals 651 and 213. The two-year-long drive was anything but a model of racial camaraderie, however, and was beset by a number of minor conflicts arising from white racism and blacks' apprehensions about collective bargaining.[36] Nevertheless, by the time of the riots, the Stockyard Labor Council's emphasis on interracial working-class solidarity made it one of the most active and effective agents of peace. Following the initial wave of assaults on July 27, 1919, the SLC immediately set out to shore up race relations in the yards. Shortly after the riots began, the SLC's leadership asserted that white workers' response to the upheaval would determine "whether colored workers are to continue to come into the labor movement or whether they are going to feel . . . abandoned by it and lose confidence in it." The SLC, therefore, urged its members to refrain from the assaults against Afro-Americans and to assist blacks wherever possible in escaping mob violence.[37]

Over the first few days of rioting, the Stockyard Labor Council's calls for peace appeared to have been well received. Although a number of racial clashes took place in Packingtown, most of the assaults in Back of the Yards, the residential community in the stockyard district, were at the hands not of unionists but Irish street gangs. Furthermore, in several instances, unionists played a proactive role in curbing violence by shielding blacks from angry mobs. Just one week after the riots began, however, the SLC's endeavors to bolster stockyard solidarity succumbed to the flames of hatred and prejudice. The union's success in soothing racial tensions ended on August 2, when arsonists torched forty-nine buildings in a Lithuanian enclave in Back of the Yards. While post-riot investigations determined Irish gangs were responsible, residents immediately blamed vengeful blacks. The immigrant press and community leaders turned against Afro-Americans as quickly as they had come to their aid, and blacks were the targets of violence in the yards.[38]

Hostilities were further exacerbated when racial conflict spilled over into labor relations. The growing tensions within the yards inspired management to seize the opportunity to undermine the packinghouse union movement. On August 8, stockyard owners tried to put an end to the union's call for a closed shop by bringing in nonunion black labor under military escort. Incensed by both the owners' decision to circumvent established mediation channels and the specter of race conflict within the yards, the SLC went on strike. Although by going on strike the SLC helped avoid a race riot at the plant, the situation deteriorated rapidly. Since the walkout violated a no-strike agreement, several hundred unionists, including a number of loyal Afro-Americans, were terminated. At the same time, the more conservative AMC effectively severed its ties to the Stockyard Labor Council, leaving it and many foreign-born workers to fend for themselves. Friction with management and the AMC soon destroyed the SLC, allowing the AMC to represent yard workers on its own.[39]

The events of August 1919 illustrated the difficulties unions faced in both promoting interracial solidarity and maintaining equanimity. Moreover, as the racial conflicts in the yards grew to influence the relationship between management and workers, the turmoil also exposed the limits of the Chicago Urban League's use for organized labor. The League's treatment of strike-breaking in this period, which it had previously identified as the second major source of tension between black and white workers, is of particular interest.

Early in its existence, the CUL acknowledged that the employment of black strikebreakers often led to turmoil at plants caught up in labor disputes. Indeed, under T. Arnold Hill's leadership, the CUL initially urged Afro-Americans to "scab" only when the striking unions discriminated against blacks. Inspired perhaps in part by the AMC's reluctant embrace of black labor, in the post-riot years the Chicago branch assisted management in its efforts to destroy the union.

Operating with a more conservative approach, the Amalgamated Meat Cutters alienated itself from the mass of unskilled foreign-born whites. Moreover, while the AMC made some haphazard efforts to strengthen Local 651, these were empty gestures. As labor historian Rick Halpern has demonstrated, the AMC's myopic approach to organizing ultimately resulted in the demise of the stockyard union movement. Between 1919 and 1921, the packinghouse district was at the epicenter of a bitter contest between management and the Amalgamated. The struggle was finally resolved in December 1921, with the failure of a major AMC walkout. Bolstered by both the high unemployment of that year and the Amalgamated's indifference to black workers, employers had little difficulty attracting Afro-Americans willing to cross picket lines. Further sowing the seeds of dissension, roughly half the strikebreakers employed by packinghouses were black. By 1922, the AMC was destroyed by scabs, company unions, coercion, and its poor relationship with the black community.[40]

During the stockyard strikes of 1921, the Chicago League continued to place blacks in the packinghouses. In fact, the CUL supplied many of the workers used to break the AMC strike.[41] The Chicago Urban League's decision to intervene on the part of employers stemmed partially from the urgency of blacks' economic circumstances. Facing sharp declines in job placements in its 1919–20 activity year, the CUL identified strikebreaking as an important entrée into industrial and commercial employment.[42] As a result, the Chicago branch eventually reassessed its strikebreaking policy. While the League had initially discouraged Afro-Americans from crossing the picket lines of unions that were open to blacks, by 1920 the Chicago group declared that it would base its decision to place strikebreakers not on union policy but on employer hiring practices. The CUL thus announced that it would assist firms in acquiring replacement workers provided the employer had previously demonstrated a willingness to hire black workers.[43]

The League's relationship with local business interests further undermined the Chicago branch's development of a firm commitment to organized labor. Stockyard companies contributed significantly to League coffers during the peak period of labor unrest. As early as 1919, grants from meatpacking interests comprised twenty percent, or $3,600, of the CUL's annual budget.[44] The Chicago League's reliance on financial support from the packinghouse industry and corporate interests in general undoubtedly enervated its embrace of collective bargaining. Not surprisingly, Chicago-area employers appear to have understood the impact their contributions would have on the CUL's labor policies. The stockyards' donations to the Chicago League ceased shortly after the defeat of the steel and meatpacking unions in 1922.

While the Chicago League did not develop a firm commitment to the principle of collective bargaining, the identification of unionization as a means of fostering interracial goodwill found even clearer expression in the National Urban League's work. This is not to imply the NUL courted organized labor simply to improve race relations. The NUL's work with unions such as the AFL was motivated to a large extent by its desire to improve blacks' employment opportunities. In a 1927 report, for example, the League stated that discrimination by "Labor Unions is keeping Negroes out of employment as plumbers, machinists and boiler makers and other important trades." It went on to assert that "unless . . . discriminatory customs and laws are lifted we shall be handicapped in our efforts, to enlarge the occupational opportunities of Negroes."[45] In order to eliminate discriminatory practices, however, the League had to appease white unionists. The NUL therefore embarked on an education campaign to reduce race tensions among workers.

The National Urban League's interest in treating unions as vehicles through which to improve Afro-Americans' job opportunities was inextricably tied to its desire to foster ethnic fellowship through interracial cooperation. The League was especially invested in addressing the impact of job competition and discrimination in wages on race relations. These concerns were explicitly expressed at a 1924 National Association for the Advancement of Colored People (NAACP) conference attended by the Urban League. The NAACP's statement to the AFL voiced the civil rights organization's anxieties about the strain discriminatory union practices placed on relations between Afro-Americans and whites. Despite the decline in immigration, the "continued and determined race prejudice of white labor" ensured that blacks would acquire semiskilled and skilled jobs most often as "scabs." The NAACP argued that the fact that blacks could acquire such jobs only as strikebreakers posed a potential "crisis in interracial labor conditions." While crossing picket lines provided Afro-Americans some short-term benefits, in the end such practices posed a "crisis in interracial labor conditions" that undermined all workers. "If there is built up in America a great black bloc of non-union laborers who have a right to hate unions," the NAACP asserted, "all laborers, black and white, eventually must suffer." The conference concluded that unions and black uplift organizations must make a concerted effort to "organize systematic propaganda against racial discrimination."[46]

One year later, the National Urban League affirmed its own commitment to securing racial harmony through the edification of white unionists. The NUL hoped to alleviate racial tensions by coordinating efforts with the union movement in order to shape the attitudes of black and white workers. The Urban League's Department of Industrial Relations, therefore, implemented initiatives designed to educate white labor as to the benefits of interracial solidarity. By 1925, the NUL's Workers' Education Bureau was circulating pamphlets among a variety of workers to inform them "as to the contributions the various races and nationalities have made to labor and to the country, generally." Ultimately, the League's project was predicated on the notion that "the relationships between the races in the ranks of organized labor could be improved" through education.[47]

Still wed to the group's general efforts to increase blacks' job opportunities, the NUL continued to treat education as a means of reducing racial animosity within the union movement through the 1920s. In 1928, the NUL's Department of Industrial Relations observed that organized labor played a crucial role in intimidating employers who were otherwise willing to hire blacks. The League concluded that in order to improve Afro-Americans' job prospects, it was necessary that "we attain a mutually satisfactory adjustment of the differences between Negroes and white labor."[48] This connection, nonetheless, highlights the League's hope that positive interactions between Afro-Americans and whites would not only increase the opportunities available to blacks but also reduce the general hostilities Afro-Americans encountered from whites.

In addition to identifying participation in the union movement with improved job performance and race relations, a number of Leaguers in the 1920s and 1930s entertained the possibility of treating organized labor as an alternative to militant political activism. Although the reports of the Urban Leagues of Chicago and New York devote little attention to this theme, essays by Leaguers such as Charles S. Johnson, T. Arnold Hill, and Ira De Augustine Reid suggest that participation in the union movement was part of the League's general strategy to adjust the political and social attitudes of marginal Afro-Americans. The works of these authors are especially significant given the positions each held within the Urban League. Reid was the director of the New York Urban League's Department of Industrial Relations during the 1920s, before he became the National Urban League's acting research secretary. Hill was the first executive secretary of the Chicago Urban League, until he was appointed director of the NUL's industrial relations department in 1924. Johnson served as the secretary of the research departments of both the CUL and the NUL. Considering the important positions held by each of these staffers, their writings provide useful insights into the ideological forces influencing the League's view of unions.

The concept of treating participation in the mainstream labor movement as a respectable alternative to radical or militant activism was neither novel nor unique to Urban Leaguers. Decades before the NUL's founding, conservative unions asserted that job consciousness had the potential to undermine the appeal of exotic ideologies. The AFL had long presented itself as an alternative to radical politics. AFL president Samuel Gompers declared his opposition to the Socialist Party in the early 1900s, asserting that "it is our duty to live our lives as workers in the society in which we live, and not to work for the downfall or the destruction or the overthrow of that society but for its fuller development and evolution." For Gompers, collective bargaining, the closed shop, and even the strike were the most appropriate tools by which labor could improve its status. He argued that a wage earner who had a stake in private property would not be swayed by revolutionary doctrines that threatened the sanctity of private ownership. As labor historian Marc Karson has argued, Gompers believed that "orderly and overt economic bargaining methods and the avoidance of radical doctrines would give workers respectability in the community's eyes, and even the employers would become more conciliatory to labor as they recognized that their rights of ownership were not being threatened."[49]

By the mid-1920s the American Federation of Labor attempted to convince black leaders of trade unionism's ability to curb the appeal of "foreign ideologies." In response to the first meeting of the communist-led American Negro Labor Congress (ANLC) in 1925, the AFL asserted, "It is bad enough to mislead those who have an equal opportunity to know, but to take advantage of the weakness of those who have a moral right to our special care is quite outside the pale of decency and ethics." As an alternative to communism, the Federation offered the "protection and experience of the Trade Union Movement." The irony of declarations of this sort could hardly go unnoticed by Urban Leaguers. Ira Reid lambasted the Federation for both its paternalistic tone and its hypocrisy in offering itself as an alternative to black radicalism. The latter point was especially vexing in light of the AFL's acceptance of discriminatory practices among its locals.[50] Nevertheless, the growth of black involvement in fringe political movements following World War I required the League to curb the tide of unrest swelling within America's urban black belts. Afro-Americans' participation in the labor unions offered a partial solution.

By the late 1910s, black nationalists, socialists, and communists actively courted the affections of ghetto residents, particularly in Harlem.[51] While Afro-American leftists hardly attracted a significant following through the early 1920s, the same could not be said of Marcus Garvey and his Universal Negro Improvement Association (UNIA). The Garvey movement's pageantry and calls for racial pride had great emotional appeal to thousands of Afro-Americans discouraged by racism and disappointed by the reality of life in the urban north. Moreover, as historian Judith Stein has argued, the movement's emphasis on the uplifting qualities of black capitalism held particular allure to aspirant entrepreneurs. In addition to inspiring legions of followers who turned out for parades and contributed to UNIA cooperatives, the organization attracted a substantial membership base. Indeed, by the early 1920s, UNIA branches in cities such as Philadelphia, Chicago, and New York would claim between 6,000 and 30,000 members.[52]

With the rise of the UNIA, Leaguers began to consider the potential ramifications of black protest activity. Nancy Weiss has convincingly argued that the Urban League's concerns about Garvey were rooted largely in its fear that Garveyism threatened the NUL's integrationist program. Leaguers believed that Garvey's separatist agenda played into the hands of white supremacists, as it conceded that peaceful coexistence between blacks and whites was not possible. These anxieties were seemingly validated by Garvey's 1922 meeting with the Ku Klux Klan. Weiss acknowledges that differences in the class backgrounds between Urban Leaguers and Garveyites accounted for some of the tensions between them; however, she ultimately contends that hostilities between the NUL and the Garvey movement were rooted in their antithetical philosophies.

Though Weiss is correct to identify a clash of ideologies as a major source of the animosities between these two groups, for many Urban Leaguers the problem with Garveyism had as much to do with what it said about the psychology of black Americans and the conditions of their urban communities as it did the nature of the UNIA's nationalist program. Indeed, Leaguers generally perceived Marcus Garvey's organization as the most salient example of the impact of unsettled minds on black politics. As they had with crime and improbity, Urban Leaguers identified nontraditional political activity as an outgrowth of maladjustment. Ira Reid, for example, viewed even "street-corner speaking" as "a symbol of . . . social disorganization." The League believed that the migration, and the dashed dreams of its participants, provided fertile ground in which such rabble-rousing easily took root. The reduced effectiveness of traditional social controls, exposure to new leisure-time distractions, urban isolation, and racial discrimination combined to alienate migrants and immigrants, making them vulnerable not only to criminal activity but also to radical and militant ideas. Reid and many other Leaguers thus believed soapbox orators and the fringe movements they spawned were the products of the unstable state of America's ghettos and the "partial assimilation" of their residents.[53]

Ira Reid argued that foreign-born blacks were especially susceptible to both left-wing economic theories and race militancy. The sway of exotic ideologies was particularly pronounced among the better-trained Afro-Caribbeans, whose inability to acquire employment commensurate with their talents resulted in reduced earnings and damaged psyches. West Indians' desire to regain status lost in the United States as well as their tradition of aggressive individual and collective agitation were viewed by Reid and others as the sources of Afro-Caribbeans' disproportionate involvement in militant and/or radical politics. The allure of fringe political movements was not unique to West Indians, however. Indeed, black American migrants were similarly disconnected from traditional social restraints and were subject to the same discouraging racial discrimination as their West Indian brethren. Urban Leaguers, therefore, viewed the Garvey movement as an expression of the bonds of oppression and stifled opportunities shared by foreign-born and domestic blacks. Thus, both Garveyism and left-wing politics appeared to be the active attempt of urbanized blacks to attain status and recognition in a world dominated by whites.[54]

After Garvey was arrested in 1923, many Urban Leaguers were concerned about what might become of his disciples. Since most believed that the Garvey movement's success owed less to its leader's charisma than to blacks' postwar psychology, they also believed it was possible that this nationalist campaign might simply be replaced by some other similarly dangerous protest movement. Charles S. Johnson, therefore, argued that "the sources of discontent must be remedied effectively and now, or accumulating energy and unrest, blocked off from its dreams, will take another direction." Johnson concluded that while the next expression of discontent could very well be harmless, the uncertainty of the future necessitated prompt action.[55]

For other Urban Leaguers, Garveyism represented both negative and positive potential for the race. In "Garvey and Garveyism—An Estimate," A. F. Elmes argued in the pages of *Opportunity* that Garvey's narrow focus on a racial politics was naive and myopic. Elmes believed that the Garvey movement stirred up racial animosity and thus stymied the cause of black uplift. In spite of its destructive implications, however, Elmes asserted that Garveyism was not without potential benefit. Perhaps the most significant and promising result of the Garvey movement, he claimed, was that it impressed upon blacks the value of self-sufficiency. Elmes hoped now that Garvey was incarcerated, his followers could be shepherded by a more intellectually stable and balanced group of leaders. This responsible leadership would, of course, attempt to uplift the race through interracial cooperation.[56]

Although Elmes was more optimistic than Johnson about the possibilities existing in the wake of the Garvey movement, both shared a basic belief in the need to fill the political vacuum left by Garvey's departure. Leaguers believed that Afro-Americans should participate in politics and even protest movements; however, the Urban League wanted blacks to become involved in activities that demonstrated their commitment to the existing political economy. Identifying Garveyism and left-wing politics as but symptoms of a pervasive social malaise, the Urban League set out to reorganize black community life. Thus perceiving social disorganization as the culprit, the League attempted to establish new, "rational" institutional outlets for collective action. Unions would provide a partial solution to this problem.

One year after Garvey was indicted and the same year that the National Urban League's Department of Industrial Relations was created, Charles S. Johnson hinted at the possibility of treating unionization as a means of combating social disorganization. Touching upon familiar themes, Johnson argued in an essay in *Survey Graphic* that the fracturing of communal norms taking place within America's ghettos stemmed from the loss of traditional social controls. He asserted that while the church had been an adequate socializing agent in the south, in the urban north it could not compete with the allure of commercialized entertainment and the cultural gap developing between the parents and children of the migration. Worse yet, the church's inadequacies had retarded, Johnson claimed, blacks' assimilation into industrial society. He chastised black ministers for their circumspection about organized labor, contending that preachers' admonitions against unions ultimately promoted an impractical individualism.[57]

For Johnson, the establishment of communal norms consistent with urban life was essential to the proper adjustment of migrants. Moreover, he argued that among the most effective ways to expose newcomers to the values that might best serve them in the city was participation in organized activities. Johnson did not believe, however, that labor unions were *currently* up to the task of promoting black assimilation. In fact, he argued that racism within unions contributed to black Americans' social problems, since such prejudice made "Negroes skeptical, untrained and individualistic." Still, Johnson's claim that organized labor's "lethargy" left blacks to "drift, a disordered mass, self conscious, but with their aims unrationalized into the face of new problems" reveals an interesting implication. The natural inference is that had labor unions been more receptive to blacks, the union movement might have assisted Afro-Americans' acculturation to urban industrial life. This interpretation is reaffirmed by Johnson's assertion that the Urban League's work rested on the view that blacks' current circumstances "required new leadership, trained in the principles of collective action, a new orientation with their white fellow workers for the sake of peace," and a "reorganization of physical and mental habits which are a legacy of their old experiences."[58] These were ultimately the same objectives undergirding the League's efforts to encourage interracial unionism. Support for unionization should, therefore, be understood as at least consonant with the League's general aim to socialize blacks to industrial society.[59]

Unions offered two means of countering the disorganization that fueled political unrest in America's urban black belts. The first was to provide blacks a toehold in the skilled trades, thus affording them greater economic stability. Ira Reid argued that the difficulty West Indians, who were overrepresented among skilled black workers, had finding work commensurate to their training was a major source of conflict as well as economic and personal disorganization.[60] The skilled craftsman employed as a mere laborer and the white-collar worker serving as an elevatorman or porter were likely to be both discouraged and on the economic margins. White-collar workers might bolster their status by securing an ethnic entrepreneurial niche such as real estate; however, Reid suggested that industrial workers could do so only through participation in unions and race boycotts.[61] Although Reid obviously voiced concerns that the foreign-born were more susceptible to militant politics and even radical labor organizations, he nonetheless continued to advocate participation in mainstream unions.[62] Unionists, he argued, had greater job security, as well as better pay. Participation in the labor movement would provide the race access to jobs that had previously been denied to them while simultaneously offering the opportunity to take advantage of the economic gains made through collective bargaining. Involvement with organized labor might thus reduce unemployment and increase blacks' earning potential, thereby alleviating the economic sources of disorganization.

Second, organized labor could promote social health in America's dark ghettos by encouraging interracial solidarity. Indeed, unionization, Leaguers hoped, might expand Afro-American political thought from a narrow racialism to a broader class vision that would stabilize black politics by bridging the divide between black and white workers. Ira Reid claimed in 1932, for example, that the nation's black communities faced social disintegration and "a breakdown of cultural controls over conduct."[63] To combat these ills, Reid offered his standard suggestion that Afro-Americans "must take some interest" in the "realignment of leisure time movements." Among the activities that he claimed required restructuring was the scope of collective action.[64]

Reid believed that the picketing of discriminatory employers and other race-conscious protest movements could not, by themselves, solve the problems plaguing ghetto communities and might even undermine integrationism. "The Negro as a group," he said, "has been thinking so long in terms of race and race alone, that many of his opinions and programs have been opportunistic, race conscious, individualistic, and complacent." Reid followed this assertion with a discussion of the state of black labor and the importance of black participation in the union movement.[65] Ultimately, Reid and the League believed that such participation would create a shared class interest between black and white workers that would help to foster harmonious relations between the races.[66] Mutual understanding between black and white workers might end or reduce byproducts of discrimination ranging from riots to unemployment.

The class interest Leaguers attempted to promote, however, had to be consistent with American values. For Urban Leaguers such as T. Arnold Hill, unions provided a means of undermining socialistic political sentiment among Afro-Americans. The mainstream labor movement thus offered a respectable outlet for those blacks bitten by the protest bug that vented their frustrations in a fashion that reinforced their commitment to American democracy and capitalism. By the mid-1920s, the need to find alternative outlets for black agitators would gain special importance.

Just as Johnson and Elmes feared, after Garvey's incarceration a new political menace threatened black communities. Responding to the growing economic despair Afro-Americans experienced during the 1920s, communist activists attempted to utilize the energies of the discontented black proletariat. In 1925, the American Communist Party, under the direction of the Soviet Comintern, organized the American Negro Labor Congress. The ANLC was intended to create "a 'united front' of black organizations and trade unions to eliminate discrimination in organized labor." It also made a panoply of radical demands, ranging from "the complete abolition of discrimination against the Negro people as a whole" to "the liberation of Haiti, Santo Domingo, the Virgin Islands, Puerto Rico . . . and all victims of American and European imperialism."[67]

By the Depression, the Communists appeared to pose a more urgent threat to order. In 1930, Communists in Harlem disrupted meetings on unemployment sponsored by the established black leadership, organized tenant associations to impede evictions, and cluttered the streets with soapbox orators and radical literature.[68] Such efforts led T. Arnold Hill and Ira Reid to conclude that the Communists were trying to take "advantage of the unsettled mind of Negro workers and promised them relief in return for their membership."[69] Hill continued to explore the sources of communist appeal in the pages of *Opportunity*. In so doing, he alluded to the labor movement's ability to curtail its sway.

In response to Representative Hamilton Fish's charges before the U.S. Congress that communism was gaining influence among Afro-Americans, T. Arnold Hill argued that blacks were less interested in radical economic theories than racial justice. According to Hill, the few blacks who were drawn to radical politics were not guided by "a Marxian theory of 'economic interpretation of history,' but by the racial concept[s] of oppression and exploitation." Although both views attested to the need for change, Hill was quick to point out that the motives behind the two were profoundly different.[70]

While Hill argued blacks were generally averse to so-called un-American ideals, he warned that the Communists were attempting to take advantage of the economic adversity Afro-Americans experienced during the Depression.[71] Since Hill assumed the desire for equal treatment was the driving force behind blacks' political activities, he held that greater participation in labor unions could help undermine communist influence among marginal Afro-Americans. Because "the chief argument communists use to bait Negro membership is that they are denied the right to work and join labor union organizations along with others," the best way to stabilize industry and to counter the threat to peace and safety posed by the Reds, Hill suggested, was to give black workers "a fair chance" in the workplace. Equal participation in labor unions might afford blacks some stake in their own economic fortunes, which Hill believed would demonstrate the efficacy of capitalism to Afro-Americans.[72]

Two months later, Hill revisited these themes, arguing in a piece on unemployment that philanthropy, government assistance, and certain types of activism might exert a stabilizing influence on a society wrought with uncertainty. Hill alluded to the mainstream labor movement's potential to redirect the energies of frustrated and disorganized workers into outlets that reinforced their commitment to American ideals. Drawing a link between social disorder and Depression-era poverty, he suggested that working conditions improved only with agitation. The Depression therefore heightened the importance of "progressive labor action." Hill warned, however, that the need to "replenish empty pocketbooks and restore morale" was urgent, for a delayed response might eventually undermine black workers' commitment to capitalism. "The time to prepare for the fire is before it happens," he asserted, since "for the moment [the masses] care not for controversial economic theories."

Hill was clear that labor unions in themselves could not hope to solve the problem. Government and philanthropic organizations would have to provide the material benefits that would in time reduce tensions and foster confidence. Nevertheless, Hill appears to have embraced a bottom-up view of social policy and political history that emphasized the need for worker activism, and he took for granted the importance of creating socially accepted outlets for those clamoring for change.[73]

An essay by Robert Isaacs, secretary of the Department House Janitors' Local Number 5 in Boston, addressed to the NUL expressed a similar faith in the ability of trade unionism to curb Afro-Americans' participation in radical politics. Isaacs likewise linked some blacks' interests in nontraditional political outlets to their belief that they had been abandoned by organized labor and the government. Responding to the AFL's charge that the American Negro Labor Congress was a Communist front organization that was a vehicle for indoctrinating black workers, he argued that the ANLC was less important than the circumstances imbuing its efforts with relevance. Like Hill, he claimed that Afro-Americans were interested not in Bolshevism but racial equality. However, because "Negroes feel that government and the labor movement have failed them," Isaacs argued, they had become more vulnerable to militant and radical ideas. "Marcus Garvey's high following . . . proved the restlessness and discontent of too large a portion of America's Negro population." The communists, Isaacs believed, were but another outgrowth of blacks' disorganization. He therefore called upon the AFL to combat this menace by assisting blacks in their quest for economic equality, which in turn would assuage Afro-American's apprehensions about organized labor.[74]

Hill's and Isaacs's appeals to the American Federation of Labor were likely intended as rhetorical devices. Leaguers hoped to nudge the Federation to increase its inclusiveness by turning the AFL's own proclamations against itself. Undoubtedly, such endeavors were designed to assist in improving blacks' job opportunities. They were, however, also consistent with the Urban League's efforts to assimilate black workers by shaping their attitudes to conform to predominant values.

■ Perceiving the problems afflicting black workers through the lens of social disorganization theory, Leaguers such as Charles S. Johnson believed that the migration eroded the communal norms and institutions that had been essential to maintaining order in rural black communities. With the reduced importance of institutions such as family and church, Afro-American newcomers were more likely to engage in any number of unwholesome activities ranging from hanging out in pool halls to militant radical political activism. The Urban League thus identified the establishment of social controls as among its chief objectives. For many Leaguers, black involvement in the union movement held the potential to establish norms and values that would adjust Afro-Americans to life in the industrial north.

In some instances, this approach accrued benefits solely to workers. By identifying Afro-American participation in the union movement as a means of improving race relations, Leaguers intended to both increase black representation in the skilled trades and reduce racial tensions. At different times, leaders of the Chicago and National Leagues believed that involvement in the union movement might foster mutual understanding between Afro-American and white workers. Shared work experience and union camaraderie held the potential to alleviate multiple sources of animosity between black and white workers. Though laudable in many respects, the Urban League's work with organized labor also illustrates the progressive limits of racial uplift ideology.

Restraints on the Urban League, particularly at the local level, prevented it from developing a firm commitment to organized labor. The Chicago Urban League's position on unionization reflected the tensions shaping local League union policy. Perhaps because the CUL's interest in unions was rooted in a desire to improve blacks' job prospects while simultaneously fostering harmonious contact between black and white workers, the allure of organized labor ended with the threat of race conflict. As racial battles in the stockyards evolved into class warfare, the Urban League was forced to choose between capital and labor. The Chicago Urban League's dependence on funding from employers made it especially susceptible to the influence of owners. Employers utilized the League's employment placement services to gain additional leverage in the collective bargaining process. Although the CUL and some prominent members toyed with the idea of participation in the labor movement, stockyard labor disputes demonstrated that the League's allegiance lay with management.

The League's belief that unions had the potential to facilitate the acculturation of urban blacks further illustrates uplift's limits. The objectives of the Urban League's union activities overlapped its vocational guidance and training programs. Early reports indicate that the NUL believed, at least in its first few years, that black unionism held the promise of improving job performance. Unions could impress upon Afro-Americans the value of developing efficient work habits while simultaneously reinforcing predominant values. Such views were by no means unique to Urban Leaguers but were shared by other progressive reformers and even prominent unionists. Nevertheless, they were indicative of the importance the League's integrationist vision placed on maintaining a disciplined workforce.

Leaguers' belief that union membership could socialize blacks politically has similar implications. Ira Reid and others perceived political activism as one of the most glaring outgrowths of Afro-Americans' maladjustment in this period. During the 1920s and 1930s, Leaguers devoted special attention to the issue of black activism. The rise of the Garvey movement and the ongoing tension with socialists and communists led the Urban League to examine sources of discontent while exploring methods of curbing protest activities. Although the League's anxieties about black political activism stemmed, at least in part, from basic ideological differences, they also reflected the social-work group's belief that activism was a consequence of the Negro's maladjustment to his environment. By attributing blacks' participation in nontraditional political movements to social disorganization, Leaguers identified such activities as a threat to Afro-Americans' assimilation. The Urban League thus pursued the adjustment of blacks through unions to combat social malaise ranging from political militancy to frivolous use of free time.[75]

5. Vocational Guidance and Organized Labor during the New Deal, 1933–1940

Prestige and advancement will of necessity go to those who are articulate and assertive.—T. Arnold Hill, 1937

By Franklin D. Roosevelt's presidential inauguration in spring 1933, the United States was in the throes of a staggering economic decline. Over the previous few years, the combination of underconsumption and inadequate fiscal policy had devastated the nation's manufacturing and financial sectors leading to widespread suffering among the citizenry.[1] Nationwide, nearly half of all gainfully employed workers were "underemployed," unemployment was a whopping 25 percent, and American workers' wages had fallen by more than 30 percent since 1929. For Afro-Americans, the situation was even more bleak than national statistics revealed. In northern cities, black unemployment was often between two and three times the rate for whites. In Chicago and New York, roughly 40 percent of black men and 55 percent of black women were unemployed, compared with just 23 percent of white men and about 14 percent of white women. Afro-Americans' wages likewise flagged. One study of 2,000 Afro-American families in Harlem found that the median income in Gotham's black belt dropped by nearly 50 percent between 1929 and 1932. Chicago's South Side residents were no better off, as black poverty rates soared in the Windy City. Beset by high unemployment and flat earnings, both white and Afro-American communities from coast to coast witnessed ballooning rates of crime, foreclosures and evictions, homelessness, and family dissolution.[2]

In response to the collapse of the nation's economic and social institutions, President Roosevelt offered America a New Deal. Roosevelt set out to stabilize American capitalism through regulation of the nation's financial and manufacturing sectors, the implementation of policies to promote both higher wages and workers' rights, and the introduction of economic stimulus packages. Though the

New Deal's overarching aim was simply to right a listing economy, the president's recovery efforts profoundly altered the meaning of American democracy. As historian Nelson Lichtenstein has demonstrated, New Dealers institutionalized a form of republican government that sought to restrain the inequities associated with industrial capital by empowering the citizenry. Through legislation such as the National Industrial Recovery Act (1933) and Wagner Act (1935), liberals in Washington attempted to equip workers with the tools necessary to advance their own interests. Myriad relief programs, the Social Security Act (1935), and the Fair Labor Standards Act (1938) likewise afforded a broad cross-section of Americans a modicum of economic stability and even personal dignity. New Dealers' vision of "industrial democracy" thus extended the rights and privileges of civil society into the workplace, effectively updating eighteenth-century notions of republican self-determination and equality for the industrial age.[3]

Influenced by broad changes in the nation's political economy, the Urban League's employment programs shifted dramatically between 1933 and 1940. As the New Deal transformed the federal government into the nation's single largest employer, the League adopted a model of economic progress that embraced the interventionist welfare state. Consequently, the Urban League's employment projects during the New Deal no longer relied simply on voluntarist arrangements with white elites and unionists but included cooperation with government. Leaguers, moreover, took steps to mobilize black workers to lobby for their own economic interests. But while the politics of the New Deal profoundly altered the scope of the Urban League's activities, the group's program did not depart fully from its past. Focusing on the League's work with private employers, government, and labor unions, this chapter demonstrates that the employment projects adopted by the NUL and its locals between 1933 and 1940 reflected the social-work group's long-standing concerns about the potential impact of maladjustment on black economic and social progress. Despite the League's decision to expand its focus, the group's efforts to address Afro-Americans' economic needs continued to evidence a vision of uplift predicated on behavioral modification.

Vocational Training and Job Placements

From the outset of the New Deal, the League's employment focus shifted from simply securing jobs for Afro-Americans in the private sector to ensuring that blacks shared fully in relief and recovery efforts. While Roosevelt's recovery program promised a kinder, gentler society, the limits of Democratic politics greatly undermined the cause of racial parity in federal programs. Despite the president's pledge to run the New Deal with "absolute equality and fairness," discrimination in recovery agencies was rampant. As Urban Leaguers and other civil rights leaders of the day noted, local control over the administration of federal programs resulted in significant disparities between blacks and whites in a range of initiatives, including the Civil Works Administration (CWA), the Works Progress Administration (WPA), the Civilian Conservation Corps (CCC), the National Recovery Administration (NRA), and the National Youth Administration (NYA). The power wielded by southern Democrats in Congress likewise led to the exclusion of the majority of Afro-Americans from the purview of the Social Security and Fair Labor Standards Acts.

. Few issues were of greater concern to Leaguers than the government's failure to provide Afro-Americans employment, through either job placements or work relief, in proportion to their needs. As early as 1933, the NUL's Department of Industrial Relations noted that discrimination on the part of both local United States Employment Services (USES) officials and employers resulted in few blacks being placed in private employment. Government agencies, Leaguers contended, were particularly negligent in their treatment of skilled blacks. T. Arnold Hill, for example, complained in 1934 that while Afro-Americans had little difficulty acquiring direct relief through the Federal Emergency Relief Administration, the CWA, the Public Works Administration (PWA), and the CCC failed to employ blacks in "skilled, unskilled, or white-collar jobs in anything like the proportion that their unemployment warranted."[4] The League claimed, moreover, when Afro-Americans did manage to gain employment through New Deal–sponsored programs such as the NRA they were frequently victims of pay disparities engendered by employers' latitude to determine wage codes and union discrimination.[5]

Urban Leaguers chronicled similar problems with state and local government aid initiatives. In 1933, the NYUL was inundated with complaints directed at Gotham's Home Relief (HR) and Work Bureau (WB) of the Temporary Emergency Relief Administration (TERA). Signed into law in 1931 by then-governor Franklin D. Roosevelt, TERA extended state subsidies to localities for both direct aid and work relief. Officially, the TERA was to be operated without bias; nevertheless, the NYUL received scores of reports of discrimination from Afro-Americans who were denied work through the HR and WB. Although the League dismissed many of these charges as unfounded, it found prima facie evidence of discrimination. The NYUL ultimately informed the administration that skilled Afro-American mechanics were underrepresented on the city's work relief rolls. Government officials attributed the small number of skilled black workers on public work sites to a dearth of projects, but the administration's ability to place skilled whites, even as it found work for no more than a token number of Afro-Americans, left the NYUL decidedly unconvinced by the bureaus' explanation.[6]

Blacks' inability to make significant gains in either work relief or private employment dismayed League officials for both practical and ideological reasons. Wages paid through work relief programs were generally much higher than direct aid benefits. Since, as mentioned above, black poverty and unemployment significantly outpaced that of whites during the Depression, Afro-Americans were in desperate need of any assistance they could acquire. By relegating blacks to direct relief rolls, government programs undercut black economic stability. Leaguers also maintained a philosophical aversion to "charity." As the NUL's mantra, "not alms but opportunity," indicated, the Urban League was dogmatically committed to the value of "work" as both an economic and social force in American life. Thus while Leaguers accepted direct relief as an expedient, they feared that dependency on the dole would vitiate blacks' moral character. Finally, League staffers, like other Americans of the era, came to identify work relief and employment generally as a right of citizenship.

With government agencies complicit in the denial of important sources of employment and aid, Leaguers set out to persuade elected officials to redress the issue of discrimination in recovery programs. To bolster the group's influence, the National Urban League and its locals immediately took steps to secure positions for prominent staffers in federal, state, and local agencies.[7] In fall 1933, NUL executive secretary Eugene K. Jones would be the first high-ranking League official to take a formal advisory position with the Roosevelt administration. For nearly four years, Jones served as director of the "Commerce Department's unit for the study of Negro problems." T. Arnold Hill—who was appointed acting executive secretary of the NUL in Jones's absence (1933–40)—likewise worked as an adviser to Washington, albeit in a somewhat limited capacity. In 1939, while maintaining his position as League executive director, Hill worked as "a consultant on Negro Affairs to the WPA and NYA."[8] Local Leaguers took positions with government agencies as well. In 1935, Sam Allen, the New York Urban League's secretary of industrial relations, left the social-work group to take a position with New York's TERA.[9] The Chicago Urban League's executive secretary, A. L. Foster, and its secretary of industrial relations, Howard Gould, also took on advisory roles with federal and state governments.

Leaguers were able to acquire positions and influence in Washington in large part because of the social-work group's lobbying efforts. Continuing to treat research as a wedge with which to pry open opportunities, Urban League officials petitioned New Dealers to redress inequities in federal recovery initiatives. Just several weeks into Roosevelt's first term, the NUL sent the president a detailed report outlining the problems blacks encountered with New Deal agencies. At the start of Roosevelt's sophomore term, the League sent him a second memorandum on blacks in relief agencies.[10] Leaguers also petitioned the president, as well as high-ranking officials in his administration, regarding specific pieces of legislation. Concerned that the National Labor Relations Act (1935) might undercut black employability, the NUL's T. Arnold Hill met with Senator Robert Wagner to draw attention to a number of challenges that Negro workers would face in light of the labor law. Urban League officials filed similar petitions regarding the shortcomings of the Social Security Act and the Fair Labor Standards Act.[11]

Local Leagues likewise petitioned government officials for greater access to work programs. NYUL executive secretary James H. Hubert, for example, actively lobbied government officials to increase black representation on New York's Public Works Administration projects. In 1933, secretary of the interior and former Chicago NAACP president Harold Ickes set minimum rates for Afro-American employment on PWA construction sites in an effort to ensure fair representation of blacks in publicly sponsored work programs. While Hubert, like most other League officials, enthusiastically supported PWA construction quotas, he was not fully satisfied with the practical implementation of the policy in New York. Hubert charged that the decision to peg representation in construction projects to the percentage of Afro-Americans in particular trades failed to adequately address blacks' suffering during the Depression. Reasoning that such programs "existed to help the needy," Hubert and the NYUL petitioned New Dealers to base racial quotas not on blacks' share of specific lines of work but on the race's "make up of the relief population."[12] Had New Deal administrators implemented Hubert's proposal, and they did not, black participation in work relief projects in New York would have ballooned.

Hubert and the New York Urban League took demands for fair employment practices to local government as well. In 1936, the NYUL criticized the New York State Employment Services (NYSES) for capitulating to employer racism. Though the NYSES placed what appeared to be an appropriate share of Afro-American job seekers, it allowed employers to specify racial preferences. Consequently, the NYSES found employment for blacks principally in domestic and personal service work. Hoping to encourage state and local officials to take legislative action, Hubert appealed to the New York State Temporary Commission on the Urban Colored Population, which had been charged with the task of investigating employment discrimination. Hubert petitioned the commission to enact legislation that "would prohibit discrimination against people on the basis of color."[13] Unfortunately, Hubert's efforts were once again fruitless.

As legislation such as the National Industrial Recovery Act helped foster interest group politics, Leaguers not only lobbied government officials but also organized Afro-American workers to demand fair treatment from government agencies. In fall 1933, the NUL took its first step in this direction with the creation of Emergency Advisory Councils (EACs). The EACs' principal target was the National Recovery Administration. The League thus discontinued the program in 1935 when the U.S. Supreme Court declared the National Industrial Recovery Act unconstitutional. Responding to complaints that blacks were systematically excluded from NRA benefits, the NUL and its locals established Emergency Advisory Councils in more than 200 cities across the nation in order to educate blacks about the ins and outs of various recovery programs. By creating an informed interest bloc, the League ultimately hoped to mobilize grassroots campaigns to persuade elected officials to remedy inequities in the administration of federal benefits.[14]

Though most EACs operated independently of local Leagues, quite a few maintained close ties to Urban League affiliates. The CUL, for example, pursued a number of initiatives in concert with the Illinois Emergency Advisory Council (IEAC). Following the National League's playbook, the CUL and the IEAC attempted to address the problem of discrimination in New Deal agencies through a series of education campaigns. The Chicago League and the IEAC collected data pertaining to the employment and reemployment trends of black workers; created pamphlets simplifying NRA codes for popular consumption; used the black press and its ties with other uplift organizations to educate black workers about their rights under the NRA; and investigated complaints. The group also instructed Afro-American workers to file complaints with elected representatives and New Deal administrators regarding the problems with local recovery initiatives.[15]

The Chicago Urban League and the IEAC appear to have achieved some rewards for their efforts. Thanks to its work with the IEAC, the CUL established close ties with local NRA administrators by the end of 1933. Utilizing personal contacts with NRA officials, the Chicago Urban League and the IEAC provided compelling evidence to New Dealers that discriminatory practices of both employers and unions prevented many Afro-Americans from receiving their fair share of employment through federal projects. While League records shed little light on the specific results of these meetings, the Chicago League claimed that NRA administrators were receptive to their efforts. In fact, the CUL alleged that state administrator Robert Dunham was so supportive of its calls for racial equality in the NRA that he issued a special appeal for fair play. The Chicago League ultimately reported that thanks to the strong support of local NRA staffers, most discriminatory charges were satisfactorily resolved.[16]

Endeavors of this sort further strengthened Leaguers' ties with local legislators, thereby enhancing the group's influence within state government. On occasion the League was able to persuade state officials to pursue measures to end discrimination in public employment. Howard Gould, director of the Chicago Urban League's Department of Industrial Relations, for example, worked with Illinois representative Charles I. Jenkins in drafting Bill No. 583 penalizing employers for discriminating against individuals on the basis of race. Capitalizing on his connections to both the Urban League and the government, Gould put together a report demonstrating the pernicious consequences of racial discrimination that was shaped by his own connection to a New Deal agency. Specifically, Gould's study relied heavily on material he gathered during his tenure with the office of the Illinois director of the Works Progress Administration to lobby for the bill. This approach, the CUL claimed, played a vital part in securing the legislation's passage.[17]

The Urban League's attempt to combine interest group pressure tactics with traditional petition politics augured a larger shift in the group's work that, by the mid-1930s, took form in the Negro Workers' Councils (WCS). The WCS, as I discuss below, identified interracial working-class solidarity as pivotal to black uplift. Institutionalizing workers' rights as an important facet of the League's agenda, the Workers' Councils evinced a new political assertiveness among Urban League officials. Still, even as the social-work group expanded its efforts to include grassroots activism through both the EACs and WCS, Leaguers did not give up the view that proper workplace conduct would enhance blacks' employability. This was especially true of the League's vocational guidance projects.

Due perhaps in part to the limits of New Deal legislation, the Urban League maintained its own initiatives to assist Afro-American workers through training and job placements. Continuing to view the proper adjustment of black labor to industrial and domestic employment as essential to black uplift, the National and local Leagues maintained active vocational mentoring and employment placement programs throughout the 1930s. The combination of budgetary constraints and the expanded role of the federal government led the Urban League to scale back these activities during the Depression. Leaguers, moreover, frequently pursued vocational guidance in concert with government. These changes in approach notwithstanding, the practical application of the Urban League's jobs programs, even during the New Deal, reflected both the group's enduring interest in the integrity of black workers and its heightened concern for middle-class Afro-Americans.

As it had before the New Deal, the Urban League conceived of vocational guidance as a means of countering employer prejudice, thereby opening job opportunities. The NUL's Department of Industrial Relations frequently attributed the high rates of unemployment among Afro-Americans to "racial sentiment," or whites' preference for whites.[18] Having ascribed black unemployment and underemployment to whites' visceral predilections, the NUL averred, particularly in the early stages of the New Deal, that efficiency offered the most effective means of securing employment.[19]

In keeping with the NUL's perspective, local Urban Leagues' employment placement programs stressed the importance of job applicants' skills and proficiency. Proceeding from the view that competition from white labor for even unskilled work was a major cause of black unemployment, the New York Urban League, for example, claimed that "quality" placements were essential to both creating new jobs and maintaining black representation in fields in which Afro-American labor had already established a firm footing. Thus while the NYUL's Department of Industrial Relations asserted in spring 1935 that it placed no limits on "the type of job for which an applicant may register," it intended to restrict its placements to the "better class of applicants." As part of an ongoing effort to engender mutual satisfaction between employers and employees, the New York League took special care to assess applicants' qualifications. It therefore rated job seekers on a three-point system that gauged applicants' appearance, self-presentation, and work experience. It also administered aptitude tests to registrants for more advanced positions in clerical and white-collar work to provide employers with tangible evidence of their skill and intelligence.[20]

Applicant screening is, of course, intrinsic to job placements. For the League, however, the implications of such efforts extended well beyond individual job seekers. Close scrutiny of prospective workers offered the Urban League a means of identifying potentially unfit as well as gifted individuals in order to demonstrate black labor's productive capacity. In this context, screening was not simply about vetting specific workers, but it served as a window onto the promise of the race. While NYUL's records do not divulge whether this led the group to assist employers in weeding out unproductive black workers as it had during the 1910s and 1920s, the desperate nature of Afro-Americans' employment situation during the Depression ultimately led the Urban League of New York to utilize new invasive techniques to exclude "undesirables" from its placement rolls.

In March 1932, the NYUL's Department of Industrial Relations established the Industrial Health Clinic. Operating for more than two years, the clinic's chief aim was to provide job seekers medical examinations in order to "satisfy the minds of the employers that our applicants were good industrial risks and free from communicable disease." Due to blacks' overrepresentation among carriers of infectious illnesses such as syphilis and tuberculosis, the Urban League had long been interested in the health of Afro-American newcomers. As early as the 1910s, local Leagues educated blacks about techniques and practices to prevent the spread of communicable diseases. By the Depression, these activities took on special significance. Leaguers believed that Afro-Americans' overrepresentation among carriers of infectious diseases caused many employers, particularly in the field of domestic work, to overlook black labor. In a context of heightened competition with white labor, League officials placed a premium on the health of its placements.[21]

For many Afro-Americans, the New York League's Industrial Health Clinic was a salutary boon. In its first two years of operation the Industrial Clinic performed physical examinations on hundreds of job seekers. Over the first nine months of 1933 alone the clinic examined 863 men and women.[22] The majority of applicants were given a clean bill of health. The League did, however, observe a significant number of "defects," including hernia, unspecified "social diseases," and tuberculosis.[23] The Industrial Clinic helped hundreds of black New Yorkers address serious medical problems since the Urban League directed applicants who exhibited signs of illness to physicians. It was, therefore, instrumental in assisting these individuals in securing treatment. Of the 106 individuals that the NYUL's Industrial Clinic referred to physicians in 1935, for example, 98 (92 percent) were prescribed some treatment regimen.[24]

The New York League's physician referral assistance undoubtedly benefited scores of Afro-Americans. Still, the Industrial Clinic's chief aim was to identify and eliminate undesirable workers. Consequently, applicants exhibiting signs of illness were not only directed to physicians but were generally excluded from the League's placement rolls. Not all visibly ill applicants were denied placement assistance out of hand, however. The New York branch reported in 1935, for example, that while it refused to assist one woman suffering from "some type of skin disease" acquire work as a "Mother's Helper," she was only excluded from the League's roll because "she was an unsuitable person for such a position and she would not consider another type of work."[25] Even so, the work of the Industrial Clinic was consistent with the League's long-standing practice of assisting employers in eliminating questionable employees in order to ensure the progress of the race as a whole.

The Industrial Health Clinic's attempts to weed out potentially "unfit" workers was not necessarily indicative of any particular class bias; nevertheless, the general job placement activities of both the New York and Chicago Urban Leagues reflected the social-work group's lingering preoccupation with middle-class blacks. The high rates of black unemployment during the Depression had forced the New York League to abandon its white-collar placements in 1930. Having quit these activities only because the better types of work were unattainable at the time, the NYUL returned to placements in more "advanced occupations" as soon as the opportunity permitted. As the local economy ticked up in 1935, the New York branch declared that its "interest in assisting unemployed professional, clerical, and other white-collar workers and those of skilled trades has been consistently maintained." The NYUL went on to assert that "at all times the League has considered its special province to lie in attempting to find positions for the specially trained or gifted individual who is handicapped in following his particular line of work by lack of proper advice or contacts, or by discrimination and race prejudice."[26]

The League's focus on white-collar and professional work was partially rooted in its lack of success in breaking into these fields. In 1934, for example, the New York League lamented that the majority of the 897 placements it made were in unskilled and domestic work. More than 70 percent of black men and 4 percent of black women the League registered were placed in unskilled positions. The vast majority of the black women, 83 percent, placed by the New York League acquired positions as domestic and personal service workers. By contrast, only about 11 percent of the New York Urban League's total placements for 1934 were in clerical, skilled, or professional work. Moreover, all five of the "professional" placements were musicians. While employer prejudice was largely to blame, the New York League's placement activities were hampered by its lack of resources. During the Depression, the New York League, like most locals, experienced a precipitous decline in contributions. As a consequence, by 1935, the New York branch's Department of Industrial Relations operated with just three staff members. The League's personnel shortage naturally constrained its placement activities, requiring it to target its efforts.[27]

Lacking sufficient staff and having little luck making its preferred placements, the League devoted a disproportionately large share of its resources to assisting applicants in securing white-collar employment. In particular, the amount of attention job applicants received from the League was contingent on the type of work for which they were applying. In 1935, the NYUL's job registration bureau was open five days a week, yet the League provided just one full day (Wednesday) to domestic placement registration. By contrast, the

NYUL registered applicants for white-collar work all day every day. Furthermore, while registrants for domestic and unskilled work were interviewed by the assistant to the acting secretary, white-collar applicants were interviewed by the acting secretary. Applicants for white-collar work were thus given priority over those applying for "run of the mill" jobs.[28]

The Chicago League's placement activities during this period also emphasized white-collar work. Though budgetary and personnel constraints had forced the Chicago Urban League to suspend formal employment assistance between 1930 and 1934, the organization did not discontinue job placements altogether. In anticipation of new employment opportunities catalyzed by both the repeal of Prohibition and the 1933–34 World's Fair, CUL executive secretary A. L. Foster worked assiduously to secure jobs for blacks in the burgeoning breweries and World's Fair pavilions. While Foster received some assistance from the Illinois and Chicago Employment Advisory Councils, his efforts were nonetheless circumscribed by an absence of staff. Consequently, Foster's placement endeavors centered on a letter campaign targeting brewery and fair officials. Foster, like the New York Urban League, was especially invested in placing Afro-Americans in white-collar positions. His work in this regard came up short, however, in that most of the blacks hired by the World's Fair were employed in menial positions. These placements were, moreover, made by an outside contractor and not the CUL.[29]

When the Chicago League reinstated its official job placement activities between 1934 and 1935, its work in this regard focused largely on expanding blacks' access to public employment. The CUL briefly pursued placements in private industry, in response to the fleeting economic recovery between 1936 and 1937. While the League was still principally interested in the "better work opportunities for Negroes," the Chicago branch announced its willingness to place Afro-Americans in all occupations, including domestic and personal service work. Still, the CUL's Department of Industrial Relations' decision to make broad placements had less to do with its commitment to such workers than its desire to maintain favorable contacts with business. Since employers invariably directed requests for domestic workers to the Department of Industrial Relations, the CUL complied principally because it feared "an unfavorable reception on [its] part might be construed as an indication that Negroes are too particular about what work they will take, and really do not want to work at all."[30] The Chicago League's decision to place menial and domestic workers was therefore made under duress. With the return of the business recession in 1937, the CUL gave up its work with private industry, resuming its focus on increasing Afro-Americans' share of New Deal work relief.

Given the limited resources of both the New York and Chicago Leagues, their decisions to target placement activities would, at first, seem a reasonable endeavor. However, in light of the general standing of black labor during the 1930s, the League's policy of devoting special attention to white-collar work is striking. As mentioned above, black unemployment rates in New York and Chicago during the mid-1930s ranged between 40 percent and 55 percent. Although Afro-American white-collar workers were hit hard by the Depression, unskilled workers comprised the bulk of unemployed blacks. By 1935, fully 84 percent of blacks receiving relief in New York City classified themselves as unskilled, semiskilled, or personal service and domestic workers.[31] The unemployment trends for unskilled workers in Chicago were little different. Considering the higher rates of unemployment for unskilled and domestic workers, the League's decision to focus chiefly on the "better occupations" was probably unwarranted.

The Urban League's emphasis on "quality" placements also ensured that the social-work group continued to pursue efforts to adjust black workers to their environments. This would be an important facet of the League's vocational training/guidance program. Since the 1910s, the League had identified job proficiency among blacks as essential to securing employment opportunities. By the New Deal, the NUL's Department of Industrial Relations argued that Depression-era unemployment rates increased the importance of proper workplace conduct. As the League asserted in 1933, "The exigencies of the day demand more than ever that [Afro-Americans] give continuous and unselfish devotion to the proven ideals and practices out of which success develops."[32] The NUL's industrial relations department went on to state that it encouraged "Negroes to make themselves proficient in new lines of work so that they may gain universal reputations of being especially suited for complete inclusion in the national occupational scheme."[33]

Perceiving efficiency as an engine of economic uplift, the NUL's Department of Industrial Relations promoted the advantages of both proficiency and job training through public relations campaigns and direct contacts with Afro-American workers. Throughout the 1930s, the National League offered vocational guidance projects in concert with black colleges and federal agencies such as the NYA, CCC, and the WPA. By 1940, the NUL even operated a training program in conjunction with the U.S. Department of Labor, affording the social-work group access to facilities and resources that had been unimaginable during the 1910s and 1920s.

Local Leagues engaged in similar activities. Throughout the New Deal, the New York and Chicago Leagues sponsored lectures and seminars designed to encourage efficiency as well as to aid the jobless in understanding the broader economic conditions leading to their unemployment. The NYUL and CUL, moreover, offered job training, albeit on a limited basis. In 1933, for example, the New York League provided adult education courses in cooperation with the State University of New York (SUNY).[34] By the mid-1930s, the NYUL operated training programs in cooperation with both the Civil Works Administration and the WPA. Forced by funding problems to suspend operation of its Employment Bureau in 1930, the CUL was unable to pursue vocational initiatives before mid-decade. In 1936, just one year after the group resumed normal operations, it followed its New York counterpart's lead by instituting its own adult education program employing 100 teachers. The CUL also sponsored "brush up classes" in concert with the National Youth Administration to assist unemployed clerical workers in maintaining their skills.[35]

The League's efforts to address the problem of black unemployment by enhancing Afro-Americans' human capital were not entirely unreasonable. Skills were hardly a panacea, but specialized training afforded individuals a modicum of job security.[36] Data compiled by the National Health Service (NHS) for 1935 and 1936, for example, revealed a modest correlation between education and unemployment among Afro-Americans. The NHS observed that the unemployment rate among blacks with only an eighth grade education was 9 percent higher than that of high school graduates and 29 percent higher than the rate for college graduates.[37] Relief rolls of the era reaffirmed the connection between skill sets and employability. In New York City during this time period, manual laborers and servants comprised about 12 percent of the workforce but accounted for 35 percent of relief recipients. By contrast, professional and semiprofessional workers made up 13 percent of the general workforce while comprising just 5 percent of relief cases.[38]

Still, while training may have afforded individuals some insulation from the vagaries of the economy, Leaguers did not see skills simply as a means of enhancing black employability. Indeed, the League's emphasis on job proficiency was wed to the group's general concerns about social disorganization. As discussed previously, Urban Leaguers feared that chronic joblessness had sapped the motivation of a stratum of Afro-Americans to work and strive for a better life. The NUL noted that Depression-era unemployment shattered many blacks' faith in the capacity of training and job proficiency to inoculate them against layoffs and poverty. As one laborer remarked to a League social worker, "They told me that I was unemployed because I didn't have a skilled trade, but when I saw all the boys who were skilled in my fix, I said 'what-the-hell.' What next? I don't know, and mister, I-don't-care."[39] Unemployment and the attendant decline in morale, the NUL claimed, fueled a host of social pathologies. More than one Urban League report during the New Deal attributed the increase in juvenile delinquency, crime, family dissolution, and even radicalism to an erosion of the work ethic engendered by chronic unemployment and dependency on the dole.[40]

League officials believed that if these trends were not addressed, they would further constrict job opportunities by reinforcing employer prejudice. As it had before the New Deal, this view led the social-work group to identify training and even public relations initiatives intended to encourage workplace diligence as essential to opening employment and remedying the social malaise threatening economic uplift. It is this perspective that shaped the focus of the third installment of the Color Line Series published by the NUL. Titled "He Crashed the Color Line!," the publication proceeded from the view that discrimination could be surmounted by skill. Series editor T. Arnold Hill asserted in the introduction, "Negro youth need not despair" over discrimination, for recent history has proven that "in almost every section of the country there are those who have achieved notable success in competition with their white compatriots by virtue of skill which is derived from sustained training and courage which will not admit defeat." To make the case, Hill's article featured accounts of individuals who managed to circumvent employment barriers by way of personal fortitude. By stressing the advantages of job proficiency through human interest stories, the Department of Industrial Relations made clear that it intended to counter the sense of apathy that it believed frequently "aborted" the Negro's "efforts to attain . . . training . . . without which" the race was "doomed to the stolid ranks of the unskilled, the underpaid and the *wretched*."[41]

Local League policy was likewise moved by concerns about the relationship between unemployment and social disorganization. Both the Chicago and New York Leagues continued to treat vocational guidance as a means of providing constructive outlets for the unemployed. The NYUL asserted in 1935 that the occupational and vocational classes the group offered not only served to provide "needed training in various lines of work" but helped to "occupy the idle workers," thereby reducing their susceptibility to unwholesome influences.[42] As a result, the League's vocational guidance programs were often tailored to the needs of both individual workers and their surrounding communities. The CUL offered courses in furniture repair, for example, that not only were designed to assist blacks in acquiring skills as woodworkers but also were intimately linked to the Chicago League's neighborhood work. In fact, the Chicago Urban League directed South Side residents with broken furniture to its home repair courses to assist trainees in developing practical experience

Eugene K. Jones (Photographs and Prints Division,
Schomburg Center for Research in Black Culture, The New
York Public Library, Astor, Lenox and Tilden Foundations)

while simultaneously providing a valuable service to their neighborhoods.[43]
These activities were therefore intended to foster a sense of community among
ghetto residents in an effort to counter personal demoralization arising from
unemployment.

The League's emphasis on vocational guidance and job proficiency as engines of uplift diminished somewhat as New Deal politics became more militant by the late 1930s. This is not to suggest, however, that Leaguers abandoned
their faith in the ability of workplace efficiency to improve Afro-Americans'
social and economic conditions. In a February 1940 report, for example, Eugene K. Jones reiterated the causal relationship between diligence on the part
of black workers and their employability.[44] Furthermore, the NUL and its locals
continued to identify job training as pivotal to black uplift into the postwar era.
Nevertheless, by the mid-1930s, the Urban League's Department of Industrial
Relations began to devote far greater attention to efforts to mobilize Afro-

American workers themselves to demand equal employment. The most salient example of this is the League's Workers' Councils.

Organized Labor

In addition to its attempts to enhance blacks' economic standing through job training and placement activities with private employers and government agencies, the Urban League stepped up its efforts to increase Afro-American participation in the labor movement during the New Deal. As discussed in Chapter 4, prominent Leaguers had long viewed unionization as a vital component of racial uplift. In the Urban League's initial twenty years of operation, two major issues shaped the group's interest in organized labor. First, Leaguers identified participation in the union movement as essential to black economic progress. Since AFL-affiliated locals and internationals represented hundreds of thousands of workers in myriad occupations, the League concluded that Afro-Americans' best hope for significant gains in skilled trades lay with unionization. Second, many Leaguers perceived union affiliation as a powerful means of adjusting both black workers' attitudes and contemporary race relations. By the mid-1930s the NUL's commitment to organized labor found institutional expression in its Workers' Councils (1934–38). Identifying both pressure tactics and interracial class solidarity as pivotal to black uplift, the WCS, according to scholars such as Jesse T. Moore, represented a radical shift in League policy.[45] The tactics and orientation of these groups ultimately revealed a new militancy within the League. Even so, the Workers' Councils continued to reflect Leaguers' entrenched concerns about the deleterious consequences of social disorganization and the status of race relations.

Established in 1934, the Workers' Councils represented both a culmination of years of effort and a bold departure from traditional League work. The WCS, which were the brainchild of T. Arnold Hill, were intended to promote black union affiliation by teaching Afro-Americans about the "problems of workers, the objectives of labor, [and] the principles of industrial organization." Hill had first advocated a program for workers' education in the mid-1920s. Indeed, shortly after his appointment as head of the NUL's Department of Industrial Relations, Hill presaged the work of the Workers' Councils when he called upon the League to develop classes to inform blacks as to the "principles and workings of the labor movement."[46] Hill's endeavor to foster mutual understanding between Afro-Americans and white unionists was hardly radical. Nevertheless, fear of offending potential employers prevented the Urban League from actively pursuing this course of action before the New Deal. Thus while the NUL consistently pressed organized labor to open its ranks to blacks throughout the 1920s, the social-work group did not sanction Hill's plan for a formal program of worker education until March 1934.

Within a month of receiving board approval, Hill—who was now acting executive secretary of the NUL—officially announced the League's plans to establish Workers' Councils in communities throughout the nation.[47] From the WCs' inception, the League made clear that the new program would operate principally as a vehicle for grassroots mobilization. Though Hill declared "the philosophy behind the Workers' Councils was that of self-determination," his model of self-reliance had less to do with the bootstraps philosophy of Booker T. Washington than the guiding principles of industrial democracy.[48] The Workers' Councils program thus proceeded from the view that interest group agitation was the key to progress in the workplace. As Hill asserted in 1934, "Only if [the Negro workers] themselves realize the necessity for action can their position be strengthened."[49]

The National Urban League wasted little time bringing the Workers' Councils from concept to reality. Initially, Leaguers organized the WCs in a kind of piecemeal fashion, extending such efforts from the work of other League projects such as the EACs. By September 1934, however, the NUL established a Workers' Bureau, under its Department of Industrial Relations, in an attempt to rationalize the program's expansion and development. Headed by Lester Granger during the high point of the WCs' activity, the Workers' Bureau provided local councils with political and organizational guidance. It educated Workers' Councils about the meaning and consequences of federal recovery efforts, New Deal labor legislation, and union politics and practice. Granger, and other bureau officials, also coordinated conferences and seminars with local WCs in their ongoing efforts to encourage black participation in the labor movement. The Workers' Bureau's efforts paid off in short order. Just one year after the Urban League announced the program, the bureau had established forty-two Workers' Councils in seventeen states, covering some 30,000 workers. After four years of the bureaus' operation, the *Workers' Council Bulletin* declared that the League had organized more than seventy councils in twenty-one states.[50]

The WCs' rapid expansion can be traced to a number of factors ranging from personnel to politics. The indefatigable efforts of Lester Granger contributed significantly to the Workers' Councils' success. Only thirty-six years old at the time of his appointment, Granger, as historian Nancy Weiss points out, was both well accomplished and highly motivated. A graduate of Dartmouth College, Granger had an impressive career in social services even before heading the Workers' Bureau. During the 1920s, Granger worked for both the Negro Welfare League of Newark and the Manual Training and

Industrial School of Bordentown, New Jersey. He had also pursued graduate studies at the Columbia University–affiliated New York School of Social Work, though he did not complete a degree program.[51]

By 1930, Granger had begun to lay the foundation for his career with the Urban League. That year the former NUL fellow helped organize the League's Los Angeles chapter. He then went on to take a position as the business manager of *Opportunity*. Granger's experience developing and supervising League projects prepared him well to head the Workers' Bureau. As a staffer, he understood the internal politics of the League as well as the group's operational structure. Granger's qualifications for the job were further enhanced by his commitment to the union movement, which he believed offered working people an opportunity to shape their own destinies. Indeed, Granger was such an outspoken supporter of organized labor that in League circles, he was often referred to as a "weekend communist." A competent administrator with a sincere belief in the value of grassroots activism, Granger not only personally supervised the organization of new chapters but he spent months at a time on the road publicizing the WCS' work. Granger's presence loomed so large over the Workers' Bureau that when he took leave from the League in 1937 for the position of secretary of the Negro Welfare Division of the Welfare Council of New York, the WC stagnated.[52] By 1938, the NUL terminated the program altogether because of both personnel and funding problems, as well as co-optation of the WCS' activities by the Congress of Industrial Organizations (CIO).

Though the Workers' Councils undoubtedly benefited from the talents of individuals such as Granger, changes in the political climate likely had an even greater impact on the program. Few issues shaped the League's interest in the union movement more than New Deal labor law. Leaguers feared that the federal government's efforts to bolster organized labor might further undermine Afro-Americans' economic standing. Section 7(a) of the National Industrial Recovery Act provided the Urban League its first glimpse onto the limits of New Deal labor policy. As part of a broad effort to enhance consumer purchasing power, Section 7(a) granted workers in industries covered by the National Recovery Administration the right to unionize. The practical effects of NIRA sanctions were often more symbolic than real. Nevertheless, Section 7(a) signaled the government's support for unionization, which in turn catalyzed a flood of American Federation of Labor and grassroots organizing drives. In the long run, the budding labor movement would spawn an important civil rights ally, the CIO. The immediate consequence of Section 7(a), however, was that it enhanced the standing of the AFL, which, as T. Arnold

Hill pointed out, made it clear that "the cause of Negro workers" was not "one of its aims."[53]

The League's apprehensions about the AFL and Section 7(a) were heightened shortly after the NIRA's enactment. In the midst of its 1933 organizing drive, the Federation rebuffed both the NUL's offer to assist it in reaching out to black workers and the League's call for a commission to redress grievances pertaining to discrimination. Despite the AFL's appalling track record on the Negro question, Federation president William Green declined the NUL's entreaties on the grounds that the great craft union had always operated without racial bias.[54] Green's disingenuous assessment of the AFL's history reflected the Federation's enduring indifference to black labor. Taking place in the wake of an NIRA-inspired union drive, the exchange affirmed the Urban League's suspicion that the status afforded the Federation by New Deal labor legislation threatened Afro-Americans' employability. As Ira Reid asserted in a 1934 essay titled the "Negro Riddance Act," numerous AFL unions receiving "the benefits of Section 7A of the Recovery Act [have] eliminate[d] Negroes from membership." "The increasing strength of the old line trade and labor unions" fostered by the NRA, Reid went on to argue, "threaten[ed] more sharply than ever before the security of the Negro worker."[55]

Section 7(a) of the NIRA was not the only labor law to galvanize the Urban League. With the Recovery Act's efficacy in doubt even before the U.S. Supreme Court declared it unconstitutional in 1935, New Dealers pursued additional measures to strengthen organized labor's hand. The National Labor Relations Act (NLRA), or Wagner Act (1935), profoundly influenced both the American labor movement and the League's approach to unionization. Like Section 7(a), the Wagner Labor Act established the right to collective bargaining as a means of bolstering wages. In contrast to earlier legislation, however, Wagner also attempted to "democratize" the workplace by granting employees influence over a number of managerial prerogatives. Specifically, the act outlawed the so-called yellow-dog contract; defined company unions as an unfair labor practice; established workers' right to a "closed shop"; denied employment to strikebreakers; and created a new and more powerful National Labor Relations Board (NLRB).[56] Functioning as the labor movement's "Magna Carta," the Wagner Act enabled workers to negotiate with capital on a more equal footing. The bill, moreover, rejuvenated the American labor movement, which more than doubled its membership—growing from just 3.8 million workers to 9 million—between 1935 and 1940.[57]

Due to the NLRA's breadth, the NUL was even more alarmed by Wagner than Roosevelt's Recovery Act. Three facets of the Wagner Act were especially "dangerous to Negro workers," according to League staffers. The absence of an antidiscrimination clause, the closed shop, and the denial of jobs to strikebreakers each, Leaguers claimed, held the potential to exclude blacks not just from effective bargaining units but also from employment in entire firms. Since Wagner contained no provisions outlawing discrimination on the basis of race or creed, union locals and internationals were free to bar Afro-Americans and other minorities from membership. Not only might blacks be confined to impotent Jim Crow organizations, but if they were excluded from collective bargaining units altogether, the closed shop would require employers to terminate Afro-Americans, along with other workers, not represented by the union. Proscriptions against hiring strikebreakers further foreclosed the race's employment options. Crossing the picket line was hardly a desirable means of accessing jobs; however, Leaguers at the national and local levels appreciated this practice both as an occasional entrée into permanent employment and as a vehicle through which to punish racist unions.[58]

Believing that the Wagner Act might legitimate discrimination in the labor movement, thereby circumscribing blacks' employment options, the League took immediate action. In 1934, the National Urban League, following the NAACP's lead, petitioned Congress to amend the NLRA. In a brief to the legislature, acting NUL executive secretary T. Arnold Hill called upon the U.S. Senate to revise the Wagner Act so as to define racial discrimination as an unfair labor practice. The League ultimately urged Congress to divest unions that barred "any worker or group of workers for reason of race or creed" of the protections afforded by the labor act. In the end, Wagner's proponents in the Senate were unwilling to attach an antidiscrimination clause to the already controversial bill for fear that such actions might scuttle the measure.[59] Congress therefore left the question of discrimination in NLRA-sanctioned unions up to the courts to decide. As a consequence, labor unions were free to deny Afro-Americans equal representation. It was not until nine years after the Wagner Act was signed into law, that the California Supreme Court ruled in *James v. Marinship* that racial bars in unions ran afoul of the Fourteenth Amendment.[60]

The Urban League's concerns about Wagner were far from abstract. Between 1934 and 1938, the *Workers' Council Bulletin*—edited by Lester Granger—highlighted numerous cases of race discrimination that were attributable to New Deal labor law. The November 1936 edition of the *Bulletin*, for example, claimed that twenty-five black electrical workers had been terminated by the Standard Electrical Supply Company of Long Island following the imposition of an AFL closed shop. According to the *Bulletin*, when the "notorious and historically anti-Negro" International Brotherhood of Electrical Workers organized Standard, it excluded blacks from admission to the union. As a result, the *Bulletin* asserted, "once the shop had been organized, management was forced to sign the contract and to discharge the Negro employees who were not permitted to become members of the union."[61]

As traditional petition politics proved incapable of swaying Congress to take steps to curb race discrimination within the union movement, the Workers' Bureau adopted a more direct, if not confrontational, approach. As mentioned previously, the Workers' Councils proceeded from the view that racial uplift required collective action. In keeping with this perspective, the Workers' Councils mobilized Afro-Americans to protest, through direct action and letter campaigns, the inadequacies of the National Industrial Recovery and the Wagner Acts, as well as discrimination in the distribution of work relief.

The League's WC locals also stepped up their work with organized labor in an effort to increase black participation in the union movement. Discrimination within the American Federation of Labor was of special concern to the Workers' Bureau. Shortly after the bureau's creation, the NUL charged the group with the task of working with the AFL. By mid-1935, the Workers' Bureau aggressively pressed the Federation to open its ranks to workers irrespective of race. Operating in conjunction with the Brotherhood of Sleeping Car Porters' (BSCP) president A. Philip Randolph, the Workers' Bureau prepared a report to be delivered to the AFL's October convention. The League intended to present its findings to the Federation's Committee of Five, an AFL subcommittee on the Negro question that was formed in response to a petition filed by A. Philip Randolph one year earlier. The Urban League's study claimed that, despite the fact that the AFL had adopted numerous resolutions condemning racism within the trade union movement since 1917, the absence of enforcement mechanisms ensured the emptiness of AFL proclamations. The report thus found that racial bars were common among Federation affiliates. After warning that unfettered discrimination would give blacks little choice but to embrace rival unions, the Workers' Bureau urged the AFL to expel racist locals and internationals. It also called upon the Federation to take steps to recruit black labor. To this end, the bureau suggested the AFL appoint black organizers and initiate a worker education program that might be run in conjunction with Workers' Councils.[62]

Doubting the efficacy of research alone to effect a change in Federation policy, bureau executive secretary Lester Granger directed Afro-American workers to voice their support for the proposed reforms in the weeks leading up to the AFL's 1935 Atlantic City Convention. "Councils, labor unions and unorganized workers," he asserted, "must use the weeks between now and the AF of L convention in demonstrating, protesting, urging and employing all other means to force favorable action on the floor of the convention."[63] Workers' Councils immediately followed up on Granger's call for action. During the week of the Atlantic City Convention, WCs organized meetings and parades throughout a number of cities demanding that the AFL stop the discriminatory practices of its affiliates. The Workers' Bureau also sponsored a delegation to the Federation's convention. Consisting of several League notables, including Lester Granger and NYUL executive secretary James H. Hubert, the group met personally with union officials in an effort to build support for the bureau's calls for workers' education and expulsion of discriminatory AFL internationals and locals. The bureau delegation, moreover, distributed a series of circulars denouncing Jim Crow unionism as a threat to the labor movement as a whole.[64]

The Federation ignored the League's calls for racial fair play; nevertheless, the convention set the stage for a development that would profoundly alter the Workers' Councils' focus. Race was not the only hotly contested issue at the convention. The Atlantic City conference would shape future of the labor movement itself. Since 1933, John L. Lewis, president of the United Mine Workers (UMW), and a host of other advocates of industrial unionism had pressed the Federation to broaden its base by organizing workers irrespective of skills. Lewis believed that the AFL's craft focus not only was anachronistic but also undermined labor solidarity by imbuing workers with a narrow trade consciousness. By the time of the Atlantic City Convention, Lewis had grown weary of what he perceived as the AFL's halfhearted commitment to industrial unionism. Indeed, while the Federation had authorized industrial drives in the steel, auto, and rubber industries over the previous year, the AFL extended little more than nominal support to these endeavors. The Atlantic City Convention reaffirmed the depth of the Federation's resistance to Lewis's goals, as delegates from conservative craft organizations voted down virtually every measure proposed by the forces of industrial unionism. Angered by the union's strategic myopia, Lewis took his first steps toward leaving the AFL. In November 1935 he—joined by such labor notables as David Dubinsky, president of International Ladies Garment Workers Union, and Sidney Hillman, head of the Amalgamated Clothing Workers' Union—established the Committee for Industrial Organizations (CIO).[65] By 1938, the group formally withdrew from the AFL and adopted the Congress of Industrial Organizations as its moniker.

Perceiving the CIO as a viable alternative to the Federation, the Urban League was optimistic about the new union. Indeed, not long after Lewis and company established the committee, the Workers' Bureau described the organization as a potential boon to Afro-Americans. Two aspects of the CIO's approach were of particular interest to League officials. Its industrial focus was, by itself, a major draw. The Urban League had urged the Federation to organize on an industrial basis since the 1920s, partly as a means of extending the benefits of collective bargaining to the mass of black unskilled laborers. Like the CIO, the Workers' Bureau believed the AFL's craft orientation undercut its efficacy by dividing workers along occupational lines. The Federation's reluctance to recruit unskilled and semiskilled labor was particularly problematic for the bureau, as these workers comprised the bulk of Afro-Americans employed outside of agriculture. The bureau therefore contended that the CIO's attempts to organize workers without concern for skills promised black labor effective, democratic representation that was beyond the reach of the AFL's craft approach. The Committee for Industrial Organization's stance on race held perhaps even greater appeal for Leaguers. As the bureau noted in May 1936, much of the CIO's leadership—including John Brophy, David Dubinsky, and Sidney Hillman—had demonstrated their willingness to organize blacks well before the CIO's genesis. Thus when the CIO stated its intention to recruit members regardless of race immediately following its creation, the assertion resonated with Leaguers with a verisimilitude that was absent in similar proclamations by the AFL.[66]

By spring 1936, the Urban League's support for the CIO had manifest in formal policy directives. Responding to the AFL's attempts to quash the CIO, the bureau instructed Workers' Councils "to use their influence so that organizations in their community shall go on record as strongly supporting the Committee for Industrial Organizations."[67] To aid the group in this endeavor, Lester Granger devoted several weeks in 1936 to promoting the advantages of union affiliation to local WCs. League branches, including the Chicago Urban League, likewise sponsored related conferences on race and unionization.[68] Workers' Councils continued these activities, which were intended to augment the CIO's recruiting endeavors, through the conclusion of the program in 1938.

The CIO's organizing drives in the steel industry reaffirmed the Urban League's expectations that the union would follow the path of racial progressivism. In spring 1936, the CIO initiated an aggressive mobilization campaign in the mills of U.S. Steel through its Steel Workers Organizing Committee (SWOC). Wresting authority from both the AFL's Amalgamated Association of Iron and Steel Workers (AA) and the company's Employee Representation Plan (ERP), SWOC secured a contract from the steel giant in early 1937. The union then engaged in an unexpectedly difficult campaign in the so-called Little Steel firms, which eventually resulted in industrywide recognition by 1943.[69] While the SWOC frequently co-opted the talent and resources of both the AA and the ERP, its mobilization drives differed significantly from its rivals'. In contrast to the Federation, SWOC organizers relied heavily on broad rank-and-file participation. As a result, the CIO affiliate actively courted black labor. Recruiting black labor proved crucial, as Afro-Americans, who accounted for between 15 and 20 percent of mill workers, were often reluctant to join the union.[70] Experience with the racist practices of the AA led many black employees of U.S. Steel, as well as a number of Little Steel firms, to perceive the ERP as the only effective means of achieving employment stability in the mills. To counter Afro-Americans' apprehensions about independent unions, SWOC not only enlisted the services of black recruiters but also coordinated mobilization campaigns with local churches and civic organizations. Organizers, moreover, targeted younger black workers who were more likely to have imbibed the ethos of industrial democracy that had given birth to the resurgence of labor militancy in the period.[71]

From the National Urban League's vantage point, the CIO's steel drive presented an unprecedented opportunity for workplace equality. Believing that SWOC's endeavors were indicative of the labor movement's "new liberal attitude" about race, the Workers' Bureau argued that CIO affiliation was essential to elevating Afro-American labor's economic standing. The SWOC, as an independent industrial union, the bureau claimed, was uniquely suited to address issues such as wage differentials and labor market segmentation.[72] This is not to suggest that the League supported the steel union without caveat. Bureau officials understood SWOC's attempts to organize black workers were motivated as much by pragmatic concerns as they were by an ideological commitment to racial fair play. The bureau therefore instructed Afro-American steelworkers to use pressure tactics, if necessary, to ensure that the CIO affiliate followed through on its pledge to organize workers irrespective of race.[73]

The CIO's approach to black labor likewise shaped League perception of the union movement at the local level. The Chicago Urban League's opinion of organized labor shifted significantly in this period. During the AFL's 1934 strikes in the mills of Chicago and Gary, Indiana, for example, the CUL openly declared its opposition to the union's campaign. The Chicago League ultimately argued that discrimination on the part of AFL affiliates meant that Afro-Americans stood to make their biggest gains in industry through alliances with employers.[74] Three years later, the Chicago branch offered a very different perspective on organizing drives in area steel mills. Inspired by SWOC's comparatively egalitarian organizing tactics, CUL executive secretary A. L. Foster publicly declared his support for the steelworkers' union. Foster even went on to work directly with local CIO organizers in an effort to increase union membership.[75]

While labor legislation and shifts within the union movement itself inten-sified the Urban League's interest in organized labor, Workers' Councils were more than pragmatic tools designed to open employment. They reflected a growing sentiment among civil rights activists that race relations in America were part of a larger class struggle. As historian Jonathan Holloway has noted, black leaders of the Depression era were driven to explore the relationship between racial oppression and class exploitation by the merger of two devel-opments—a surge in radical political activism and the simultaneous decline in the popularity of scientific racism. Throughout the 1930s the Communist Party of the United States (CPUSA) aggressively courted Afro-Americans in its attempt to transform the race into the vanguard of the proletarian revolution. Although the depth and breadth of the CPUSA's ideological appeal among blacks was often unclear, its ardent defense of the Scottsboro Boys (1931), along with the its drive to organize Afro-Americans into unemployment and tenant councils, afforded the Communist Party both real and symbolic gains among working-class blacks. At the same time, the efforts of social scientists such as Robert Park and Franz Boas to illuminate the fallacies of eugenics had begun to gain intellectual traction in America. Consequently, much of the liberal intelligentsia of the 1930s adopted the view that race was a social, as opposed to biological, category.[76]

In a context of rising class appeals and a growing belief in nurture's preemi-nence over nature, Afro-American political activists came to understand race oppression as an outgrowth of economic exploitation. In the mainstream of the civil rights community, the ideological and political realignments of the era first materialized in the NAACP's Second Amenia Conference. Organized by Association president Joel Spingarn, the 1933 conference called for a rein-terpretation of the problems confronting blacks "within the larger issues facing the nation." Participants, including the NUL's Ira Reid and Elmer Carter, argued that race leaders had focused too narrowly on the so-called Negro question, leading them to overlook the relationship between the poor working condi-tions thrust upon Afro-Americans and "black economic social and psychologi-cal depression."[77] Reasoning that blacks were an exploited class of laborers, conference attendants identified interracial working-class alliances as essen-tial to Afro-American uplift. Though Amenia eschewed specific program-matic prescriptions, the NAACP's Committee on the Future Plan and Program attempted to rectify this matter one year later. Headed by black economist Abram L. Harris, a former NUL fellow and staffer, the committee encouraged the NAACP to transform itself into a center for workers' education and agita-tion. Harris thus urged the Association to develop courses to assist blacks in making sense of their place in industry while simultaneously promoting interracial solidarity. He also called upon the civil rights group to educate workers as to their rights and the importance of political participation.[78]

While the NAACP chose, at least initially, to shelve the recommendations of both the Second Amenia Conference and Harris's committee, the Association's proposals appeared to chart the basic course of the NUL's Workers' Councils. Like Amenia, the WCS proceeded from the view that the social and economic problems afflicting Afro-Americans had as much to do with class exploitation as they did racism. Presuming that blacks were "a working group first of all, and members of a race second," Workers' Bureau publications generally argued that Afro-Americans would "make real progress on their problems as Negroes" only when "their problems as workers [were] solved."[79] The Workers' Bureau therefore identified interracial working-class solidarity as pivotal to racial uplift. Since working men and women of both races were exploited by capitalists, the Urban League claimed, the way to equality closely followed the road of common ground. This was especially true in the context of the New Deal broker state, which had proved highly sensitive to interest group pressure tactics.

The Workers' Councils' official calls for collective agitation and interracial solidarity were unquestionably indicative of a new militancy within the League. Although some prominent Leaguers had expressed an interest in interracial unionism dating back to the 1920s, as mentioned previously, little came of these calls prior to the WCS. The League's decision to formalize a program of workers' education and collective agitation during the New Deal should therefore be understood as a product of the times, arising organically from a leftward shift in American and Afro-American politics. Still, the Urban League's identification of interracial unionism as an instrument of uplift was neither altogether novel nor indicative of a commitment to left-wing politics. Indeed, the WCS' calls for biracial unionism were shaped, at least in part, by the social-work group's long-standing preoccupation with race-relations theory and even social disorganization and reorganization.

Since the 1920s League officials had explored interracial unionism's potential to promote goodwill between blacks and whites. As discussed in Chapter 4, Charles S. Johnson alluded to this issue in the famed Chicago Commission on Race Relations Report. According to the CCRR, labor market segmentation and union discrimination were among a number of issues contributing to the 1919 Chicago race riot. In its efforts to stave off similar conflagrations in the future, the CCRR suggested that greater equality in the workplace might, in time, reduce racial animosity. "Through contact and association with Negroes during working hours," the commission argued, "white workers may come to look upon Negroes, not as members of a strange group with colored skin, but as individuals with the same feelings, hopes, and disappointments as other people."[80] Although the CCRR only implied that interracial unionism might counter ethnic prejudice, in 1925 the NUL took a small step toward fostering racial harmony within the union movement through a program of worker education. The League's overarching aim was to elevate "the relationships between the races in the ranks of organized labor."[81] By promoting a sense of camaraderie between black and white workers, the League hoped to defuse racial tensions. The above perspectives were hardly radical. Johnson and the NUL were influenced not by Marx or Lenin but rather by sociological models of assimilation such as ethnic cycle theory. The social-work group thus simply set out to facilitate blacks' assimilation into the American mainstream, socially and economically.

Assimilation theory continued to influence Leaguers' perspectives on unionization even during the New Deal. T. Arnold Hill, the Workers' Councils' founder, for example, left little doubt that he perceived interracial working-class solidarity as a means of developing a sense of mutual empathy between blacks and whites. In a 1937 publication, Hill identified unions as a potent means of combating apathy among blacks while simultaneously defusing racial tensions. In tones reminiscent of W. E. B. DuBois's *Black Reconstruction*, Hill argued that since slavery, the ruling class had used race as a wedge to prevent black and white workers from allying against their common enemy. During the era of the New Deal, Hill claimed that organized labor, particularly the CIO with its comparatively liberal racial policies, showed the promise of interracial class alliances. To be sure, Hill argued that such coalitions would enhance black workers' economic standing. Even so, he was clear that these efforts might likewise engender racial amity. Seemingly influenced by ethnic cycle theory, Hill asserted that organized youth groups had already shown their capacity to neutralize racial animus. Groups that brought black and white youth together for a common aim, he argued, "have not only inoculated others with the germ of good-will toward their fellow men, but have marshaled a new force of militant opinion for economic reform and cooperative efforts in social welfare and social reorganization."[82]

The Workers' Bureau's assessment of the CIO's union drives in the south echoed Hill's views. As the Steel Workers' Organizing Committee attempted to unionize southern steel mills in late 1937, the bureau argued that black participation in industrial unions held the potential to create "a new type of interracial relationship." Successful organization, the League claimed, required that the trade union movement take steps to protect labor's rights. Integrated CIO affiliates would therefore "find themselves . . . defending the civil liberties of Negro workers even at the risk of supporting 'social equality.'"

Though the *Workers Council Bulletin* eschewed discussion of specific public policy issues, it indicated that CIO affiliation might foster a sense of fellowship between Afro-American and white workers, thereby profoundly altering civil society. According to the Workers' Bureau, if SWOC did organize blacks "on a basis of democratic equality," race workers would necessarily play a vital role in local unions. In a context in which organized labor represented a powerful interest bloc, union affiliation could afford Afro-Americans real influence over "outside politics." "Thus, for the first time since Reconstruction," the bureau asserted, "Negro citizens of the south will have a chance to join in large numbers with white citizens in democratic efforts for civic improvement."[83]

Two years later, in the pages of *Opportunity*, the League revisited the topic of SWOC's southern organizing drives and their potential to adjust race relations. In "The Negro Worker and His Union," Alfred B. Lewis, reiterating the Workers' Bureau's assessment, argued that the CIO's campaign in Birmingham, Alabama, not only demonstrated SWOC's racial progressivism but augured a fundamental shift in race relations. Like the bureau, Lewis claimed that since blacks in the Alabama SWOC were admitted to the union on the same footing as whites, they had an opportunity to shape policy in both the CIO and civil society. Lewis ultimately argued that the experience of working toward a common cause held the potential to engender fealty between black and white workers, thus chipping away at Jim Crow. "It would seem clear that, in the long run, the best attack on segregation," he asserted, is organizations "including both whites and Negroes," in quest of "economic advantage for the group as a whole." He went on to say that "unions are a perfect example of such groups."[84]

Leaguers also continued to suggest that unionization might be used to adjust black workers' attitudes. As with race relations theory, League officials indicated well before the New Deal that participation in the union movement might counter social disorganization among blacks. League officials such as T. Arnold Hill and Ira Reid were especially keen on treating union affiliation as an alternative to both radical and militant nationalist political movements. In a series of essays appearing in *Opportunity* in 1930, Hill tied Communist agitation among blacks to the frustrations and difficulties engendered by protracted unemployment and union discrimination. Similarly, Ira Reid described pre–New Deal racial protest campaigns such as "don't buy where you can't work" as products of a narrow race consciousness rooted in maladjustment. Attributing the appeal of nontraditional political movements to the collapse of institutional social controls, both Reid and Hill identified interracial unionism as a promising antidote. They hoped that union affiliation would not only draw blacks' attention to structural sources of inequality but also, in the long run, eliminate tensions between black and white workers.

During the New Deal, Hill and the League continued to advance these perspectives. In a May 1933 publication assessing the Depression's impact on black America, for example, the NUL claimed that chronic unemployment lessened the sway of institutions such as church, school, and family, resulting in escalating rates of personal demoralization. The report, which was based partly on fieldwork performed by T. Arnold Hill, devoted particular attention to the relationship between joblessness and political radicalism among blacks. The League claimed that "discouragement caused by discrimination in employment" was "promoting a feeling of rebellion." Such sentiments, it observed, were most common among highly trained and intelligent Afro-Americans whose "deep sense of injustice" made them susceptible to new political ideas. Echoing views articulated by Hill before the New Deal, the NUL alleged that Communist organizers preyed upon the alienation gaining momentum among more industrious Afro-Americans. Offering workers the "social camaraderie of the meetings of the Council of the unemployed," Communists enticed unemployed blacks with a sense of belonging. The NUL concluded that political movements provided a social wage to workers in the form of a "reassuring joy of having found a solution in the efforts of a new movement."[85]

The NUL's 1933 report did not mention unionism. Nevertheless, given that Leaguers such as Hill had previously alluded to the promise of organized labor as an alternative to radicalism, the publication's observations are significant with respect to the issue of biracial unionism. Indeed, the implications of the May 1933 report in this regard are made all the more tantalizing by the fact that the study noted that radical sentiment among blacks had given rise to calls for interracial solidarity. As one unemployed Afro-American laborer informed a League social worker, "In the future we are going to have a class conscious group of Negro workers who with white workers are going to demand among other things assurance against just such a circus as we have had for the last four years."[86] When one considers that the study was authored less than one year prior to Hill's proposal for the Workers' Councils, it seems likely that a desire to counter maladjustment as manifest in, among other things, radicalism played some role in his thinking about the practicality of the WCS. This suggestion is further buttressed by the fact that Hill consistently instructed Lester Granger to take steps to prevent communist infiltration of the Workers' Councils.[87]

Hill revisited the union movement's capacity to counter social ills among Afro-Americans in a 1937 study, this time offering a broader assessment of

black culture. Reflecting upon lingering circumspection about organized labor among Afro-Americans, Hill argued that many blacks suffered from a
deep fatalism rooted in the cultural legacies of slavery and Jim Crow. During
slavery, Hill argued, planter paternalism had divested blacks of faith in their
ability to bring about change. In the postemancipation era, philanthropists
and employers' domination of black life reinforced Afro-Americans' "trusting
reliance upon something unforeseen" for solutions to their problems. Reasoning that in the era of New Deal liberalism "prestige and advancement will of
necessity go to those who are articulate and assertive," Hill claimed that lack of
self-confidence, if unchecked, would consign blacks to the bottom rung of
economic and social life. Hill ultimately argued not only that participation in
groups such as the CIO would bolster blacks' employment prospects and
wages, but that collective agitation based on economic needs and citizenship
rights might assist Afro-Americans in throwing off entrenched feelings of
inferiority.[88]

The Urban League's greater interest in the labor movement during the New
Deal was indicative of the complex issues shaping the group's uplift vision.
The Workers' Councils, the clearest institutional expression of the League's
embrace of the union movement during the 1930s, sprung from both pragmatic and ideological imperatives. A direct response to the political and economic importance of unions during the New Deal, WCs embodied the social-
work group's basic desire to ensure that blacks received their fair share of
decent jobs. Such practical concerns eventually led the League to dissolve the
Workers' Councils in 1938, as the CIO's own initiatives to recruit Afro-Americans obviated the work of the WCs. The tangible and immediate advantages of
unionization notwithstanding, Leaguers also conceived of black participation
in the labor movement as a means of soothing racial tensions and redressing
the cultural pathologies they believed were prevalent among Afro-Americans.
The group's acceptance of labor militancy in this period was thus consistent
with the League's belief that the acculturation of black workers was pivotal to
the racial uplift.

■ The New Deal greatly influenced the scope of the League's employment
work. Because of the federal government's increased role in the nation's economic affairs during the 1930s, the NUL and its locals de-emphasized voluntarist arrangements in favor of efforts to secure government assistance. In many
respects, this shift marked a new militancy within the League. National and
local Leagues worked closely with government officials to shape public policy,
and even occasionally encouraged protests against racial injustice in federal
programs. But while there is little doubt that such efforts constituted a signifi-

cant change in approach, the League's basic philosophy and concerns differed little from its pre–New Deal endeavors. Believing that joblessness might vitiate blacks' character, thereby reinforcing employer prejudice, Leaguers pursued policies to counter the deleterious effects of social disorganization. The social-work group's vocational guidance and union activities thus continued to reflect the League's desire to foster harmonious relations through mutually satisfying contacts between blacks and whites. The heightened racial and economic liberalism of the decade mitigated many of the least egalitarian aspects of this approach during the New Deal. Even so, League policy—particularly in the realm of vocational guidance—continued to stress both the elimination of black undesirables and the simultaneous elevation of the so-called Negro better classes. These tendencies would be even more evident during and immediately following the Second World War.

6. Employment from the March on Washington to the Pilot Placement Project, 1940–1950

We must be alert to guide the interest of the Negro community along constructive channels of activity.—Lester Granger, 1941

During the 1940s, the Urban League continued to perceive government assistance as essential to achieving its traditional goals of helping blacks obtain employment while adjusting them to the economic realities of the day. The combination of expanding employment opportunities and the swelling tide of left-wing politics ultimately strengthened the League's commitment to a kind of militancy that generally muted the class implications of the group's program through the first half of the decade. Even so, Urban Leaguers shed neither their concerns about social disorganization nor their special interest in the plight of the black middle class. The Urban League's calls for state intervention on behalf of Afro-Americans in this period were, as was the case during the New Deal, consistent with the group's general emphasis on the proficient performance of black labor and the integrity of the Afro-American community. Moreover, by the end of the decade, League employment initiatives, influenced partly by the postwar downturn, again prioritized the needs of the so-called Negro better classes. This chapter thus contends that despite major changes in the League's orientation, in the group's political stance, and in its focus during and following the Second World War, the acculturation of black workers was still a vital element of the social-work group's uplift program.

World War II

Following the outbreak of the Second World War in Europe, League officials were alarmed by the growing gulf in employment separating black and white workers. As policies such as the Lend Lease Act revitalized America's economy, unemployment rates dropped drastically. Indeed, between 1940 and 1942, national unemployment declined from 8,120,000 individuals to just 2,660,000. Despite the return of economic health, however, blacks' job opportunities during the early stages of World War II remained grim.[1] Not long before the Japanese attack on Pearl Harbor, the United States Employment Service (USES) reported that more than half the firms it surveyed refused to employ blacks.[2] Racism within the labor movement further checked Afro-Americans' employment prospects, particularly in construction and the burgeoning aviation industry. Confronted with entrenched discrimination, Afro-American workers had little luck breaking into the booming defense industries.[3] As late as 1942, Afro-Americans comprised just 3 percent of all workers employed in firms engaged in war production.[4] Furthermore, the few defense contractors willing to hire blacks rarely utilized race men and women in skilled or even semiskilled positions, relegating those fortunate enough to acquire jobs in munitions production to manual labor, irrespective of their training.[5]

With blacks virtually excluded from defense jobs, unemployment among Afro-Americans remained at Depression levels. As a result, Afro-Americans continued to be overrepresented among relief recipients. As white representation among Works Projects Administration (WPA) workers began to fall nationally, for example, blacks' proportion increased. In April 1941, about 237,000 blacks were certified for WPA work. This meant that Afro-Americans, who were roughly 10 percent of the general population and 13 percent of the labor force, comprised 16 percent of WPA workers nationally. Leaguers believed that Afro-Americans' disproportionate representation among the unemployed and relief recipients posed a threat to the future of black labor. Since many New Deal programs were simply emergency measures that were to be dismantled once unemployment returned to acceptable levels, League officials feared that blacks' failure to secure private employment would reinforce the race's standing as a reserve army of labor. In a bifurcated employment structure of this sort, Afro-Americans would naturally bear the brunt of both unemployment and underemployment for the foreseeable future.[6]

The Urban League's experience with New Deal agencies taught it the potential advantages of federal intervention. Thus Leaguers not only continued to court government officials, but they occasionally advocated protest action on a national scale. In the fall of 1940, A. Philip Randolph, the NAACP's Walter White, and the NUL's T. Arnold Hill met with President Roosevelt to urge him to take action against discrimination in the defense industries. Dissatisfied with Roosevelt's response, A. Philip Randolph decided on a more confrontational approach. Thus in January of 1941, Randolph organized the March on Washington Movement (MOWM).[7]

Randolph proposed to lead between 10,000 and 100,000 Afro-Americans on a protest march through the then racially segregated Washington, D.C. The labor leader hoped to secure federal assistance in eliminating the color bar within unions, defense employment, public agencies, and the military. These issues garnered broad support from Afro-Americans, who were largely unenthusiastic about the war. As a 1942 survey performed by the Office of War Information (OWI) asserted: "Resentment at Negro discrimination is fairly widespread throughout the Negro population." In fact, disillusionment among blacks ran so deep that most blacks surveyed by the OWI indicated that they were likely to be treated the same or better under Japanese rule. Though a clear majority conceded they would be worse off under Nazi rule, only 11 percent of respondents imagined that an American victory over the Axis would improve blacks' socioeconomic standing in the United States.[8]

With significant numbers of blacks indifferent to the war effort, Randolph's movement attracted a large, heterogeneous following. Afro-Americans ranging from former Garveyites to prominent members of the NAACP such as Walter White joined the MOWM. The NUL's Lester Granger, who was appointed assistant executive secretary of the National League in fall 1940, likewise declared public support for the March on Washington Movement and even participated in its sponsoring committee. Granger served with Randolph's group as a private citizen rather than as an Urban League official; nevertheless, his presence in the MOWM represented a bold departure from the cautious approach that had characterized the League's work prior to the Depression. Many whites, including the president, criticized the proposed march on the grounds that it posed a potential threat to national security. In this context, the NUL was compelled to withhold formal endorsement of Randolph's movement. Even so, Granger's involvement in the MOWM had the potential to tarnish the League's reputation with both business and the government.[9]

Historians Paula Pfeffer and Beth Bates have demonstrated that mainstream uplift organizations' support for the MOWM was largely owed to a combination of Randolph's efforts to woo them and the movement's mass appeal.[10] Pervasive discontent among blacks, as scholar Lee Finkle has shown, compelled "responsible" black leaders to encourage Afro-Americans to tie the fight for democracy abroad to the extension of equality at home. The Detroit race riot, according to Finkle, led much of the mainstream black leadership class to sour on Randloph's movement by summer 1943. Still, the early support for the MOWM offered by leaders such as White and Granger was one of the most salient examples of the so-called Double Victory Campaign (victory over Hitlerism abroad and at home) that dominated black politics during the war. The seemingly interminable poverty and discrimination encountered by Afro-Americans, even in the midst of an expanding economy, ensured a rapid decline in morale that pushed the old-line civil rights organizations to back mass protest politics in order to maintain their relevance.[11] But while the quest for vitality was an important aspect of League officials' involvement in the MOWM, Leaguers' support for Randolph's movement also reflected a growing sentiment within the social-work group that direct assistance from the federal government had become essential to Afro-American economic uplift.

In exchange for Randolph's pledge to call off his march, Roosevelt finally attempted to tackle discrimination in the war industries by issuing Executive Order 8802 in June 1941. Executive Order 8802 did not achieve all of MOWM's objectives; nevertheless, Roosevelt's decree laid out the federal government's opposition to discrimination based on "race, color, creed, or national origin" in federal agencies and in firms and unions contracted by the federal government for war production.[12] The centerpiece of the presidential order was the creation of the Fair Employment Practices Committee (FEPC). Functioning under the auspices of the Office of Price Management (OPM), the FEPC's main task was to "receive and investigate complaints of discrimination in violation of the provision of this order and take appropriate steps to redress grievances which it finds valid."[13]

Though many black leaders were initially skeptical about Executive Order 8802 and the FEPC, the Urban League gave them its unabashed support. Echoing A. Philip Randolph's sentiments about the order, CUL president Earl Dickerson likened Roosevelt's directive to a second Emancipation Proclamation: "This order has given new meaning, new vitality to the Emancipation Proclamation. Lincoln's proclamation of 1863 freed us physically; Roosevelt's proclamation of 1941 is the beginning of our economic freedom."[14] Lester Granger likewise argued that Roosevelt's order had the potential to significantly improve the economic lives of Afro-Americans.[15]

The League's enthusiasm about the presidential order is by no means surprising. The FEPC's primary goal of opening war industries to all workers irrespective of race, creed, color, or national origin was, of course, consistent with the Urban League's general objectives. The League and the Fair Employment Practices Committee, however, shared more than a common aim. Aided by connections established through its work with New Deal agencies, the Urban League maintained operational ties to the FEPC. Prominent Leaguers like Granger and CUL director of industrial relations Howard Gould worked as liaisons between the social-work group and President Roosevelt's committee. A number of Urban Leaguers, moreover, secured appointments to the FEPC board. Earl Dickerson was a member of the original Fair Employment Practices Committee (1941–43). A University of Chicago–trained lawyer, Dickerson was a seasoned politician—having been both attorney general for the northern Illinois district and a Chicago alderman.[16] By 1943, however, Dickerson was unceremoniously discharged from the FEPC following President Roosevelt's reorganization of the committee. Though Dickerson was the only original member of the FEPC who hoped to continue on with the board, his militancy doomed his bid for reappointment.[17] Still, the CUL president's departure from the FEPC did not eliminate the Urban League's presence on the board. In fact, Dickerson was replaced by another CUL associate, Sara Southall. Lester Granger also participated in board decisions in the reorganized FEPC.[18]

The League believed that its connections to the Fair Employment Practices Committee afforded it an opportunity to exert real influence over national policy. Arguing that the FEPC's efficacy depended "largely upon the kind of intelligent follow-up that is developed," the NUL announced its intention to assist the committee through the fulfillment of a number of "unexciting" day-to-day tasks in keeping with its general approach to black uplift. Leaguers thus took great pains to provide the FEPC and the Office of Price Management with reports and data to inform them about discrimination in employment. Between 1941 and 1942 this work was sometimes augmented by privately established Fair Employment Practices Councils that many local Leagues, including the CUL, helped to create in order to assist regional divisions of the FEPC in their quest for accurate data on job discrimination in the war industries.[19]

The committee's early efforts in Chicago suggest the League did, in fact, enjoy some measure of influence over board policy. Sharing the Urban League's belief in the importance of "information" in combating racial discrimination, the first major task confronting the FEPC was "educational." The organization, therefore, spent much of 1941 and 1942 engaged in a massive publicity drive to outline its objectives to employers and workers. The centerpiece of the committee's educational work consisted of a series of public hearings held in Los Angeles, Chicago, New York, and Birmingham. Much like the Urban League's private endeavors to combat job discrimination, these hearings were designed to demonstrate the pervasiveness of racial prejudice in the workplace in order to educate employers and workers about the importance of complying with Executive Order 8802. The lack of any enforcement mechanism ensured the committee's meetings were not always efficacious; however, by the time the FEPC opened its Chicago hearings, it had adopted a more aggressive stance that both complemented the activities of the Chicago Urban League and demonstrated the advantages of the League's ties to the committee.[20]

Even before President Roosevelt issued Executive Order 8802, the war economy had a discernible impact on black Chicagoans' employability. The

Illinois State Employment Service reported that blacks comprised more than 16 percent of the workers it placed between August and September 1940. Six months later, Howard Gould asserted that the war emergency induced nearly three dozen employers who had previously refused to hire Afro-Americans to open their doors to blacks. In spite of these noteworthy advances, however, the majority of the city's industries continued to deny employment to Afro-Americans. Consequently, black Chicagoans remained overrepresented among the city's unemployed and relief cases.[21]

Faced with entrenched job discrimination against Afro-Americans, the Chicago Urban League worked diligently to try to win the hearts and minds of employers and white labor. As it had from its inception, the CUL attempted to improve the employment opportunities available to Afro-Americans through voluntarist arrangements with local firms. The growing war economy did provide the League with some success, particularly with companies that had previously employed Afro-Americans. Nevertheless, most employers were moved by neither the Chicago League's attempts to demonstrate black workers' productive potential nor its pleas for racial fair play. Management at General Motors' Buick airplane engine plant in Melrose Park (a Chicago suburb) proved to be one of the CUL's toughest foes. The Melrose plant refused to hire Afro-Americans in spite of a labor shortage. Howard Gould, therefore, spent many months trying to persuade the plant to employ black workers. To show the potential advantages of employing black labor, Gould collected data from the Illinois Institute of Technology (IIT) demonstrating that blacks who had acquired technical training sufficient to merit employment were consistently denied jobs by the Melrose Park plant. He thus informed Melrose that the racial bar contributed to the company's labor shortage. Receiving no response from Buick, Gould eventually turned to the Office of Price Management for assistance.[22]

When the OPM took no steps to redress this matter, Gould sent his findings directly to the FEPC, which made Buick one of its chief priorities in Chicago. At its initial hearings in the Windy City, the FEPC summoned six Chicago-area employers: Stewart-Warner, Majestic Radio and Television, Bearse Manufacturing, Simpson Construction, Studebaker, and Buick.[23] Adamantly denying any wrongdoing, Buick—whose placement practices the CUL challenged just a few months earlier—was perhaps the most obstinate firm at the hearings. Using information supplied by the CUL, the FEPC adduced a mountain of evidence demonstrating that Melrose's employment policies were in violation of Executive Order 8802. Following in Gould's footsteps, the FEPC reviewed the placement records of the IIT and found that none of the 309 graduates employed by Buick were Afro-American. Given that Melrose required applicants to divulge their race and religion, the fact that none of the recent hires was black suggested that this practice was discriminatory.[24]

Buick ardently denied charges that its hiring policies were discriminatory; nevertheless, the Fair Employment Practices Committee was not convinced. The FEPC directed Buick's Melrose plant and the other Chicago-area companies it investigated to change their employment policies. It not only ordered management to "cease and desist" requests to employment agencies specifying applicants' race or religion, but it also required offending firms to inform all employment agencies of their intention to comply with President Roosevelt's directive. Perhaps most importantly, each company was ordered to submit "monthly reports to the FEPC demonstrating its progress in hiring without regard to race, creed, color, or national origin."[25]

The second round of FEPC hearings in Chicago tackled the issue of discrimination in organized labor. The building trades were of particular interest to the committee, since racism within these unions had long undermined black construction workers' ability to find employment. In an ironic turn of events, the plight of Afro-American workers was further exacerbated when the Office of Price Management gave the AFL a near monopoly over construction work in exchange for a no-strike pledge. Because Afro-Americans were rarely admitted to the building trades, this agreement effectively barred black workers from a large portion of construction projects. Like their national parent organizations, the Chicago chapters of both the Urban League and the NAACP negotiated in vain with the building trades to open their ranks to Afro-Americans. Frustrated by their inability to secure employment in their chosen professions, members of the American Consolidated Trades Council, "an organization of black plumbers and steamfitters," telegrammed Earl Dickerson in early 1942 requesting the FEPC's assistance.[26]

Perhaps because of his familiarity with the issues at hand, Dickerson chaired Chicago's second series of FEPC hearings in April 1942. A number of black plumbers and steamfitters reported to the committee that the discriminatory practices of the Pipe Trade Council (PTC) of Chicago prevented them from obtaining employment in publicly funded projects.[27] The testimony of representatives from Chicago's Pipe Trade Council only confirmed allegations of discrimination. William Quirk of the Chicago Journeyman Plumbers' Union Local 130 stated that the only blacks on union projects would be those "passing for white." He went on to say that until unemployment was eliminated among white unionists, whites would "come first." Wilson Frankland, president of the Steamfitters' Protective Association Local 597, was more conciliatory than Quirk but was no more receptive to integrating his membership. Ultimately, Frankland argued that he could do nothing as long as the union's core membership was against integration. Furthermore, pointing to rank-and-file opposition to black union membership, Frankland claimed that attempts to integrate the workforce would result in dangerous work stoppages that were detrimental to the needs of the nation's war economy.[28]

Dismayed by the Pipe Trade Council's testimony, the FEPC again took action. Just as it had with business interests, the FEPC "issued directives and cease and desist orders." The committee ordered both the Steamfitters' Protective Association and the Chicago Journeymen Plumbers' Union to open their doors to black craftsmen and to permit them to work on government projects. The FEPC also required the unions to file monthly reports demonstrating their compliance with Executive Order 8802.[29]

The Chicago hearings reaffirmed the League's assumptions regarding the potential value of its ties with the FEPC. Just as the NUL speculated before the hearings, Dickerson's presence in the FEPC meant that the committee had full "access to the fund of information and social wisdom that the League has accumulated during the past thirty years."[30] The importance of this connection was evinced most clearly by the committee's handling of Buick. As significantly, the Chicago hearings also gave Dickerson and, to a certain extent, the League, an opportunity to shape the methods the committee used to achieve its aims well beyond the hearings.

When questioning Wilson Frankland of the Steamfitters' Protective Association, Dickerson asserted his belief that the committee should not use strict quotas to define and redress discriminatory practices. Though quotas had been used successfully in a number of New Deal projects, Dickerson believed strict quotas ran counter to American ideals of fair play. Instead, he proposed a system of "case method" work that was strikingly similar to the Urban League's. It called for investigating complaints, which would allow the FEPC to gauge employers' and white labor's attitudes as well as employment and membership practices in specific firms and unions. Assuming a violation was uncovered, the committee would share its report with the accused in a private meeting in order to persuade the offending party to comply with the executive order. The case-method approach became the signature of the FEPC's investigatory work and remained its primary method of combating discrimination even after Dickerson left the committee.[31]

Influence over the committee provided the League but a means to an end. The Urban League was first and foremost interested in the FEPC's ability to broaden blacks' employment vistas. While the hearings' final results were mixed, they had provided grounds for optimism. In spite of the fact that the FEPC lacked any real enforcement mechanism, most of the companies it investigated in Chicago followed through, to varying degrees, with pledges to comply with the executive order. The directives, therefore, appear to have played some role in opening many new fields of employment to Afro-Americans.[32]

The Urban League's placement activities for 1942 confirmed the FEPC's worth as a means of enhancing Afro-Americans' employability. The number of men and women registering with the Chicago League's West and South Side offices doubled between 1940 and 1942. The South Side office alone registered more than 19,000 job seekers in 1942. The deluge of applicants was so great that the Chicago Urban League was forced to reestablish its job placement bureau before year's end. In response to the increased demand for black labor, the CUL's Department of Industrial Relations made 598 field visits and conferred with fifty-one labor leaders in 1942. The Chicago League claimed these efforts were reasonably well received. It persuaded 278 firms to open new work opportunities to blacks, helping the League find jobs for more than 12,500 black men and women.[33]

The Brooklyn Urban League (BUL)—which would become part of the Urban League of Greater New York by 1944—experienced a similar improvement in its ability to make placements. In just two months, from June 1 to August 1, 1942, the Brooklyn League's placement office interviewed 2,054 men and women. Nearly 30 percent of these individuals were referred directly to jobs in industry, while another 25 percent were directed to either government or union placement offices. Perhaps more striking was the change in demographics among job seekers visiting the BUL. The Brooklyn League noted that war production and the FEPC facilitated black men's ability to find industrial employment to such an extent that the majority of those seeking the League's job placement assistance were now women.[34]

In spite of these significant accomplishments, however, black workers continued to face stiff employment barriers. A year after FDR issued Executive Order 8802, the directive had yet to expand employment opportunities in key areas of defense production such as the aircraft industry. Moreover, firms that had been named in the FEPC's hearings often ignored the Committee's directives. Buick's Melrose Plant and the Pipe Trade Council of Chicago, for example, both refused to file monthly reports with the FEPC as they had been ordered during the Chicago hearings. Furthermore, when employers chose to comply with Executive Order 8802, they rarely considered Afro-Americans for skilled positions. The situation was far worse for Afro-American women. The Brooklyn Urban League lamented that even employers who had been willing to hire black men in skilled occupations generally remained opposed to hiring black women in such fields.[35]

Keenly aware of the Fair Employment Practices Committee's limitations, the Urban League and the FEPC board itself called on President Roosevelt to increase the committee's powers at the conclusion of the public hearings in the spring of 1942. Dickerson and his fellow board members urged President Roosevelt to expand both the committee's jurisdiction and its powers to sub-poena individuals and records. They also called for a larger budget and staff, as well as "additional legal means to adjust difficult cases." To the disbelief of Leaguers and FEPC members alike, however, Roosevelt responded to these requests by pursuing steps to actually weaken the Fair Employment Practices Committee.[36]

In the winter of 1942, the president transferred jurisdiction over the FEPC from the Office of Price Management to Paul McNutt's War Manpower Commission (WMC). An outspoken critic of the FEPC, McNutt not only slashed its budget but also limited its access to the WMC's facilities and refused to increase its staff.[37] The FEPC was dealt perhaps its most severe blow when President Roosevelt, advised by McNutt, indefinitely postponed the highly anticipated railroad hearings. The League, like most uplift and civil rights organizations, believed this postponement was an affront to Afro-Americans. Job uncertainty during the Depression intensified already virulent racism within the railroad brotherhoods and the industry generally. Whites thus began to displace blacks even from the few unskilled railroad jobs in which Afro-Americans had established niches.[38]

Though incensed by President Roosevelt's decision, the Urban League responded cautiously, eschewing public confrontation. In fact, as A. Philip Randolph organized a new round of MOWM-sponsored protest campaigns, called the "Save the FEPC" rallies, in Chicago and New York, NUL executive secretary Lester Granger actually distanced himself from the MOWM. Granger, it should be noted, remained at arms length from Randolph's movement even as the labor leader's efforts resonated with a great many Afro-Americans.[39] Advancing the view that America could not successfully wage a war against tyranny abroad while denying millions of its own citizens the rights and privileges accompanying citizenship, Randolph's "Save the FEPC" campaigns inspired wide support among blacks through spring 1943, breathing, at least for a time, new vitality into the flagging March on Washington Movement. Backed by dozens of civil rights organizations and thousands of Afro-Americans, Randolph ultimately urged President Roosevelt to reinstate the Fair Employment Practices Committee not simply to fulfill the promise of democracy to America's loyal black citizens but to increase the nation's moral and material capacity to prosecute the war.[40]

The MOWM's popularity notwithstanding, Granger's decision to maintain some distance from Randolph's FEPC campaign was, in many ways, understandable. The Fair Employment Practices Committee's official function was,

Lester Granger, center, conversing with U.S. Naval personnel (U.S. National Archives, 80-G-33398. Reproduction by Photo Response)

by itself, controversial. Employers and unionists alike often opposed the FEPC's activities on the grounds that its work infringed on their rights to determine the composition of their workforce and membership. White southerners likewise found the specter of a federal antidiscrimination agency menacing. Alabama governor Frank Dixon's assertion that "the war emergency should not be used as a pretext to bring about the abolition of the color line in the South," typified southern antagonism to the FEPC.[41] Granger and the League believed that at a time in which many white Americans not only opposed black equality but also perceived efforts to integrate the workforce as a threat to national security, Randolph's methods were too "radical." As mentioned above, following the 1943 Detroit riot, Granger and other so-called responsible black leaders came to see Randolph's movement as a potential threat to social order and, by extension, the cause of equality in the workplace.

Though the League's reservations about the MOWM led it to eschew ties with Randolph's rallies, the social-work group's own campaign in support of the FEPC bore the imprint of the black labor leader's influence. The Urban League's behind-the-scenes efforts to encourage the committee's reinstatement hammered at the very themes explored in Randolph's rallies. In a letter to Paul

McNutt, for example, the NUL's William Baldwin decried the WMC's decision to postpone the railroad hearings as "a serious disservice to the cause of victory." Baldwin argued that discriminatory policies by the railway brotherhoods and management undermined the war effort by creating labor shortages that threatened the supply of men and materials. Moreover, Baldwin claimed, discrimination of this sort was a blow to blacks' morale. He asserted that the NUL board frequently observed "the bitter disillusionment and cynicism which the War Manpower Commission's action has occasioned among our Negro citizens."[42] One month later, Lester Granger echoed these sentiments at a FEPC conference on the committee's future. Like Baldwin, Granger asserted that the WMC's decision to postpone the railway hearings sapped Afro-Americans' morale. By reinstating the railway hearings, he concluded, the government would demonstrate its goodwill to the nation's black citizens.[43]

Randolph's and the League's attempt to use the war as a pretext for building popular support for the FEPC was a shrewd political strategy.[44] Given the broad opposition to the committee's work, attempts to base claims for blacks' workplace integration on war production requirements was an effective means of countering white antagonism. Moreover, this strategy carried considerable weight with liberal politicians. Indeed, when Roosevelt signed Executive Order 8802, he declared that because of the war emergency, the nation could no longer countenance the inefficiency in production engendered by thousands of workers' exclusion "from employment in industries engaged in defense productions solely because of race."[45] Thus FDR's decision to reinstate the FEPC in May 1943 under Executive Order 9346 is a testament to the brilliance of Randolph's approach.

But while Randolph's and the League's efforts to "shame" the president into action may have been illustrative of their political acumen, in the case of the League these endeavors also reveal the continuities between the Urban League's prewar reliance on petition politics and its wartime militancy. Granger's and Baldwin's attempts at moral suasion were ultimately consistent with the League's practice of basing calls for black inclusion on the conduct and contributions of Afro-Americans. It is therefore not surprising that the League's support for the committee was rooted in part in its faith in the FEPC's ability to foster mutually satisfying relations between blacks and whites.

Although whites often charged that the committee's work was divisive, the Urban League believed that the FEPC had the potential to bring the nation together. As with its private endeavors, the League hoped to use the committee to integrate Afro-Americans into mainstream society socially as well as economically. In a 1941 National Urban League report on the FEPC, Lester Granger alluded to the committee's ability to help "guide the interests of the

Negro community along constructive channels of activity." Identifying social disorganization as a threat to individual probity as well as race relations, the report implied that the committee's efforts to improve blacks' employment options had the potential to help young Afro-Americans see the connections between their own economic and political interests and the nation's as a whole. Granger was especially concerned that poor job prospects might lead blacks to engage in separatist politics, asserting that "we must stand staunchly against the unwise 'racialist' programs that are being offered in our communities by neighborhood 'medicine men.' " Just as the League had argued even before the Depression, vocational training presented an alternative to such activities. According to Granger, however, vocational guidance could only fulfill this role if blacks were provided assurances that training would be rewarded with employment.[46] The committee's work thus offered a means of demonstrating to Afro-Americans that their best hope for progress lay not in separatist programs but in hard work and self improvement.

Similarly, Leaguers believed the FEPC's efforts might also foster goodwill between black and white workers. Although blacks' integration into new fields of employment frequently erupted into conflict, the League had reason to believe that the FEPC's work would, in the long run, mollify tensions at the job. By engaging in careful negotiation that emphasized black workers' productive capacity as well as the democratic value of integration, the committee not only might facilitate the introduction of blacks into new fields but also could help quell racial hostility in the workplace. When Detroit's Packard Motor Company introduced two black workers to new fields of employment in October 1941, for example, 600 whites staged a sitdown strike until the black employees were removed. Over the next several months, the FEPC negotiated successfully to have them reinstated, and, according to the League, tensions were eventually eased at the plant.[47] Such experiences led Earl Dickerson to conclude that careful integration of Afro-Americans into the workplace would make clear that blacks and whites could, in fact, work together, which he believed was pivotal to encouraging employers to use Afro-American labor in skilled positions during and after the war.[48]

While the Urban League supported the Fair Employment Practices Committee on the grounds that it might facilitate the integration of Afro-Americans both socially and economically, it did not believe that the FEPC's activities obviated voluntarist, self-help endeavors. In fact, the League's commitment to social engineering ultimately undermined its faith in the ability of coercive measures alone to solve blacks' employment problems. Lorenzo Davis, director of the Brooklyn Urban League and an active supporter of the FEPC, spoke for most Leaguers when he argued that the federal government's antidiscrimination programs were inadequate because their methods were mainly "suppressive and remedial measures rather than basic or curative."[49] Believing that the committee's work, by itself, would do little to increase business owners' willingness to hire Afro-Americans, the League continued to identify demonstrations of black labor's versatility and efficiency as essential to expanding Afro-Americans' job prospects. The National Urban League and its locals, therefore, tried to ease blacks' transition into industry by helping them "adjust" to industrial employment.

Illustrative of the enduring influence of ethnic cycle theory, the League encouraged employers and unionists, as it had even before the New Deal, to think of their black employees and shift-mates as *workers* first and *Negroes* second.[50] The National, New York, and Chicago Leagues sustained their prewar efforts to adjust the attitudes and habits of black workers while negotiating behind the scenes with union leaders and personnel managers. The Urban League surveyed plants to determine employer satisfaction with black labor as well as blacks' sentiments about their jobs; it negotiated directly with personnel managers and union leaders to create job openings; it provided vocational guidance to Afro-American job seekers to help match the "right worker" with the "right job"; and it used union drives, handbills, the black press, and company personnel offices to advise black workers of their rights and duties as paid employees of particular plants.[51]

While the extent of the League's impact on Afro-Americans' employment prospects is unclear, the Urban League's voluntarist efforts were, in fact, relevant.[52] The FEPC was hardly a panacea. Because its scope was limited to defense and federal employment, many jobs were beyond its purview. Furthermore, since the reorganized committee could take action only against companies that were brought to its attention by official complaint, many defense firms operating in violation of Executive Orders 8802 and 9346 could escape the FEPC's attention.[53] Finally, the Fair Employment Practices Committee had no effective enforcement mechanisms as it could only broker voluntary agreements with employers that were not actually binding. Thus, given the FEPC's limitations, the League's own efforts may likely have had some influence.

Whether as a consequence of the expanding war economy or the work of the Urban League and the federal government, the League's placement work continued along an upward trajectory through 1943. Of 300 plants the NUL surveyed that year, 288 claimed to have employed more blacks than in the past. Moreover, blacks were employed as skilled and semiskilled workers in 154 and 247 firms, respectively. Afro-Americans also made significant gains in the defense industry. The War Manpower Commission reported that blacks comprised 9 percent of Chicago's defense workers by November of 1943. Of some 559,000 workers employed in 686 Chicago plants, 49,515 were listed as nonwhite. This marked an increase of more than 10,000 Afro-American workers in just six months.[54]

In a striking turn of events, employers now actively sought the League's placement assistance. Seven hundred and eighty three firms placed more than 4,500 requests for black labor with the CUL in 1943. Most of these requests, 4,169, were for industrial or commercial employment. The increase in manufacturing employment was the most promising aspect of this development. Nearly 60 percent of the firms seeking the Chicago League's assistance requested Afro-Americans for positions in mechanical trades and manufacturing.[55]

Despite apparent advances, the Urban League believed that there was much room for improvement. In particular, Leaguers were concerned about blacks' inability to make significant gains in skilled occupations. While federal agencies such as the WMC and the FEPC created thousands of new openings in industrial work, the government was unable to break down all the obstacles confronting blacks in skilled employment. As Lester Granger noted, Afro-Americans' ability to acquire skilled and semiskilled jobs was hampered by "hidden or overt management resistance, and also by discriminatory policies in such unions as the International Brotherhood of Boilermakers, Iron, Shipbuilders and Helpers of America and the International Association of Machinists." Though the majority of their placements between 1942 and 1945 were for unskilled jobs, the difficulties blacks encountered in securing the "better types of employment" led the Urban Leagues of both New York and Chicago to scale back their placements in domestic and personal service work while simultaneously increasing their emphasis on "upgrading" blacks' job opportunities. The League, therefore, focused greater attention on assisting Afro-Americans in acquiring employment in semiskilled, skilled, and white-collar jobs.

As with its general placement work, the Urban League held that demonstrations of Afro-Americans' job proficiency were essential to gaining access to the better occupations. Believing that blacks' success in semiskilled and skilled jobs depended on getting them started "on the right foot," the Urban League devoted special attention to easing Afro-Americans' entry into new fields of employment. Following its tried-and-true formula, the League administered aptitude tests to job applicants to increase the likelihood of employer satisfaction with placements in semiskilled and skilled positions.[56] During the war, however, the League was also able to use such tests to break into entirely new fields. The Brooklyn League, for example, claimed that proficiency tests had greatly improved Afro-American women's efforts to acquire industrial employment. According to the BUL, aptitude tests helped to assuage employers' misgivings about black women's qualifications, which ultimately enabled the League to place a number of women in semiskilled jobs that had previously been beyond their reach.[57]

The Urban League also continued to use testing and "brush-up" courses to assist its placements in white-collar occupations. The League administered tests to gauge the clerical skills—including typing, filing, and accounting—of prospective white-collar workers, and offered refresher courses to assist those whose skills had deteriorated due to inability to work in fields for which they were trained. While such efforts convinced few in private industry to employ blacks as clerical or professional workers, the federal government provided thousands of Afro-Americans with white-collar employment. In fact, the League reported that in fields such as departmental services, 49 percent of Afro-American workers were classified as "clerical—administrative and fiscal," with another 9.9 percent as "clerical—mechanical," and 1.1 percent as professional and sub-professional."[58] For Leaguers such as the NUL's Julius Thomas, these figures reaffirmed the value of both the FEPC and the League's own attempts to prepare black workers for the better types of employment.

When tests failed to breach the ramparts of racism that repulsed blacks' advance into skilled and semiskilled work, the League often attacked the discriminatory bulwarks from their flanks. To counter many owners' apprehensions about employing blacks in semiskilled and skilled positions, the Urban League frequently used its unskilled placements as a means of gaining access to more advanced fields. For example, Lester Granger reported that after representatives from the National and local Urban Leagues encouraged the Bell Aircraft Company of Buffalo to hire black workers in production work in 1941, management expressed its willingness to hire some "big, husky [black] men" for manual labor but refused to consider Afro-Americans for either skilled or semiskilled positions. Disappointed but undeterred, the Buffalo Urban League complied with the company's request and referred thirty black men to Bell "to crash the color line and establish a bridgehead for further placements." According to Granger, the Buffalo League's patience and efforts were quickly rewarded. Thanks to the satisfactory performance of these initial hires, the Bell plant accepted five black trainees for semiskilled production jobs. Granger argued that the Bell plant's positive experience with black labor catalyzed a chain reaction in the aircraft industry. Glenn L. Martin, North American Aviation, Consolidated, and Brewster Aircraft "all began to use Negroes at production jobs." More importantly, Lockheed-Vega employed more than 350 blacks in skilled and semiskilled positions.[59]

Breaking into new fields also required that the Urban League address the issue of resistance from white workers. The Chicago League found that its ties with management and the government were among the most effective tools at its disposal for circumventing white employees' opposition to "upgrading" black labor. When the CUL, in coordination with the USES, attempted to move a promising young black man from the yards to a semiskilled job in the mill at a local firm, white workers shut the plant down for forty-five minutes and threatened to walk out. At the Chicago Urban League's urging, the foreman stuck by the black worker and informed his men that "this was the man the USES sent them and this was the man the company was going to use." Management was even more adamant about continuing this experiment with Afro-American labor. As the strain of breaking the color line eventually led the young man to contemplate quitting, the personnel director encouraged him "to do something for his people by staying on the job, and sticking the thing out until the barriers were broken down." The man stayed on and apparently performed so well in his first two weeks that the League was able to send more blacks from the yards to the mill.[60]

Once Afro-American workers crossed the color line, the League assisted management and unions in ensuring both the best use of black semiskilled and skilled labor and harmonious race relations. In contrast to the 1910s and 1920s, however, the growing war economy mitigated the pressure the League felt to assist employers in terminating less productive workers. Nevertheless, the mutual adjustment of black and white workers continued to occupy a crucial place in the Urban League's uplift vision. Hoping to reduce workplace hostilities resulting from the abrupt introduction of black labor to new fields of employment, the Urban League worked directly with union leaders and management to ease blacks' transition into better jobs.[61] The CUL, like the Urban League generally, believed that antagonism toward the "upgrading" of Afro-American labor could be checked by both impressing upon white workers the importance of workplace solidarity and appealing to their sense of fair play. The Urban League, therefore, coordinated activities designed to foster racial harmony with local union leaders in the building trades, the United Auto Workers, and sundry other locals, to both reduce workplace tensions and increase black representation among supervisors, foremen, and skilled and semiskilled workers.[62]

The League's meetings with union officials stressed not only the negative consequences of discriminatory union practices but the humanity of black workers. Lamenting in 1944 that local unions often failed to support the promotion of even "a good [black] union member" to skilled jobs, it informed the city's labor leaders that such actions necessarily undermined blacks' commitment to the union movement. Playing on the self-interest of union leaders, the CUL warned them that low black morale might adversely affect organized labor's bargaining power. Since "management takes its cue from labor," the Chicago branch argued, union representatives "could not afford to let management know that the union will not back up the Negro workers." The League therefore urged white unionists to think of the integration of the better occupations as consistent with every worker's desire to earn a decent wage based on his talents.[63]

To assist in its attempts to sell the integration of skilled and semiskilled jobs to white workers, the Urban League also coordinated information sessions with both unions and management. The Chicago League thus encouraged employers to offer "introduction meetings" for black and white workers. Orientation sessions were particularly important for blacks entering skilled and semiskilled fields, since they were often at the vanguard of the assault on the color line. Introduction meetings' greatest value was providing plant officials the ability to identify potential sources of conflict between Afro-American and white workers, so that they might prevent racial unrest at the plant. By offering a forum for a prejudiced worker to air his/her grievances, the Chicago League asserted, "personnel managers can talk the matter out with him," thereby defusing a potential powder keg. Though League records offer little specific information, the Brooklyn Urban League claimed that its contacts with several CIO locals helped the group place a number of skilled black workers in jobs in radio and electronics.[64]

As in previous decades, the Urban League's emphasis on breaking into semiskilled, skilled, and white-collar jobs was largely rooted in the realities of the employment opportunities available to Afro-Americans. The League scaled back its placements in less glamorous positions in part to address the demands of workers. As the Brooklyn League noted, most men and women visiting its placement offices eschewed domestic and personal service work in favor of better-paying industrial jobs. Because black workers naturally desired jobs with higher pay, the Urban League's attempts to elevate black labor were in many respects a response to the needs and expectations of Afro-American job seekers. "Upgrading" was also indicative of the pattern of black industrial employment. Since employers were willing to hire blacks as unskilled labor, Afro-Americans had little difficulty acquiring such work, even on their own, during the war. Consequently, even the FEPC's work often focused on efforts to "upgrade" black workers. Therefore, from the League's perspective, the relative ease with which Afro-Americans acquired unskilled positions reduced the need for assistance in acquiring these types of jobs.

Equally important, the League's endeavors to facilitate Afro-Americans' transition into the better occupations were part of a long-term strategy for expanding blacks' job opportunities after the war. Aware that most industrial employers had hired blacks only because of a combination of wartime labor shortages and pressure from the federal government, the Urban League viewed black labor's job record during World War II as essential to shoring up their postwar employment prospects. As Lester Granger asserted as early as 1943, Afro-American labor was "on public trial so far as postwar employment policies are concerned." Granger believed this was especially true of the better occupations, declaring that "unless there is standing proof of a praiseworthy record, there is danger that an end of the war emergency can mean an end of extensive industrial employment for Negro workers of semiskilled and skilled production jobs."[65]

While the Urban League's attempts to ease Afro-Americans' transition into skilled and semiskilled placements represented a clear response to socioeconomic realities, these activities also reflected the enduring belief among many Leaguers that the race's progress hinged on the creation of a stable black middle class. The Urban League of Greater New York argued in a 1944 report that the limited opportunities available to elite Afro-Americans posed a threat to blacks' advancement. The NYUL lamented that "job exclusion in some fields and low wage levels in others" resulted in great disparities in income between black and white workers. In fact, the New York State Department of Commerce's report on black wage earners in New York City found that the bottom 50 percent of Afro-Americans earned only 46 percent as much as the bottom 50 percent of whites. The New York League argued that black poverty was a major obstacle to racial uplift not simply because of its attendant social ills but because it prevented the black middle class from uplifting the masses. "Negro wage earners in high income brackets are so few," the report asserted, "that there is no substantial middle class to carry the load of the great mass below them."[66] Though the NYUL did not expound on how a more vibrant black middle class would benefit the race as a whole, insight into this issue may be found in the pages of *Opportunity*.

In an article exploring the social consequences of unemployment and segregation among Afro-Americans, Floyd Reeves and Robert Sutherland argued that opening the talented tenth's access to more advanced occupations would shore up the integrity of the black middle class and by extension the economic and social progress of the race in general. The authors lamented that the difficulties educated and cultured Afro-Americans experienced acquiring the skilled or professional jobs for which they were trained caused many to become discouraged. Consequently, job discrimination and segregation often led even middle-class blacks to "behave in a manner typical of a lower social class which has become accustomed to lower standards." The authors found declining standards among the black better classes troublesome because they believed the economic successes of middle-class Afro-Americans benefited the race generally by offering poor Afro-Americans positive role models. Reeves and Sutherland therefore argued that opening up professional jobs to the talented tenth was necessary to improving standards for all Afro-Americans. "If the number of Negro youth living in middle and upper-class conditions . . . were increased," the authors claimed, "their standards would immediately be raised and with them those of many members of the lower classes." "These youth, seeing the opportunity for advancement," the piece went on, "would strive for higher position, and so striving would accept the stricter standards of educational and economic achievement, of personal and moral conduct that the next higher position requires."[67]

Its lingering concerns about the integrity of the black middle class notwithstanding, the Urban League's uplift program of the Depression and the Second World War had grown in significant ways. Though the Urban League continued to identify the proper conduct of blacks as essential to collective progress, its experiences with New Deal agencies and the FEPC demonstrated the potential long-term advantages offered by government assistance. The League, therefore, no longer relied exclusively on voluntarist action. In fact, the group's interest in easing blacks' transition into new occupations was wed to its support for government assistance during the war. Fearing that many employers would overlook their positive experience with black labor, Leaguers advocated the continuation of these programs into the postwar era.[68] Thus as early as 1941, the Urban League suggested the need for a permanent Fair Employment Practices Committee.[69] By 1944, Lester Granger asserted that in order to maintain the ground Afro-Americans gained during the Second World War, the FEPC's work must be carried out after the war either through amendment or through the National Labor Relations Act or other means.[70]

Leaguers also supported the adoption of antidiscrimination legislation at the state level. By the war's conclusion, the League was aware that the FEPC would in fact be terminated with the surrender of the Axis forces. Disappointed but not discouraged, Leaguers called for the enactment of state laws barring workplace discrimination. The Chicago League actually claimed to have influenced the scope of the first such law passed in Illinois in the early 1940s. Like the Illinois act, New York's Ives-Quinn Law, enacted in the summer of 1945, forbade discrimination based on race, color, creed, or national origin. The League hoped that state antidiscrimination laws would fill the void created by the conclusion of the Fair Employment Practices Committee.[71]

The League did not believe that the government's role in economic affairs should be limited to those effecting racial minorities, however. As the war drew to a close, many Leaguers called on the U.S. government to play a more active role in ensuring the nation's economic health generally. As one might expect, the League enthusiastically supported the GI Bill for its ability to provide talented individuals, irrespective of race, with the education necessary to improve their economic status. The Urban League's interest in "color blind" government programs, however, was not limited to "training" and education.[72] In fact, some Leaguers went so far as to suggest a need for economic planning.

As Congress debated the merits of the Full Employment Bill of 1945, Lester Granger publicly declared his support for the pending legislation. In a series of speeches to college students, Granger asserted that enduring economic security requires "full, stabilized and constructive employment that gives outlet for the ambitions and talents of the individual and also serves the welfare of the whole community." Granger's calls for a full-employment economy were, of course, intimately tied to his vision of black economic uplift. While Granger sincerely supported endeavors to improve standards for working people generally, he considered full employment vital to blacks' economic progress. Experience taught him that employers tended to ignore Afro-American labor except in tight job markets. This practice, Granger believed, had much to do with the high rates of poverty that plagued black communities across the nation. Full employment would naturally reduce employers' ability to use Afro-Americans as a labor reserve, thereby enhancing black employability and wages while simultaneously defusing a major source of racial tension. His particular interest in black economic progress notwithstanding, Granger's support for a full-employment economy represented a major expansion of the League's vision of racial progress.[73]

Postwar

Although the New Deal and the war imbued the League with a new assertiveness and an expanded class vision, this would change as Afro-Americans' economic prospects declined in the years immediately following VJ Day. Just as the League had feared, the conclusion of the Second World War brought about a reversal in blacks' economic fortunes. Between 1948 and 1950, black unemployment grew from 5.9 percent to 9.0 percent. These figures were significantly higher than the unemployment rates for whites. In 1947, for example, black joblessness was 64 percent higher than that of whites. Three years later, blacks were nearly twice as likely to be unemployed as whites. Skilled Afro-Americans were especially hard hit by postwar layoffs. Most Afro-American white-collar and technical workers during the war were employed in war agencies or defense production.[74] In fact, more than 60 percent of black federal employees were employed in either the Department of War or the Department of the Navy. With the cessation of global conflict, the government reduced the size of these agencies, forcing many Afro-American white-collar workers to take unskilled positions. Most skilled black industrial workers were likewise employed in firms engaged in defense production. These individuals faced a similar fate when war production cooled off after the war.[75]

Remarkably, even as unemployment levels rose among Afro-Americans generally, the League narrowed the focus of its jobs programs. What seemed to trouble the NUL most about its placement work in the wake of the war was that its "efforts to break-down discriminatory employment practices against Negro professional and technical workers in private industry" had been largely ineffective. Ultimately, the difficulty well-trained blacks had obtaining employment commensurate with their talents in a shrinking postwar economy led the National Urban League to redouble its effort to secure new openings for Afro-American white-collar workers. By the late 1940s, the Urban League's endeavors to place Afro-Americans with special training and skills in the "better occupations" had evolved from disorganized practice among League branches to a comprehensive national program called the Pilot Placement Project.

Established by a special grant from the Rosenwald Fund (a philanthropic organization that had supported many League initiatives over the years), Pilot Placement would become the chief priority of the industrial relations departments of the National, New York, and Chicago Urban Leagues. The project was initiated by the NUL in January 1948. Its general approach and overarching objective were not altogether different from the placement policies developed by the National and local Leagues during the 1920s and 1930s. Like many of the jobs projects that preceded it, Pilot's mission was to demonstrate the "job potentialities of specially trained" black workers. The League hoped that by placing "qualified Negro workers in occupations where Negroes were formerly excluded," it might "clear the way for employment of more persons through regular channels without direct intercession." The Urban League thus once again identified the competent performance of Afro-American workers as essential to dispelling racial stereotypes and ultimately demonstrating the practicality of employing blacks in a greater variety of skilled occupations.[76]

Not surprisingly, with Pilot, the League set out to achieve its objectives through the fulfillment of four familiar tasks. First, it attempted to locate well-qualified Afro-American workers trained in a number of fields requiring technical and professional education. Second, it aggressively courted private business concerns in need of technical and professional workers in order to encourage them to open their doors to qualified blacks. Third, it screened and placed Afro-Americans possessing such technical and professional skills in jobs equal to their talents. And finally, it performed follow-up examinations that determined not only its placements' job performance but also the attitudes and sentiments of their white coworkers and employers.[77]

Despite its basic similarities to earlier placement programs, Pilot differed from its predecessors in two significant ways. First, Pilot represented the first successful attempt to standardize the job placement activities already being carried out by League locals. During the 1920s, the National Urban League had attempted to rein in the placement efforts of its branches. As early as 1927, T. Arnold Hill and the NUL began encouraging Urban League locals to provide a database of job openings that would assist the National League in finding employment for Afro-American college graduates in cities and towns across the nation. Like Pilot, the Department of Industrial Relations' initial efforts to reorganize its locals' jobs activities were predicated on the desire to create a comprehensive program with a national scope. By the 1930s, the Depression and poor funding curtailed the League's skilled placement initiatives. It was only able to resume such placements with any success in the 1940s, when new possibilities were engendered by the combination of expanding job opportunities heralded by the Second World War and the League's improved financial status.

The Pilot Placement Project finally equipped the NUL with the tools to erect a national system of "clearance" allowing the League to direct skilled Afro-Americans to jobs equal to their talents and training, irrespective of location. In addition to providing a database of job openings, the National Urban League established clear guidelines shaping both the tone and the type of questions that locals asked employers and employees during the interview process. The Chicago and New York Leagues appear to have complied willingly with the NUL's standards. Both locals established files for "appropriate candidates" to provide a profile of applicants' credentials as well as their personal conduct and grooming. The New York and Chicago branches were also responsible for acquiring the names of black seniors and recent graduates of local colleges who possessed special skills and training that fit Pilot's purview. Moreover, through the Pilot Placement Project, the League developed contacts with prospective employers believed to be receptive to opening professional and white-collar positions to black workers. Pilot thus marked the fulfillment of a dream that was more than two decades old.[78]

The second aspect of Pilot's work distinguishing it from earlier placement efforts was the character of the jobs it targeted. The Urban League had always placed special emphasis on finding employment for blacks in the "better types of jobs." Such employment generally included skilled and semiskilled blue-collar jobs as well as sundry white-collar occupations. Unlike many of the League's earlier efforts, however, the Pilot Project narrowed the League's placement focus by explicitly targeting its efforts to white-collar jobs. Pilot ultimately offered well-educated Afro-Americans an important tool for acquiring professional employment. Though some black architects, engineers, and secretaries managed to secure employment in their chosen professions during the war, the end of the Second World War reduced the production and even governmental pressures on employers to place black workers in positions requiring high levels of education. The League, therefore, treated Pilot as a means of persuading employers to hire skilled black white-collar workers at a time when the material incentives to do so were fading.

Pilot's early activities seem to have been well received. In February of 1948, after just one month of operation, the National Urban League declared that Pilot was a success. The National office interviewed twenty-five black job seekers, including a Massachusetts Institute of Technology–trained engineer, a Harvard Business School graduate, a chemist, and a woman who was a recent Yale Law School graduate. Although NUL records do not specify what kind of employment these individuals acquired, the League claimed to have secured a number of jobs for specially trained blacks in private industry. In fact, the National Urban League was so enthusiastic about Pilot's initial efforts that the organization's goal was to place some fifty applicants a month in professional and white-collar positions.[79]

Perhaps the most encouraging job openings secured by the Pilot Program in its first two years were with the General Electric Company. In January 1949, the NUL's Department of Industrial Relations arranged for representatives of General Electric to visit Howard University, which at the time was the only historically black college in the country with an engineering program. At the conclusion of this first meeting, General Electric was persuaded to offer engineering positions to five black seniors for the "first time ever."[80] League records reveal nothing about these employees' performance; however, indirect evidence indicates GE's general satisfaction with its experiment with skilled Afro-American white-collar labor. Just one year later, the Chicago Urban League reported that General Electric's director of personnel, Maynard Boring, returned to Howard with Julius Thomas, director of the NUL's Department of Industrial Relations, in quest of more black engineers. Boring inspected Howard's facilities, met with faculty, attended classes, and interviewed fifteen seniors. To the delight of all, Boring and GE offered seven of the Howard students employment on terms equal to the company's white employees.[81]

As the Urban League had hoped, GE's experience with Afro-American white-collar workers triggered a chain reaction. In its 1950 report, the Chicago League claimed General Electric's decision opened a floodgate of job opportunities for black college graduates. Following Boring's visit, Dupont, RCA, General Cable, Westinghouse, and General Motors each sent recruiters to Howard and other universities in efforts to recruit promising black students. According to the CUL, it managed to place no fewer than forty Howard University engineering graduates with leading manufacturers between 1949 and 1950.[82] On the heels of this success, the NUL declared its intention to expand the Pilot Placement Project's work to target minority students already in universities to help direct their course of study in order to facilitate their placement in skilled occupations upon graduation. Consistent with the program's general aim, the overarching objective was to alleviate the pressure these young men felt to take jobs that were beneath their talents and training.

Although the Pilot Project's mission was to find employment for blacks in the better occupations, due in part to the labor market segmentation of black men and women, these placements were not limited to high-tech or glamorous professions. Indeed, Pilot and other postwar League efforts to secure the "better jobs" for blacks devoted a fair amount of attention to clerical and sales positions. Most of the Urban League's attempts to create openings in these fields appear to have been directed toward securing employment for black women.

The year the Urban League of Greater New York began its own attempts to fulfill the promise of the Pilot Placement initiative, it boasted that its efforts had a profound impact on the representation of black women in clerical and sales positions. The NYUL claimed that its attempts to educate both employers and black labor, combined with the establishment of the new State Commission Against Discrimination, had much to do with the employment gains Afro-American women experienced between 1940 and 1947. In 1940 the New York Urban League found that white women outnumbered Afro-American women by thirteen to one in clerical and sales jobs. Black women, on the other hand, outnumbered white women in domestic and personal service work by eight to one. Though their prospects were far from ideal, by 1947 black women's job opportunities were significantly better. Between 1940 and 1947, the percentage of black women employed as domestic workers dropped from 64 percent to 36 percent. In the same period the percentage of gainfully employed black women in sales and clerical jobs grew from 3 percent to 13 percent.[83] In addition to claiming partial credit for these general advances, the NYUL asserted that it was responsible for the placement of more than 500 black phone operators at New York Telephone Company, as well as the employment of countless black women as secretaries and stenographers in various businesses. In fact, one-third of the NYUL's placements in 1947 were clerical.[84]

While Pilot represented a laudable attempt to find employment for well-educated black men and women in private industry, its focus on white-collar employment was indicative of the class leanings of the League's approach. In particular, the Pilot Placement Project's work draws attention to the League's enduring view that the race's advancement could best be secured by first taking care of the economic needs of black America's best and brightest. Pilot was actually part of a general trend within the Urban League to target its efforts to better-trained Afro-Americans, a practice that reached back to the League's inception.

Even before Pilot, many League locals scaled back their placement work after World War II. The Chicago Urban League, for example, narrowed the scope of its placements more than a year before it was able to implement its Pilot program. Between 1946 and 1949 the number of job placements the Chicago branch made dropped dramatically. In 1946 it conducted more than 11,500 interviews and made some 6,300 placements. Two years later the CUL conducted just under 11,000 interviews and made more than 3,500 place-ments. By 1949, however, the year before the Chicago branch implemented its own Pilot Placement Project, it conducted fewer than 4,000 interviews and placed just 744 applicants. According to the CUL, the source of this decline stemmed largely from the fact that the number of "Job Opportunities"—the number of job openings of which the League's placement office was made aware—dropped precipitously in this five-year period from a high of 6,741 to only 949 in 1949. This drop corresponded with an increase in black unem-ployment. Yet as the demand for black labor declined, the Chicago League— as the New York and National Urban Leagues had done just prior to the Great Depression—"de-emphasized indiscriminate mass interviewing and placing" in favor of skilled and white-collar applicants.[85]

Budgetary concerns played an especially important role in shaping this trend. The Chicago League argued that the Illinois State Employment Service was better suited to the task of mass placements because the state had more extensive resources. Given that financial problems prevented the Chicago branch from officially implementing Pilot Placement until 1950, funding un-doubtedly offers a partial explanation for the CUL's and even the National and New York Urban Leagues' shift in priorities.[86] Financial concerns, however, do not explain why Pilot, a national program with its own budget, became the chief priority of the National and most local Urban Leagues' industrial rela-tions departments. Instead, the League's decision to narrow the range of job placements it made appears to have had just as much to do with its belief that the ascendancy of the better classes was essential to the race's progress.

As with its earlier placement efforts in semiskilled and skilled trades, the Urban League's interest in securing employment for black professionals was partially rooted in its concerns about the negative psychological and material impact that poor job opportunities might have on well-educated, middle-class black Americans. Decades before sociologist William Julius Wilson identified "urban isolation" as a major source of poverty and despair within America's ghettos, the League argued that blacks faced great difficulties finding decent jobs because of segregation and labor market segmentation. In a summary of Pilot's work in New York, the Urban League asserted, "Within [New York City's] four main boroughs are isolated communities of Negroes and Puerto Ricans who receive few opportunities to exchange experiences and knowledge with persons from other groups in other localities. . . . This situation is a serious handicap to Negro and Puerto Rican youngsters in the formative stage of life who must essentially compete in the economic arena with youth from more advantaged groups and areas." "In the case of most minority youth," it continued, "channels for the interchange of experiences are virtually non-existent except for occasional interracial events." Pilot was therefore conceived as a means of directing minorities, who were generally outside of "the job loop," to better employment.[87]

For proponents of the Pilot Project, the difficulty well-educated blacks living in ghetto communities had securing employment equal to their talents not only undermined their immediate material status but also posed a threat to their drive and determination. In expanding employment opportunities for Afro-Americans, Pilot was intended both to enlighten whites and to encourage black achievers to continue to strive for excellence. As the NUL asserted in 1948, "The acid test of the usefulness of this project lies in the continuing effect which such initial placements were proven to have upon the employment attitudes of management and upon the determination of aspirant Negroes to secure the ultimate in training." That same year, the Chicago League was ecstatic over the increase in the number of white-collar placements it made over the previous twelve months. Forty-four percent of the CUL's placements in its 1947–48 activity year were in white-collar, skilled, and semi-skilled positions, with white-collar work comprising more than half of these jobs. For the CUL, what was most encouraging about the increase in white-collar placements was that it demonstrated "to the fine young men and women of the Negro community who have sacrificed to 'get ahead'" the value of hard work and determination. The negative impact that racial discrimination might have on the psyches of well-trained Afro-Americans was a long-standing concern for Urban Leaguers. Pilot and similar programs were, there-fore, essential to ensuring the status of the Negro better classes by providing them outlets for their skills. Without such outlets, Leaguers feared that these Afro-Americans might become susceptible to a variety of unwholesome in-fluences.[88]

The creation of job opportunities for black professionals was a crucial component of the League's integrationist vision and the advancement of the race. In explaining why it focused on skilled white-collar placements, for example, the Chicago League explicitly stated in its 1949 annual report that it could "best serve the interest of Negro workers and the community by open-ing up new job opportunities in higher occupational categories."[89] Although the CUL did not expand on the importance of "higher occupational catego-ries" to black community life in this particular report, some insight into its meaning may be provided by a similar issue raised by the Urban League of Greater New York. In a discussion of its own job placement work, the NYUL implied, in tones consonant with ethnic cycle theory, that improved employ-ment opportunities might help to undermine racial stereotypes. Although whites often derided blacks for maintaining lower standards of living, the New York branch argued, the poor conditions in which Afro-Americans often lived could be attributed to low wages. Afro-Americans generally earned less than whites, the League argued, because of their disadvantaged position in the workplace engendered by racial discrimination. The NYUL claimed that the best way to prevent a sense of discouragement from setting in among black workers was to assist them in finding employment in advance occupations through training and placement.[90] In securing better-paying and more stable employment, the League indicated, black professionals might advance the race's cause by providing proof of the Afro-American's potential, thereby undermining racial stereotypes.

■ League employment policy during the 1940s bore the clear imprint of the broad political and economic shifts taking place within the nation over the decade. Drawing upon the lessons of the first two Roosevelt administrations, League officials continued to identify the American welfare state as pivotal to Afro-American uplift. This was especially true during the Second World War, as black leaders wed the quest for racial equality at home to the extension of democracy abroad. Influenced by both the black protest campaigns of the era and the blossoming of industrial democracy, Leaguers, through much of the 1940s, maintained the militant political posture they adopted during the New Deal. As a result, not only did the Urban League forge an active partnership with government, but some high-ranking officials even advocated direct-action protest campaigns that challenged the racial status quo. At the conclusion of the war, Leaguers would, moreover, advocate an extension of the welfare state. Urban League officials thus called for federal and state protections against discrimination as well as measures, such as the Full Employment Bill of 1945, intended to provide every American, irrespective of race, the right to a decent living.

These issues notwithstanding, the League's expanded vision during World War II—its militancy and commitment to an interventionist state—deviated little from the group's belief in the importance of proper behavior as a vehicle of uplift. Urban League officials supported black protest politics as well as federal initiatives to combat discrimination in order to enhance blacks' economic standing while simultaneously addressing the principal sources of personal demoralization and social disorganization. Indeed, Leaguers believed that the March on Washington Movement and the Fair Employment Practices Committee bolstered black morale as each gave Afro-American workers incentive to identify their own interests with those of employers and the nation as a whole. The Urban League's greater political militancy and its related support for an interventionist welfare state were therefore bound to the sociological models of assimilation that had guided the group's philosophy since the 1910s.

The class implications of this approach were mitigated during the war by the expansion in opportunities brought about by military Keynesianism. Though the Urban League continued to prioritize job placements for skilled and white-collar work, during World War II these endeavors were inspired largely by comparatively low rates of unemployment. As the postwar era made clear, however, the Urban Leaguers' greater interest in professional work also reflected the social-work group's general preoccupation with the so-called Negro better classes. As black unemployment swelled during the late 1940s, the League stepped up its investment in white-collar placements with the creation of the Pilot Placement Project. Pilot reflected Leaguers' long-standing belief that programs targeting the talented tenth were essential to the progress of the entire race as these individuals best exemplified black workers' potential and versatility. Successful placements, Leaguers hoped, would not only disabuse whites of racial prejudice but also motivate large numbers of Afro-Americans to excel in work and in the classroom. As in earlier periods, this approach could be interpreted as a response to contracting job opportunities. Still, the more democratic uplift vision adopted by Leaguers from the 1930s through the 1940s continued to reflect the class interests and anxieties of the black petite bourgeoisie.

7. Housing and Neighborhood Work in the Age of the Welfare State, 1933–1950

The more that Negro families become distributed throughout the city in public housing projects, and the more that white families are allowed to demonstrate their desire and ability to live amicably in projects located in areas such as Harlem, the more we lay the groundwork for amicable living together of whites and Negroes in other than public housing situations.—Lester Granger, 1945

The great demographic, political, and economic shifts taking place during the 1930s and 1940s exerted significant sway over the Urban League's housing and neighborhood development initiatives. The impact of migration and unemployment on blacks' living conditions was, as it had been in the group's first two decades, of some concern for the NUL and its locals in this period. While the Depression had slowed the pace of migration, the Afro-American populations of Chicago and New York grew steadily through the 1930s. To be sure, the growth of black New York and Chicago had tapered off significantly when compared with that of the previous decade; nevertheless, the Afro-American communities in each city experienced absolute increases during the era of the New Deal. Between 1920 and 1930 black Chicago and New York grew by more than 110 percent. By contrast, between 1930 and 1940 black Chicago grew by less than 20 percent, from 233,903 to 277,731 individuals. New York's black population, on the other hand, grew from 327,706 people to 458,444, or by about 71 percent.[1]

As the nation's economic fortunes turned around following the outbreak of the Second World War, the pace of black migration to northern cities picked up. Race discrimination prevented Afro-American workers from acquiring their fair share of the fruits of military Keynesianism, ensuring that blacks continued to feel the sting of depressed wages and comparatively high rates of unemployment. Still, the combination of industrial expansion and a modest surge in racial liberalism greatly enhanced Afro-Americans' employment prospects during the 1940s.[2] Hoping to take advantage of new opportunities in northern industry, southern blacks, as they had two decades previously, poured into cities like New York and Chicago. Between 1940 and 1950, black New York grew from fewer than half a million individuals to more than 700,000. Over the same decade, Chicago's Afro-American population expanded by 78 percent, from 277,731 persons to 492,265.[3]

The confluence of economic instability and constant growth, League officials believed, ensured that urban blacks would continue to experience the effects of social disorganization that had plagued these communities in previous decades.[4] Harlem and Chicago's South Side black belt remained overcrowded. Both communities were beset by racial tensions, crime, juvenile delinquency, and neighborhood decay. Moreover, blacks in New York and Chicago still faced difficulties acquiring affordable housing. Since these were the same issues with which the League was concerned in the years before the New Deal, it should be of no surprise that the social-work group continued to take steps to enhance the quality of life in America's black communities through the years immediately following World War II.

This chapter explores the Urban League's attempts to improve the character of neighborhood life and to increase the stock of available housing from 1933 to 1950. The League's housing efforts, like its employment activities, reveal a shift in the group's vision of collective progress as Urban League officials embraced the welfare state as a means of shoring up black neighborhood life. Still, the Urban League's approach to community development and housing in this period continued to pivot from the view that social disorganization posed a threat to the material and political advancement of the race. Thus, even as the League's housing approach reflected an expanded vision of collective progress, it remained tied to the notion that mutually satisfying contacts between the races was pivotal to black uplift. This perspective would lead Urban League officials to advance militant calls for housing integration that presumed Afro-American advancement required that blacks demonstrate their acceptance of mainstream values.

Community Development

In the early 1930s both the New York and Chicago Urban Leagues had little choice but to scale back their housing activities. The national and local Urban Leagues' coffers atrophied during the Depression as charitable contributions to the groups diminished substantially. The combination of shrinking budgets and rapidly increasing unemployment led many League affiliates to target their efforts more narrowly. Consequently, housing and neighborhood work took a back seat to the League's employment and jobs placement programs in the 1930s and 1940s. The CUL made clear that housing would play only a secondary role in its activities when it abolished its civic improvement department in late 1930. By the mid-1930s, the NYUL likewise announced its plans to step back from housing. Nevertheless, the Urban League remained invested in improving black urban life.[5]

As they had prior to the New Deal, Leaguers believed neighborhood neglect cause for concern. They feared that local governments' failure to provide services and facilities, ranging from adequate policing to parks and recreation, posed a major threat to the stability of black community life. In fact, the New York Urban League asserted in 1941 that "a discouraging record of neglected opportunities and indifference" on the part of the Mayor Fiorello La Guardia and his administration was largely responsible for the 1935 Harlem riot.[6] Prominent NUL officials echoed these perspectives.

Lester Granger, the National Urban League's executive secretary from 1940 to 1961, frequently voiced concern that neglect engendered a sense of apathy among residents of ghetto communities that further fueled the disorganization of urban life. In "Manhattan and Beyond," an installment of Lester Granger's regular column in the *Amsterdam News*, the NUL executive declared that "Harlem is, in general, a filthy area," due to overcrowding, residents' ignorance of urban living conditions, and poor sanitation services. For Granger, perhaps the most disheartening consequence of decay in Gotham's principal black belt was its impact on the residents themselves. Many Harlemites, he declared, "just don't give a hoot about their neighborhoods." "It doesn't take many shiftless, prideless residents in a city block," he continued, "to drag down standards that their neighbors try to keep up."[7] Like Charles S. Johnson and Earl Moses before him, Granger argued that antisocial behaviors, ranging from criminality to rudeness, were partially rooted in the anonymity of urban life.

Though Urban League officials generally attributed ghetto disorganization to deficiencies in social services and even law enforcement, the national and local Leagues continued to pursue efforts to acculturate black newcomers to urban life. As they had in the 1920s and 1930s, the Chicago and New York Leagues set out to provide constructive outlets for maladjusted and/or vulnerable black belt residents in an effort to counter social disorganization. Identifying education as essential to improving black community life, the CUL pursued efforts to foster civic awareness among black Chicagoans. To aid it in this endeavor, the Chicago League sponsored a series of "block clubs." These organizations disseminated information through bulletins and newspapers and established personal contacts with neighborhood residents in their efforts to improve "personal and group behavior." While the League's records reveal few details about these groups, the CUL claimed that they did indeed promote community awareness. In 1937, the Chicago League declared that "in two years time, we have succeeded in making the city of Chicago realize that something must be done to improve this community[,] and individual residents within the area have become more and more community conscious and are lending their support for improvement."[8]

The New York Urban League was similarly engaged during the 1930s and 1940s. Just as it had in the years prior to the New Deal, the NYUL emphasized the remedial effects of wholesome activities for young people. Beginning in 1930, the New York League operated a nursery and play school to assist working mothers. More than just a childcare facility, the nursery and play school was also intended to help reduce juvenile delinquency by providing wholesome guidance to children.[9]

Juvenile delinquency and criminality were of special concern to Leaguers during the Depression and World War II. The National Urban League reported in 1935 that some 200,000 children passed through the juvenile court system annually. In Chicago, roughly 43 percent of all arrests made in 1935 were of youth under twenty-five, with teenagers comprising the bulk of these offenders. Particularly startling to Leaguers was the fact that blacks, who comprised less than 10 percent of the city's population, accounted for more than 18 percent of incarcerated youth ages fifteen to twenty-one. Worse yet, Afro-Americans tended to have longer criminal careers than whites. While the largest share of white criminals was between fifteen and twenty-one years of age, the largest group of black offenders was between the ages of fifteen and twenty-nine.[10] The situation was no better in the 1940s. By 1943, the New York Urban League reported that criminality and juvenile delinquency were five times higher among blacks than whites.[11]

The League offered a familiar explanation for black delinquency and criminality. A 1937 NUL report argued that the poor quality of black neighborhoods, the anonymity of urban life, and lack of proper supervision brought about by the prevalence of working mothers in ghetto communities left blacks susceptible to unsavory influences. Just as it had prior to the New Deal, the League identified the establishment of wholesome outlets as essential to combating social disorganization among black youth. Citing statements from both J. Edgar Hoover and the warden of Alcatraz, the League argued in a *Color Line Series* article that the most effective way to combat the problems confronting black ghetto residents was to "organize around church, school, labor union or social agencies." The report went on to state that "[the Negro] could lend his collective support to those forces that are seeking to correct these conditions."[12]

The Urban League pursued a variety of means of creating wholesome outlets for black youth. Recreational work had been a major component of the League's neighborhood work well before the Depression. Though the NYUL's annual budget for such activities shrank to a paltry $324 by 1930, the New York League continued its recreational program in a diminished and even haphazard fashion. Operating within the NYUL's Department of Industrial Relations, the League's recreational activities consisted chiefly of classes offered to underprivileged children designed to both occupy their time and impart proper values.[13]

In its ongoing effort to combat juvenile delinquency, the Urban League sponsored meetings and supervised clubs for Harlem's youth. Programs such as the Harlem Big Brothers movement, which the League helped to organize, provided mentoring for at-risk children. To this end, the NYUL continued to operate summer camps for black youth. In 1933 and 1935, the League ran the Farley Camp for children. In the summer of 1934, the NYUL also re-opened its Fresh Air Home in Verplanck. While gaps in the League's records preclude a thorough exploration of the NYUL's work in this regard, the New York League appears to have maintained these activities through the 1940s. Working with the Citizens Committee on Harlem, the League urged the improvement of recreational facilities such as playgrounds and parks, an expansion of community centers, and that additional facilities be made available for summer camps for black children.[14]

Unfortunately, the NYUL records offer little direct information as to the overarching objectives of such activities during the 1930s. Nevertheless, these programs appear to have been an attempt to reorganize the lives of ghetto residents. As the Urban League of Greater New York argued in a 1947 report on its neighborhood work and its camps for young people, the purpose of the League's activities in this area was "to develop a program for the participants which will provide a constructive outlet for the energies" of ghetto residents as well as "opportunities for personal growth, and developing social responsibility."[15] This was, of course the same rationale for such activities prior to the Depression.

In addition to creating organized outlets for ghetto residents the Urban League challenged public policy and private real estate interests that had a negative impact on ghetto life. In fact, Leaguers not only worked with public officials to improve conditions in Afro-American communities, but they encouraged black belt residents to take action themselves. Believing that the problems facing ghetto residents stemmed in part from insufficient resources, the Urban League mobilized Afro-Americans to press for better public services. City governments not only frequently failed to provide adequate recreational facilities, but they also neglected services such as policing and garbage pick-up.[16]

In some respects, the League's strategy of treating organized activities as a means of improving the character of black neighborhoods was an accommodation to residential segregation. The CUL, for example, stated that it established its program of civic improvement in 1934 in response to the fact that the expansion of black residential areas into neighboring white districts had been curtailed by restrictive covenants. Consequently, Afro-Americans' housing options were greatly limited. The Chicago League initially responded to this reality by attempting to increase black belt residents' personal investment in their own neighborhoods. As the CUL asserted in 1935, the chief objective of its neighborhood work was "to develop a common mind on the fact that for many years people are going to be living within this area and it is up to them to decide on the future value of their property and present moral conditions of the neighborhood, and the very fact that they are citizens, there is encumbered upon them a responsibility to work for the improvement of their community."[17]

In this sense, the civic departments of League locals reflected the social-work group's enduring concern about the absence of barriers between upstanding Afro-American citizens and their "maladjusted" brethren. Lester Granger's emphasis on the degrading affects of neighborhood decay on the psychology of ghetto residents in his "Manhattan and Beyond" essay, for example, mirrored the concerns voiced by Leaguers such as Charles S. Johnson and Ira De Augustine Reid twenty years earlier. Prevented by residential segregation from fully escaping ghetto communities, "respectable" Afro-Americans continued to be forced to live cheek by jowl with the vicious elements just as they had during the 1910s and 1920s. Granger believed the lack of viable social controls in ghetto communities led many residents to accept even violent criminal behavior as a normal part of urban life. One of the clearest examples of this, according to Granger, took place on a Harlem bus. In response to the bus driver having missed a stop, a young man allegedly smashed a bottle over the driver's head, and passengers failed to intercede. Granger concluded that only in Harlem would such an event be tolerated.[18] Thus for Leaguers such as Granger, violence, filth, and vandalism were becoming all too commonplace in Harlem and in America's black belts generally.

Anxieties of this sort revealed the League's continued commitment to the capacity of respectable behavior to undermine race prejudice. Reflecting on an incident involving a particularly crass individual on a Harlem street corner, Granger asserted in his column in the *Amsterdam News* that "every one of my readers has undoubtedly had the experience of watching some brother of the race conduct himself in public in such a way as to make almost every Negro within hearing distance earnestly wish the offender could be locked up—for a long time if not for good." He went on to declare that "vile profanity in a subway car give[s] our neighborhoods a black eye almost as conspicuous as the 'crime waves' avidly reported in the metropolitan press."[19] Granger thus believed that widespread disorganization in America's black belts reaffirmed whites' prejudices, thereby fortifying the bulwarks that confined blacks to urban enclaves.

Given Lester Granger's history with the League, such perspectives are particularly striking. In the period preceding the modern civil rights movement, Granger was generally considered to have been one of the Urban League's most politically progressive officials. Indeed, his thirty-year tenure with the National Urban League was distinguished by a pronounced political militancy. In 1934, just four years after Granger started with the social-work group, T. Arnold Hill appointed him executive secretary of the League's Workers' Bureau, which, under Granger's leadership, identified interracial working-class solidarity, rather than voluntarism, as pivotal to black social and economic progress. After a contentious power struggle with Hill, Eugene K. Jones appointed Granger executive secretary of the National Urban League in 1940. In contrast to previous League executives, Granger did not eschew controversy. In 1941, Granger declared his personal support for A. Philip Randolph's March on Washington Movement even as the NUL failed to formally endorse Randolph's group. Moreover, he consistently called upon the federal government to redress both racial and economic inequality throughout the 1940s. Despite his attention to structural sources of inequality, however, Granger was no less invested in the relationship between adherence to normative values and uplift than more moderate Leaguers.

None of this is to suggest that the League's housing and community development projects in this period were limited to creating wholesome outlets for ghetto residents. After all, attempts to improve the character of black neighborhood life would have no direct impact on the number of homes available to Afro-Americans. During the 1910s and 1920s race discrimination profoundly limited blacks' housing options in both Chicago and New York. The Depression exacerbated an already deplorable situation. Rather than relying entirely on ghetto residents themselves to fix the problems endemic to America's black belts, Leaguers again took steps to increase the number of homes available to blacks. As I discuss below, however, the League's efforts to improve the physical environment within ghetto communities reflected both the major changes taking place in American political economy and its lingering emphasis on social engineering. While the Urban League's housing strategy from the New Deal through the immediate postwar era differed in significant ways from its pre–New Deal endeavors, it also reflected important continuities with its earlier activities.

Housing

As it had since its first decade of operation, the Urban League tried to attract responsible real estate investors to black communities. The Depression and the New Deal, however, brought about a major shift in the Urban League's work in this area. Whereas prior to the New Deal the NUL and its locals hoped to attract private investors, by 1933 the League came to view government assistance as essential to improving housing conditions for blacks. Thus, during the 1930s and 1940s the National, Chicago, and New York Urban Leagues not only actively courted government intervention, but they worked to combat discriminatory practices by government agencies.

The League's decision to turn to the state for assistance was, in part, a reaction to the federal government's expanding role in the nation's economic affairs. In 1933, Franklin D. Roosevelt signed the National Industrial Recovery Act (NIRA) into law. A major component of Roosevelt's economic stimulus package, the NIRA was part of a broader effort to increase industrial production and the earning power of working people. To achieve this end, the NIRA not only lent modest government support to the union movement, but it also set new standards for wages, hours, and child labor. As significantly, the Public Works Administration (PWA), which administered NIRA resources, targeted government spending to key sectors of the economy in order to stimulate growth. This facet of the program would lead the government to play an active role in the creation of affordable housing.

In response to the demands of charitable organizations such as the National Conference of Catholic Charities, Senator Robert Wagner included a provision in the National Industrial Recovery Act enabling the government to finance the construction of urban housing as a component of the bill's public works program. Title II of the NIRA called for "a comprehensive program of public works" accompanied by "construction, reconstruction, alteration, or repair under public regulation or control of low-cost housing and slum-clearance projects." The public housing provision of the PWA made significant contributions to the nation's housing stock during the 1930s. Under the supervision of Interior Secretary Harold Ickes, the PWA financed and/or built fifty-eight housing developments containing some 25,000 units in its first four years.[20]

With the PWA's commitment to improving housing evidenced by the rapid growth in publicly funded units, the League had reason to believe that the federal government offered at least a partial solution to the problem of black housing. Housing was of paramount importance in the 1930s. Harlem's population, for example, grew by 146 percent between 1920 and 1934, doubling the population density in many black neighborhoods.[21] Moreover, as discussed in Chapter 2, rents in black Manhattan were excessively burdensome. Not surprisingly, high rents resulted in a large number of evictions. In desperation, many black New Yorkers responded to the housing crisis in Harlem through radical protest. Assisted by the Communist-led Harlem Tenants League, mass protests were a regular part of life in Harlem by the mid-1930s.[22] Perhaps the clearest examples of the discontent in this period were the Harlem riots of 1935 and 1943, which Leaguers believed highlighted the urgency of the housing conditions in Gotham.

Afro-Americans in Chicago faced a similar housing dilemma. Prior to the Second World War, black Chicago experienced an acute housing shortage. While the number of apartment units in the Windy City grew by more than 287,000 in the 1920s, the Depression brought an abrupt end to housing construction. In the decade following the stock market crash, only about 15,500 homes and apartments were constructed. This was slightly more than 5 percent of the total built the previous decade. Chicago's black belt witnessed no appreciable increase in housing. Since construction ceased as the black population grew, rents soared during the Depression. In fact, the Chicago Urban League noted that the lack of new construction produced the "peculiar phenomena of increasing rents during a depression period." Moreover, housing in the black belt often lacked basic amenities. A CUL investigation of one black neighborhood found that many homes lacked even "ordinary conveniences," such as water, toilets, and centrally radiated heat. Consequently, tuberculosis and infant mortality rates were significantly higher in the black belt than in the city generally.[23]

The combination of the decline in the number of units built by private investors, neighborhood decay, and the increasing role of federal intervention ultimately led the New York and Chicago Leagues to turn to the government for assistance. The Chicago Urban League, in particular, aggressively courted government action. One of the CUL's earliest efforts in this regard focused on the Ida B. Wells housing project. Construction of the project began in the summer of 1939 on the heels of controversy. Though the United States Housing Authority (USHA) first attempted to secure the site in 1936, opposition from neighborhood associations and even the courts slowed the development of the government housing project. Property owners in the adjacent white neighborhoods of Hyde Park, Kenwood, and Oakland allied with business interests to oppose the construction of Ida B. Wells. Moreover, questions pertaining to the constitutionality of eminent domain forced the USHA to alter its procedures for acquiring properties used for public housing.[24]

Identifying the apartments as having the potential to provide an important source of housing, the CUL weathered the controversy and played an active role in the struggle to get the publicly financed homes built. As historian Arvarh Strickland has demonstrated, the Chicago League mobilized support among blacks and whites for the project. As early as 1936, the CUL launched an information campaign designed to dramatize blacks' housing plight while making the public aware of the issues being debated behind the scenes by the city council and state government. The League's newly reinstated civic department also coordinated activities with a number of other groups working in support of the Ida B. Wells project.[25]

In addition to coordinating efforts with civic organizations, the Chicago Urban League worked directly with politicians. After 1937, a major point of contention was how the project was to be financed, and this posed the greatest challenge to the Wells apartments. In response to a federal court's decision in a Louisville, Kentucky, case questioning the legality of eminent domain, the Chicago division of the PWA ceased its efforts to acquire land through condemnation and instead moved to purchase property directly from owners. When the USHA took over responsibility for the Ida B. Wells project in 1937, it determined that the added expense of land purchases required that low-cost projects be exempted from state and city taxes in order to keep the rental rates down. Many representatives opposed this approach because of the loss of revenue that would naturally result. Consequently, the project's construction was delayed until August 1939 and was not completed until 1941.[26]

Fearing that delays in construction might doom the Ida B. Wells project, Leaguers looked beyond appeals to the general public and turned their attentions to local officials. Representatives from the Chicago Urban League appeared before both the city council and the state legislature urging swift completion of the project, going so far as to implore them to petition Washington for greater assistance. The League's work with local officials did not end there. A number of CUL officials converged on the state capital to lobby for the housing bill's passage. In fact, Urban Leaguer Amelia Sears lobbied in Springfield until the bill was finally passed. When the housing bill stalled in the statehouse, the CUL's executive secretary, A. L. Foster, met personally with Governor Henry Horner. Governor Horner eventually pledged his support to the project. Foster also met with the mayor of Chicago, who not only pledged his support but vowed to enlist the support of other city leaders.[27]

The New York League likewise encouraged local officials to increase the number of publicly financed homes available to blacks. By the mid-1930s, the NYUL and the NAACP joined forces with the Consolidated Tenants League to lobby for government housing assistance in New York's black belt. The NYUL met with prominent realtors and architects in order to influence the location of future housing sites. The League and the North Harlem Community Council implored officials in the La Guardia administration to consider Harlem as a site for federally funded housing. By 1935, the Consolidated Tenants League succeeded in persuading La Guardia and Harold Ickes to locate a site in Harlem. In an ironic twist of fate, the new project—the Harlem River Houses—was to be located at the site of the now bankrupt Dunbar Apartments.[28]

Although the League's interest in public housing was partly a response to changes in the nation's political climate and housing structure, the philosophy behind public housing was ultimately consistent with the Urban League's broad vision of racial uplift. The NUL and its locals had long held that modern housing had the potential to mitigate many of the harsher aspects of urban life. Leaguers continued to perceive housing through this lens during and following the New Deal. The New York League, for example, claimed in the 1940s that housing and neighborhood design were essential to fostering a healthy community. In particular, the NYUL asserted that planned communities could have a salubrious affect on both family life and residents' immediate environment. Several years after Harlem River opened for business the League asserted, "A process of housing again is more than construction, important as that is. It is also dwelling design, neighborhood layout, materials manufacture and distribution, mortgage finance, city and regional planning, public controls . . . and enterprises."[29] "The usefulness of housing," it continued, "depends in part on its proper location . . . its relation to transit and transportation to places of work and recreation, to hospitals and medical centers, to educational and religious institutions, to the open countryside." In other words, "housing is the physical environment, largely man-made, in which families live, grow and decline." Decent housing, the NYUL concluded, "contributes to a sense of human worth and dignity and thus to mutual respect and companionship."[30]

Many prominent proponents of public housing shared the League's belief that attractive affordable homes were essential to fostering community life in urban neighborhoods. As historian Gail Radford has demonstrated, pioneering architects such as Lewis Mumford and Catherine Bauer hoped to create low-income housing that was on a par with most middle-class housing in the 1930s. Bauer and Mumford both set out to create planned communities that, much like the Dunbar Apartments, were designed to combat the alienation that allegedly characterized urban life. To provide homes for residents of moderate means, however, trailblazing architects such as Mumford and Bauer argued that government assistance was necessary.[31]

Public Works Administration officials often echoed these views. In an article in *Opportunity* on the advantages of public housing, Robert Weaver, the PWA's aide for Negro affairs, stressed the social benefits of affordable, attractive housing. Weaver argued that government-sponsored apartment projects would not only provide homes for some 10 million American families in need of inexpensive housing (defined as costing $7 per room per month) but also improve the quality of ghetto life.[32] Weaver asserted that affordable rents in planned communities were essential to the proper acculturation of low-income city dwellers. In particular, "the whole theory behind public housing is that the individual is affected greatly by his environment. . . . Not only does the person develop more fully if he is given better surroundings but society benefits because a better citizen is produced."[33] Thus many of the principles behind public housing in the 1930s meshed tightly with the League's vision of uplift.[34]

Though budgetary constraints often forced the Public Works Administration to sacrifice aesthetics for quantity, a number of PWA planned communities were designed to foster civic virtue and pride among their residents. Harlem was the site of only one major apartment project in the 1930s; nevertheless, this PWA project incorporated many of the best aspects of reform-minded public housing. On October 23, 1937, the Harlem River Houses opened to tenants. Like the Dunbar Apartments it replaced, Harlem River was designed to provide residents both comfortable living quarters and a socially salubrious environment. The buildings incorporated the style of both the American garden apartment tradition and "European-derived classicism." The complex, therefore, consisted of a series of "low-rise structures set around the perimeter of a lot, enclosing a landscaped interior." The apartments also came standard with an array of amenities, including hot and cold running water, steam heat, and private bathrooms. Since the designers were, in the words of one of the architects, "interested in housing, *not* housing for the poor," they settled on this approach, in part, because the blend of aesthetics and function that Harlem River would embody had been popular among reformers in the 1920s and 1930s. The housing offered to the tenants of the Harlem River complex was, therefore, free of the aesthetic stigma attached to most low-income units.[35] Designers hoped that this would, among other things, aid in fostering a sense of commitment to the apartments.

The actual layout of the apartment buildings was also designed to improve residents' sense of community. Though the complex's 574 units were generally more attractive than most rentals available to Harlemites, the rentals differed little physically from those in privately owned buildings. What distinguished the complex from others in Harlem, however, was that the Harlem River Houses utilized physical space in a fashion that both created social cohesion within the complex and maintained the buildings connection to the surrounding neighborhoods. Much like Dunbar, the buildings of Harlem River were organized around a number of courtyards. The complex also provided residents a nursery school with its own outdoor play area, a clinic for diagnosing tuberculosis and another for assisting mothers with their babies, a branch of the New York Public Library, numerous social rooms, and a large sports field. The complex's location between West 151st Street, West 153rd Street, and 7th Avenue ensured that renters would have easy access to the surrounding neighborhood.[36] Ultimately, the design and facilities were intended to offer tenants both beauty and avenues for communal interaction.

As part of this overarching effort to create a healthy environment for renters, prospective tenants at the Harlem River Houses were screened by an application board. When the complex opened in October of 1937, management was inundated with applications. Some 14,000 families applied for the admission to just 574 apartments. The plethora of potential renters required that the application board develop a rigorous admissions process that considered the character, needs, and financial means of hopefuls. Applicants were screened first by an "impartial" point system based on "merit and need." Those who made the first round were evaluated by a New York Housing Authority investigator who rated candidates based on the character of their home lives, including "cleanliness" and family structure.[37]

It is not clear if the New York Urban League played any part in this process; however, the board's criteria were nonetheless in line with the League's attempts to create model communities. In fact, Leaguers had long complained that the failure of absentee landlords to screen their tenants had much to do with the social disorganization that plagued many ghetto communities.[38] Given both the NYUL's emphasis on community building and the importance it placed on screening applicants, it is likely that it supported these efforts in the case of the Harlem River Houses.

The New York League was initially enthusiastic about the Harlem River development, but it was by no means fully satisfied. The NYUL was particularly disappointed in Harlem River's inability to influence the general housing market for black New York. For the League, the most important aspect of public housing was its promise to provide homes for families of moderate means. As Robert Weaver argued in the pages of *Opportunity*, public housing had the potential to improve the housing available to low-income families in two ways. First, publicly funded projects would ameliorate housing conditions directly by providing those who qualified with affordable, attractive homes. Second, by increasing the supply of desirable housing, publicly funded projects would pressure private real estate interests to improve the quality of the units they provided. Moreover, competition with public units could exert downward pressure on the rents charged by private landlords, further improving the housing conditions in America's black belts.[39] Not long after Harlem River's completion, however, Leaguers lamented that the project was incapable of fulfilling either of these objectives.

In 1944, just seven years after the Harlem River projects were built, the Urban League of Greater New York explored the impact of federal housing policy on Harlem. The League argued that in spite of the presence of Harlem River, residential "congestion" in Harlem was unbearable. In fact, the NYUL found that Harlem averaged more than 3,800 individuals per block. Population density naturally drove rents in Harlem higher, with blacks continuing to pay higher rents than whites. Part of the problem was that Harlem River was the only publicly funded apartment project available to black Manhattanites. Since Harlem had more than 300,000 residents in 1944, Harlem River's 574 units could not have possibly influenced the overall state of housing for Afro-Americans in Manhattan.[40] One apartment complex could not alleviate overcrowding and high rents in Harlem. Irrespective of the amenities it offered, the project's mere 574 new units would not constitute sufficient competition to galvanize private investors to take action.

Adding insult to injury, the rent structures in the Harlem River Houses were too high for the average Harlemite, further undermining its ability to positively affect housing for black New Yorkers. Ironically, the criteria employed by Harlem River's application board undermined its ability to achieve its primary objective, providing housing for those of moderate means. The New York City Housing Authority was especially interested in the financial status of renters. The PWA and the Housing Authority developed a rent structure based on the minimum rent required to "pay back fifty-five percent of the capital costs to the federal government over 60 years." The rents were then scaled to ensure that they would not exceed 20 percent of tenants' earnings.[41] The New York Housing Authority also mandated that tenants could earn no more than five times the maximum rent plus utilities. The income maximum notwithstanding, the rent criteria all but ensured the renters in the Harlem River Houses were generally better off than the average Harlemite. In fact, according to historian Gail Radford, the yearly earnings of residents was more than $1,300 "at a time when median income for black families in New York was $837."[42]

The small number of publicly financed apartments and high rents were not

the only problems the League identified with Harlem River. Like other federally financed housing complexes in the United States, the Harlem River
Houses were segregated. Fearing that a federally sanctioned policy of segregated public housing was detrimental to black community life, Leaguers advocated integration of public housing.

In a 1945 report, Lester Granger argued that "in most cities public housing
has been set up on a basis of racial segregation even in neighborhoods where
under private ownership white and Negro families have lived together amicably for years." Lamenting the exclusion of blacks from New York's Redhook
and Queensboro Projects during the war, Granger argued that barring or
limiting blacks' admission to public housing was unacceptable for a number
of reasons. The same "indifference and contempt" that created segregation,
Granger asserted, were responsible for the neglect and deprivation of public
services such as building inspections, policing, and health and sanitation that
characterized the nation's urban black belts. This was especially problematic
for Leaguers, who believed that the poor conditions engendered by residential
segregation undermined the morale and moral integrity of ghetto residents.[43]

For the League, public housing presented new possibilities for improving
blacks' housing options. One advantage of publicly financed housing over
private units, for example, was that Afro-Americans could exert greater influence over the political process than they could the market. Adopting one of
the civil rights movement's most important strategies, the NUL and its New
York local argued that as taxpayers blacks were just as entitled to publicly
financed housing as whites. League locals thus engaged in many battles for the
integration of public housing units.[44]

The CUL spent much of the late 1930s and 1940s working with both local
and federal government to open public units to blacks. Around the time that
the construction of Chicago's Ida B. Wells was under way, the government
opened three other South Side projects. The Jane Addams Houses, Julian
Lanthrop Homes, and Trumbull Parks Homes were all open for occupancy in
1937. For Leaguers, these projects represented an opportunity to lobby for the
integration of public housing. The Chicago League's first effort in this regard
focused on the Jane Addams Houses. Leaguers encouraged blacks to apply for
admission while the Addams Houses were still under construction. The Jane
Addams Houses' administrators discouraged prospective Afro-American
renters from applying. The CUL was not deterred, however. In fact, Chicago
Urban League executive secretary A. L. Foster wrote Secretary of the Interior
Harold Ickes to request that he take measures to ensure that blacks would
have an equal opportunity to "live in projects outside of the 'black belt.'" In
response to Foster's request, Ickes sent a special field agent to investigate the

situation in the Windy City. Eventually, the government gave its assurances that the project would not be "lily-white."[45]

Unfortunately, Ickes' pledge did not resolve the controversy. To avoid conflict with white tenants, the Jane Addams project manager announced that black renters would be confined to just thirty apartments in one building. The Chicago Urban League opposed this plan and vowed that it would not compromise on the issue of integration. The CUL continued its two-pronged approach of tenant mobilization and behind-the-scenes negotiations with government officials. As historian Arvarh Strickland has demonstrated, Leaguers went so far as to meet with applicants "who had been rejected to hear their grievances and to gather information." Furthermore, in light of the Housing Authority's obstinacy on racial integration, Leaguers called for black representation within the Housing Authority itself. The CUL and other Chicago civic organizations' protests eventually paid off.[46]

The first dividends of the League's protest activities came in the form of the appointment of Robert Taylor, an Afro-American, to the Housing Authority. The impact of Taylor's presence was not immediately apparent. In fact, the first black families admitted to Jane Addams were confined to racially restricted units. By the summer of 1939, however, Taylor had successfully lobbied to end discrimination in admission to the Addams Houses.[47]

The integration of the Chicago housing project was by no means uncontested. Many white tenants threatened to move; others took out their hostilities on their new black neighbors. In fact, the first black families to move into the integrated section of the projects were greeted by angry mobs, who hurled both epithets and bricks at them.[48]

The Jane Addams was not the only housing project that witnessed racial violence triggered by integration. Incensed by the Chicago Housing Authority's policy of nondiscrimination in the selection of tenants for veterans' emergency housing, many white communities protested both the construction of apartment projects in their communities and the admission of black tenants to two other Chicago-area apartment projects. Black tenants in Chicago's Airport Homes and the Fernwood Park projects were targets of intense mob violence between 1946 and 1947. Taking place for more than a month, the Airport Homes events were particularly vicious. Protesters overturned cars, vandalized buildings, and even attacked police. Fernwood Park residents were the victims of similar actions, though riots there lasted just a few days.[49]

While housing was a low priority for the Chicago League, the local offered moral if not material support to black families who were at the vanguard of housing and neighborhood integration. Rumors abounded that the CUL offered financial assistance to black families to break the color barrier in public housing. The CUL board denied the allegation, but many prominent Leaguers publicly declared their support for the integration of apartment projects. When Elizabeth Wood, the Chicago Housing Authority's executive secretary, was criticized and eventually demoted for her commitment to the CHA's open-occupancy policy, CUL president Earl Dickerson and Executive Secretary Sidney Williams rushed to her support. In fact, Dickerson and Williams went so far as to denounce the only black member of the CHA board, John Yancey, who led "the movement to curtail Miss Wood's powers." Though Dickerson and Williams appear to have made this move without consulting the Chicago Urban League board, their decision to chastise Yancey is especially striking since he was a former CUL board member.[50]

Without a doubt one of the main reasons Leaguers were so invested in increasing blacks' share of public units was the desperate nature of housing in the 1940s. As the Second World War drew to a close, Chicago's South Side was dangerously overcrowded. In 1945, the Chicago Planning Commission estimated that 300,000 men, women, and children were crammed into an area on the South Side that could reasonably accommodate only 225,000. At the same time, blacks' greatest gains in housing came in the form of publicly funded units. By the end of the war, the Chicago Housing Authority operated 7,644 permanent low-income housing units. This included some 4,000 blacks-only apartments in Ida B. Wells, Robert H. Brooks, and Altgeld Gardens.[51]

Chicago was not unique in this regard. The National Urban League argued that federally funded projects provided more homes for blacks than private developments in the 1940s. A 1948 NUL report stated that Afro-Americans did not benefit to any great extent from the nationwide construction boom following the war. In fact, the League claimed, "of 4,400 privately financed units built [in New York] since 1940, only 200 were available to Negro occupancy." By contrast nearly 2,200 of the 5,462 publicly financed units constructed during the same period were available to Afro-American renters.[52]

The Urban League had enough faith in the ability of progressive federal housing policies to improve blacks' and the nation's housing stock that it eventually advocated the passage of the Taft-Ellender-Wagner Act, or the Federal Housing Act of 1949. In declaring its support for Taft-Ellender-Wagner, the NUL stated that "if there is not a publicly financed housing program, our nation's slums will continue to expand because average and low-income groups and racial minorities have no other source of shelter." The League went on to argue that a disproportionately large number of Afro-Americans had incomes too low to pay for the full cost of standard housing. The situation was so bleak, according to the NUL, that "an increasing number of Negroes in the average income groups . . . are not adequately served by private enterprise."[53]

The National and local Leagues' emphasis on the importance of federal housing policy represented a significant departure from its pre–New Deal voluntarism. In fact, the Urban League's support for comprehensive housing policy occasionally revealed a growing militancy within the uplift organization. Believing that publicly financed homes provided a democratic alternative to the private market, prominent Leaguers often issued sharp criticism of private real estate interests. By the 1940s many Urban Leaguers came to view private housing interests as perhaps the most significant contributing factor to the housing problems confronting Afro-American renters and homeowners. Leaguers feared that the discriminatory practices of private interests had begun to affect public policy.

By the mid-1940s, Lester Granger, for example, complained that federal housing policy often treated public apartment projects as a means of warehousing blacks who had been excluded from the purview of the Federal Housing Administration's (FHA) long-term mortgage programs. Giving banks incentive to provide first twenty- and then thirty-year mortgages, the FHA transformed a nation of renters into a nation of homeowners. Unfortunately, federal housing policy also institutionalized discriminatory lending practices through "redlining," which ensured that most Afro-Americans would not benefit from this important initiative.[54] Granger argued that the FHA's discriminatory policies stemmed largely from its close ties to private real estate interests.[55] According to Granger, under the FHA, the real estate interests and banks that had contributed to ghetto decay further undermined blacks' housing prospects by preventing them from acquiring loans for homes "in residential areas . . . open[ing] up on the outskirts of the city." Granger believed that "this is the reason why the Federal Housing Administration, owned by the American people but controlled by private real estate interests, has been one of the most sinister enemies to the housing interests of Negroes that have been developed during the past decade."[56]

Despite the pernicious influence of private interests, Granger believed that a comprehensive federal housing policy provided an important means of circumventing intransigent real estate and banking groups. The public sector's susceptibility to protest afforded the League, and blacks generally, greater leverage over public housing policy than they had over private interests. The end result was blacks' greater gains in public housing. For Granger and other Leaguers, irrespective of its shortcomings, public housing was crucial to meeting blacks' immediate needs.[57]

Expediency, however, was not the sole reason Leaguers pushed for the expansion of public housing and its integration. Urban League locals weathered the controversy surrounding the integration of public apartment complexes, in part, because they hoped to use public housing to foster mutual understanding between blacks and whites. Indeed, in keeping with ethnic cycle theory, Leaguers identified the desegregation of public housing as essential to improving both black community life and race relations.

League officials argued that integration was crucial to combating social disorganization that stemmed from social isolation. In an appeal for planned communities in New York City, for example, the NYUL called on the government to implement "color blind" housing policies in order to "decentralize" the black populations of New York and other major cities. Pointing to the growing concentration of Afro-Americans in Brooklyn between 1930 and 1940, Granger asserted that the isolation of blacks in ghetto communities was cause for alarm. He argued that the concentration of blacks in a given area promoted neglect, due at least in part to the decline in public services that accompanied a neighborhood's transition from white to black. Though Leaguers were quick to point out that racial discrimination was responsible for decline in services, as discussed previously, this was invariably accompanied by social decay. To combat this tendency, the NYUL called for New York City to develop a building plan for low-cost housing that would determine eligibility on the basis of need rather than race.[58]

Not surprisingly, the Urban League of Greater New York echoed Granger's concerns about social decay and his calls for neighborhood planning and fair housing policy. In a report produced in the late 1940s, the NYUL stated plainly that housing was more than just attractive homes with modern conveniences. "Housing," the League declared, "is the physical environment, largely manmade, in which families live, grow, and decline." Proceeding from the view that decent housing contributed to "a sense of worth and dignity," the NYUL expressed great concerns about the impact of poor housing on black life in New York. Like Granger, the New York League noted that discriminatory housing policies had limited the housing opportunities available to Afro-Americans, confining blacks to bad housing in overcrowded neighborhoods. The "filth, lack of personal cleanliness and family privacy" in these homes "breaks down family morale," the group asserted, "and has a profound and evil influence upon the happiness, welfare and health of the people." The Taft-Ellender-Wagner Act was the principal remedy the New York League identified to counter the social disorganization and personal demoralization afflicting many black New Yorkers. The NYUL claimed that the pending legislation, which was supposed to finance some 500,000 new public housing units, held the potential to alleviate the overcrowding that had caused so much misery among urban blacks. While the NYUL did not emphasize the need for integrated public housing here, it was clear that FHA loan discrimination and

Elmer Carter and Nelson Rockefeller (Photographs and Prints Division, Schomburg Center for Research in Black Culture, The New York Public Library, Astor, Lenox and Tilden Foundations)

restrictive covenants had much to do with blacks' housing crisis.[59] The report thus implied that open housing policy would greatly enhance black life.

Expanded public housing was, of course, more than a counter to social disorganization. League officials appear to have perceived the desegregation of public housing as a wedge, opening the way to the integration not just of public units but also of privately owned residences. Indeed, for Leaguers such as Lester Granger, housing policy held the potential to engender mutual understanding between the races. Much as Charles S. Johnson argued in the 1920s, Granger believed that integration would mitigate racial prejudices by humanizing both blacks and whites. "The more that Negro families become distributed throughout the city in public housing projects, and the more that white families are allowed to demonstrate their desire and ability to live amicably in projects located in areas such as Harlem," he asserted, "the more we lay the groundwork for amicable living together of whites and Negroes in other than public housing situations."[60]

In conceiving of public housing as a wedge, Leaguers identified, just as they did prior to the New Deal, black respectability as a necessary precondition to eventually ending racial discrimination. Specifically, the League continued to view maladjustment as a major stumbling block to racial uplift. Ironically, the League clung to the notion that racial hostilities erupted over housing when lower-class blacks or black migrants moved into previously middle-class white neighborhoods. Poor blacks and middle-class whites had different expectations regarding neighborhood upkeep and appropriate behavior, resulting in tensions that were based less on racial characteristics and more on disparities in values. "It has been the clash of culture far more than the clash of race," the League asserted, "that has promoted many of the widely held fallacies regarding the effect of Negro residence on property values."[61]

Leaguers believed that integrated public housing promised an effective means of quelling such tensions. Even after the conflicts over the integration of public housing in Chicago, Urban Leaguers asserted that publicly funded units were especially well suited to defuse racial tensions. Lester Granger argued, for example, that by maintaining admission standards designed to ensure that residents, irrespective of race, were from comparable backgrounds, publicly funded projects reduced an important source of racial friction. Because admission standards ensured that "the cultural and economic backgrounds of Negro and white families are most closely comparable," integrated low-cost housing was crucial to demonstrating blacks' and whites' ability to live together in peace.[62]

Thus while the League's emphasis on the integration of public housing policy was indicative of a significant shift in strategy, the social-work group remained invested in the proper conduct of blacks. In particular, the Urban League's belief in the acculturating affects of integration was consistent with its traditional emphasis on respectability as an engine of uplift. It was likewise indicative of the sometimes unrealistic expectations the League had of education and interracial interaction as means of eliminating racial stereotypes.

■ The Urban League's neighborhood improvement and housing activities from the New Deal to 1950 reflected the group's dynamic approach to uplift. As was the case with its employment work, the League's approach to housing was fairly militant during this period. The group assisted black tenants in pressuring city officials to improve services in ghetto communities. It likewise organized blacks and worked with government officials to increase blacks' share of public housing while simultaneously throwing its support behind a general expansion of federal housing programs. These activities were without question indicative of the group's pragmatism. The NUL and its locals seized new opportunities made available to blacks as a result of the expansion of the welfare state. However, considering that the League did not simply accept housing policies as they pertained to Afro-Americans but encouraged re-medial action when necessary, pragmatism does not suffice as an explanation. Indeed, Leaguers embraced the expansion of the American welfare state, like many other Americans, as an essential element of democracy in the age of industry.

But while the League's uplift program shifted dramatically, its housing and neighborhood work in this period revealed important continuities with its pre–New Deal program. Continuing to identify maladjustment as a potential threat to racial uplift, Leaguers tried to create mechanisms for social control for ghetto residents much as they had in the 1910s and 1920s. The League thus remained invested in the creation of wholesome outlets for "disorga-nized" blacks. Likewise, the national and local Leagues hoped to treat federal housing policy as a means of acculturating urban blacks. Providing tenants attractive homes and a variety of amenities, planned communities, the League believed, were the foundation for social cohesion. Integrated neighborhoods stood to impart greater stability to black life by reducing social isolation among Afro-Americans, thereby increasing the likelihood that blacks would have full access to the services to which they were entitled.

More striking, however, was the fact that the League continued to identify the proper behavior of blacks as essential to group progress. In fact, even the Urban League's attempt to treat the integration of public housing as a first step toward ending residential segregation evinced the group's enduring com-mitment to Chicago School models of assimilation. In identifying biracial public housing as a means of demonstrating blacks' and whites' ability to live together in peace, the League revealed its lingering concerns about mal-adjusted blacks. The maintenance of housing admission standards was, of course, essential to ensuring peaceful coexistence. For Leaguers, blacks who threatened to reaffirm prejudice also threatened group progress. Thus the League's community work and its forays into government housing policy reflected the organization's ongoing apprehensions about ghetto residents.

Conclusion

From the National Urban League's inception, political activists ranging from Marcus Garvey to former Urban League staffer Abram L. Harris criticized the group for its failure to adequately address the real-world concerns of the Afro-American masses. Garvey, a black nationalist, and Harris, a left-leaning economist, occupied different niches in Afro-American politics; nevertheless, both claimed that the League's ties to white business and philanthropic organizations led the group to pursue a conciliatory agenda that benefited only a select few. By the conclusion of the modern civil rights movement, the charge that the National Urban League's vision was far removed from the concerns and dispositions of most blacks resonated well beyond the bounds of political activists. The League's reliance on corporate sponsorship led it to eschew the protest campaigns of the 1950s in favor of more aggressive job placement and social work projects. The NUL would participate in direct-action initiatives during the 1960s, including the 1963 March on Washington; but even then, it continued to stress the importance of proper behavior, in political demonstrations as well as in the workplace, as crucial to racial uplift.[1] In the era of black power and beyond, the social-work group's emphasis on respectability and moderation reaffirmed the perception that it was out of touch.

As this study shows, the aforementioned characterizations are not entirely without merit. Still, whatever the group's shortcomings, the story of the NUL and its locals is far more complex than the common charge that it was detached and bourgeois would have us believe. While the League was firmly embedded in the conservative wing of the modern civil rights movement, the group's cautious tactics during its first four decades were a direct outgrowth of the fundamentally liberal presumptions driving its work. Indeed, the Urban League's identification of proper behavior as an engine of uplift was not only consistent with the efforts of other reformers; it also mirrored important trends in liberal social science research.

Among progressive social scientists, behavior and culture would be the dominant lenses through which to view issues such as poverty, urbanization, and race relations for most of the twentieth century. The Chicago School of Sociology cast a particularly long shadow over such studies. Although the Chicago School encompassed a range of approaches, the research it generated pivoted, as sociologist Dennis Smith has noted, on the question of how one might realize liberal values and goals in a modern society. Focusing largely on issues related to urbanization, Chicago sociology thus established theories intended to determine how the nation might combine material prosperity, peace, social justice, and individual happiness with industrial capitalism.[2]

In its heyday, the study of race and ethnicity played a major role in the Chicago School's examination of life in the industrial city. As previously discussed, sociologists coming out of the university established theoretical frameworks such as social disorganization, urban ecology, and ethnic cycle that challenged eugenicists' claims that the so-called new immigrants and Afro-Americans were biologically inferior and therefore unassimilable. While scientific racists pointed to upsurges in crime, vice, and political radicalism as proof of those groups' biological deficiencies, the Chicago School attributed problems afflicting urban communities to particular structural influences such as migration. Individuals, in this view, were not hardwired to be delinquents, criminals, or malcontents, but they engaged in such behavior only when traditional avenues for personal fulfillment were no longer viable. Assimilation and the social harmony it engendered simply required the creation of effective institutional outlets for self-expression that were compatible with the existing social order. Thus, most social scientists influenced by Chicago sociology in the first half of the twentieth century perceived civil unrest and even racial prejudice as mere stages of a metabolic cycle that would inevitably resolve into equanimity and mutual understanding.[3]

In the context of the interwar period, the Chicago School's theories on race relations and assimilation were undeniably progressive. Nevertheless, the conceptual lenses developed and refined by pioneers such as W. I. Thomas, Robert Park, E. Franklin Frazier, and Charles S. Johnson were not without their own problems. Even as the Chicago School orientation traced social ills such as juvenile delinquency and crime to particular structural sources, it perceived such issues in terms of personal maladjustment, sidestepping the impact of political economy. The reason for this was, as historian Alice O'Connor has argued, that Chicago sociology accepted the hegemony of industrial capitalism. Consequently, any behavior that did not complement the process of capital accumulation was necessarily deviant, evidencing the absence of viable social outlets or, in other words, social disorganization. Thus perceiving the instability inherent to capitalist development as part of a kind of natural order, social scientists influenced by Chicago sociology presumed that appropriate remedies for social malaise would necessarily center on adjusting *people* rather than their *environments*.

For the League, the Chicago School's vision offered real advantages. Chicago sociology proceeded from the belief that race was socially constructed, a perspective that assisted reformers in developing optimistic frameworks through which to view and even shape race relations. The Chicago School's reification of the order imposed by the manufacturing city was also palatable to benefactors, some of whom, including John D. Rockefeller Jr., funded both the Urban League and the Chicago School. The plusses afforded by Chicago sociology notwithstanding, its theories and concepts ultimately provided the intellectual scaffolding for the Urban League's limited class model of collective progress. The group's commitment to attitudes and values as engines of uplift led it to develop housing, jobs, and union programs designed to either contain or acculturate Afro-Americans who appeared to threaten black equality. Leaguers therefore not only attempted to reorganize Afro-American institutional life in order to counter the pernicious effects of social disorganization, but they also occasionally assisted landlords and employers in dispatching those who failed to conform to mainstream values. The need to demonstrate blacks' capacity to assimilate likewise inspired the NUL and its locals to devote greater attention to the immediate material expectations of the black petite bourgeoisie. Indeed, the social-work group's efforts to establish mutually satisfying contacts between the races required that it prioritize projects intended to enhance the standing of individuals who best exemplified Afro-Americans' potential.

To suggest that the Urban League's application of Chicago School models of assimilation played a part, along with the influence of benefactors, in constraining the social-work group's vision is to undercut neither the organization's significance nor its legacy. Leaguers, like all of us, were products of their historical moment. They used the intellectual and institutional tools at their disposal both to understand their world and to try to create a more democratic society. They pursued these goals, moreover, with intelligence and dignity, tailoring their initiatives to the realities of the day.[4] That said, the inability of the NUL and its locals to deliver on their goal of uplifting *the race* is by no means an unflattering reflection on the integrity of the group's officers. Instead, the problems arising from the League's uplift approach can be traced to two matters: the difficulties inherent to challenging the barriers impeding integration through voluntarism and the hegemony of industrial social order. The limitations of the Urban League's work should therefore be understood as evidence of the shortcomings of liberal social reform generally, since any attempt to simply slot Afro-Americans, or other groups, into a system predicated on economic inequality would necessarily replicate class divisions within the larger society.

From this vantage point, what is perhaps most striking about the direction the NUL's work took between 1910 and 1950 is not the group's failings per se but the extent to which the League's agenda foreshadowed public policy initiatives of the modern civil rights movement and beyond. Due partly to the enduring significance of Chicago sociology, many of the problems associated with the Urban League's early work would be evident in later generations of social reform. In the second half of the twentieth century, the Chicago School's emphasis on urban studies and race relations held special appeal to a broad community of social scientists and activists. Chicago sociology appeared to offer well-honed tools with which to address some of the most pressing problems of an era encompassing the Cold War, the civil rights movement, and deindustrialization.[5] As a result, ethnic cycle, social disorganization, and urban ecology recurred in liberal efforts to redress racial and economic inequality over the past several decades.

In an age of liberal consensus, the Chicago School's race relations models were reasonably effective vehicles through which to press for black equality. Ethnic cycle theory, for example, played a prominent role in the NAACP's successful challenges to de jure segregation in education during the 1940s and 1950s. The NAACP's case in *Brown v. Board of Education* was, moreover, aided by the research and support of prominent social scientist and former League staffer Ira Reid.[6] But while Chicago sociology offered activists and policymakers a potent means of challenging formal racial hierarchy, the failure to adequately account for the political and economic forces contributing to inequality ensured that Chicago School–inspired reform projects would fall short of the material needs of Afro-Americans and other out-groups.

Even as concepts such as urban ecology and social disorganization have provided valuable insights into some of the problems afflicting American cities, they have not been up to the challenge of redressing the sources of inequality. In fact, urban ecology's focus on neighborhood integrity has frequently led policymakers to look past the actual sources of poverty and social unrest. The Community Action Programs (CAP) of the War on Poverty (1964–68) are instructive in this regard. Proceeding from the view that issues such as delinquency and crime were largely "expressions of temporary cultural and social 'disorganization,'" CAP attempted to reorganize institutional life of ghetto communities.[7] The architects of Community Action therefore set out to use government and indigenous leadership to revitalize neighborhood institutions in order to connect ghetto residents to mainstream society. By enhancing both access to government services and "community culture," policymakers ultimately hoped to create stable black neighborhoods that would foster productive, well-adjusted members of society.[8]

For the Johnson administration Community Action's approach, at least in its earliest incarnations, was appealing for a number of related reasons. CAP appeared to offer comparatively cheap solutions to the urban unrest of the 1960s. The programs also posed a minimal threat to the existing social relations, despite the ire CAPs provoked among mayors, as they attempted to add new vitality to ghetto communities rather than calling for major economic or social change.[9] Still, the problems plaguing central cities in the 1960s had less to do with institutional decay than with a shift in the nation's economic footing. Specifically, deindustrialization—which was itself a product of federal policy—had begun to transform the economic function of American cities from manufacturing sites to centers of service and commerce, thereby eliminating important sources of employment. Consequently, efforts to revitalize neighborhoods that even reformers understood to be hemorrhaging decent-paying blue-collar jobs were destined to fail, as provision of new outlets for personal fulfillment could counter neither the material consequences of economic collapse nor the inadequacies of federal housing policy.

Despite the obvious problems with Community Action, ecological frames continued to influence discourse about racial and economic inequality well beyond the 1960s. With the rightward shift in American politics in the 1980s, social scientists and policymakers devoted even greater attention to the alleged cultural deficiencies of impoverished minorities than they had previously. Over the past thirty years, conservatives and liberals have, for different reasons, gravitated to the idea that many poverty-stricken blacks and Latinos are part of an "underclass" possessing values detrimental to assimilation. Liberal sociologist William J. Wilson, an intellectual descendant of the Chicago School, is one of the most influential students of the Afro-American "underclass."[10] Examining Chicago's black belt through the lens of urban ecology, Wilson has argued that deindustrialization, housing discrimination, and black middle-class flight have isolated poor Afro-Americans in communities bereft of both good jobs and viable institutions. As a consequence, Wilson claims, many impoverished blacks have developed a "ghetto-specific culture" that not only fuels aberrant behavior but also undercuts participation in legitimate economic pursuits.[11]

A self-described social democrat, Wilson has advocated massive government works projects to facilitate the integration of the so-called underclass into civil society. In the era of federal retrenchment, however, policymakers have taken the work of Wilson and other urban ecologists as justification to dislocate poor minorities. Federally sponsored programs such as Hope VI have wed underclass ideology and ecological concerns about neighborhood organization to publicly financed redevelopment schemes intended to replace public housing with mixed-income communities. If efforts of this sort were genuine attempts to assist poor people, they might go a long way toward extending the promise of American democracy, if for no other reason than such communities might offer low-income residents better services. As Chicago's Near North Redevelopment Initiative (NNRI) has shown, however, Hope VI and similar mixed-income housing schemes displace many more poor people than they directly assist. Worse yet, in the case of the former residents of Cabrini-Green—the apartment project razed by the Chicago Housing Authority to make room for the NNRI development—those who did not qualify for low-income housing in the Near North community were scattered throughout Illinois and neighboring states. Since the ecological models shaping the NNRI and similar projects presume that impoverished minorities are victims of pathological cultures rooted in local community structures, many policymakers perceive the destruction of these neighborhoods and the dislocation of their residents as necessarily positive.[12]

Though the Urban League was in no position to challenge the political economic structures of inequality, the tradition of liberal reform in which it was grounded would not have thought to do so anyway. The group's philosophy was, in keeping with the Chicago School, the product of liberal capitalism. Its objective was simply to ensure that blacks shared equally in the fruits of American liberty. From the vantage point of the early twentieth century, this was, by itself, a bold and laudable goal. When one considers that Leaguers such as George E. Haynes, T. Arnold Hill, and Ira Reid lobbied for integration in an era marked by scientific racism and a Jim Crow social order extending well beyond the Mason-Dixon Line, it is hard not to admire the Urban League's efforts to advance the cause of black rights through scientism. Still, in viewing the League's work within a broader context of social reform, one point stands out beyond all others: calls for cultural assimilation as part of a narrow focus on ethnic-group integration cannot deliver. "Acting right," even if it does not hurt an individual's chances at upward mobility, is hardly a panacea. Behavioral models of uplift not only downplay or even ignore root causes of poverty, but they may reproduce other forms of inequality, undercutting any project to uplift the race.

Notes

Abbreviations

CUL Papers   Chicago Urban League Papers, University of Illinois, Chicago

NUL Papers   National Urban League Papers, Library of Congress, Washington, D.C.

Schomburg   Schomburg Center for Research in Black Culture Collection,
    Collection   New York Public Library, New York, N.Y.

Introduction

1. Booker T. Washington, *Up from Slavery* (New York: New American Library, 2000), 152–55.

2. James D. Anderson, *The Education of Blacks in the South, 1860–1935* (Chapel Hill: University of North Carolina Press, 1988), 35–40, 73–78.

3. W. E. B. DuBois, *The Philadelphia Negro: A Social Study* (Philadelphia: University of Pennsylvania Press, 1996), 6–8, 15, 55, 67, 192–96, 389–90.

4. Ibid., 195–96; Adolph L. Reed Jr., *W. E. B. DuBois and American Political Thought: Fabianism and the Color Line* (New York: Oxford University Press, 1997), 29–33, 34–37, 40–41.

5. Kevin Gaines, *Uplifting the Race: Black Leadership, Politics, and Culture in the Twentieth Century* (Chapel Hill: University of North Carolina Press, 1996), 31–32, 34–43.

6. In her study of the National Baptist Convention, Evelyn Brooks Higginbotham argues that Afro-American women's uplift endeavors were characterized by prioritizing collective progress over personal gain. Denied access to traditional political avenues, black churchwomen set out to uplift the race through the "politics of respectability." Afro-American churchwomen, according to Higginbotham, encouraged blacks to embrace middle-class values such as thrift, industry, and temperance in order to challenge the perception of the race as inherently debauched. Though Higginbotham acknowledges that this approach was not altogether free of class tension, she ultimately contends that black reformers' racial "nationalism" muted the class anxieties of even middle-class black churchwomen. The combination of Evangelical communalism and whites' failure to acknowledge class and cultural differences among Afro-Americans, Higginbotham argues, prevented middle-class black Baptist women from making sharp distinctions between themselves and their poor sisters. Their uplift strategies were therefore characterized by a greater egalitarianism than Progressive Era reform generally. See Evelyn Brooks Higginbotham, *Righteous Discontent: The Women's Movement in the Black Bap-*

tist Church, 1880–1920 (Cambridge: Harvard University Press, 1993), 56–58, 58–65, 67–72, 190–93, 195–97, 213–15.

7. Though Stephanie Shaw's multigenerational study of black professional women differs significantly in focus from Higginbotham's, her *What a Woman Ought to Be and Do* echoes many of Higginbotham's conclusions regarding the interplay between racial and class identification on the uplift vision of middle-class black women. According to Shaw, Afro-Americans' attempts to counter the debilitating affects of racism during the Jim Crow era required the use of far-flung social networks—neighbors, distant friends and family, and even loose acquaintances—to nurture the talents and aspirations of black girls and boys. Shaw claims that the importance of communal ties in fulfilling professional goals led middle-class black women to develop what she calls a "socially responsible individualism" in which Afro-American professional women linked their personal advancement to the race's generally. While Shaw does acknowledge the existence of parallels between black and white reformers, she nonetheless contends that middle-class black women developed a vision of racial progress that generally overrode the class biases that shaped the reform endeavors of their white counterparts. See Stephanie Shaw, *What a Woman Ought to Be and to Do: Black Professional Women Workers during the Jim Crow Era* (Chicago: University of Chicago Press, 1996), 4, 6, 54–56, 60–61, 66, 74, 170.

8. In contrast to most students of uplift, Kevin Gaines sets out to make sense of racial uplift ideology by situating black uplift in a broader nexus of reform. Gaines explores the influence of issues such Social Darwinism and eugenics on black thought in more than simply reactive terms. Products of their moment, black reformers, according to Gaines, perceived race relations through the lens of behavioral models of collective progress shaped by contemporary race theory. In this respect, Gaines's work differs significantly from the other works cited in that Gaines leaves little doubt that black reformers imbibed many of the conservative ideologies of their day. Gaines's *Uplifting the Race* offers a compelling and sophisticated account of the class biases undergirding uplift philosophy. Nevertheless, his focus, which centers on biographical accounts of black reformers' ideology, does not reveal the full implications of uplift.

9. I have chosen to focus on the League's activities between 1910 and 1950 largely because this period encompasses a number of monumental events in black history. Indeed, during the Urban League's first four decades of operation, Leaguers would be forced to develop programmatic responses to the Great Migration, the Depression and New Deal, World War II, and two postwar economic downturns. Though some might believe the 1954 *Brown* decision to be a logical point to conclude the study, the book's focus on the Urban League's housing and jobs programs undercuts *Brown*'s relevance to this project. The study thus concludes in 1950, because the late 1940s would witness major shifts in the League's housing and employment projects.

10. Nancy J. Weiss, *The National Urban League, 1910–1940* (New York: Oxford University Press, 1974), 59–63.

11. Jesse T. Moore, *A Search for Equality: The National Urban League, 1910–1961* (University Park: Pennsylvania State University Press, 1981), 32–34, 54–60.

12. Weiss (*National Urban League*) and Moore (*Search for Equality*) set out to

address a significant issue in the context of both Urban League historiography and Afro-American politics. Nearly from its inception, radicals and militants have charged that the League's commitment to job training and its close ties to business were indicative of a fundamental conservatism. With the rise of the black power movement of the 1960s and 1970s, allegations of this sort would be wed to the contention that the Urban League was out of touch. Weiss's and Moore's efforts to place the League's ideology within historical context therefore serve an invaluable function. Each examines a charge that is often made reflexively through the lens of historical empiricism, attempting to assess the NUL's work and ideology within a broader context of black politics.

13. Weiss's contention (*National Urban League*) is based on the author's equation of black self-help with the Wizard of Tuskegee. As a result, she understates the appeal of vocational and moral guidance among a spectrum of black political activists of the era, including DuBois. Moore (*Search for Equality*) errs antithetically. Though he correctly identifies the League as a social work group, his attempt to place the NUL within a tradition of black militancy leads him to overlook the League's predilection for self-help nostrums.

14. NLUCAN Bulletin, "Report 1911–12" (October 1912) NUL Papers, Series 13, Box 1.

15. It ultimately identified mutually satisfying interactions between disparate peoples as an indispensable element of assimilation—a subordinate group's integration into mainstream society.

16. Placing particular emphasis on the impact of migration and urbanization on the social structure of ethnic groups, social disorganization theory attributed issues such as crime, vice, and even radical politics among migrant populations to the collapse of traditional mechanisms of social control.

17. While the NUL did not formally initiate the Pilot Placement Program until 1948, the New York League adopted the approach that would characterize Pilot, which emphasized job placements for skilled white-collar workers, as early as 1947.

Chapter One

1. It is important to note that sociologist Robert Park had a relationship with Booker T. Washington. While working as a journalist, Park not only spent time with Washington at Tuskegee but he was the ghost author of Washington's *Up from Slavery*. There is little doubt that Park's thinking about race was influenced by his time with Washington. Still, this should not be taken as evidence that Park's views on race and ethnicity were simply an elaboration on Washington's accommodationist philosophy. Washington's perspectives on blacks arose organically from a nexus of ideas that reflected both the hegemony of industrial philanthropy and contemporary race theory. The same can, of course, be said for Park, who was influenced by theories of group assimilation bearing the intellectual imprint of both the German conflict school and concepts pioneered in the natural sciences. As historian Alice O'Connor has argued, models of assimilation pioneered by Park and the Chicago school's were, moreover, well liked by philanthropists who were disposed to fund studies that validated their interests in

America's budding industrial cities. Given that Park and Washington were shaped by many of the same broad social and intellectual forces, one would expect some overlap between the two. This does not mean, however, that Park's and Washington's views on group progress were one in the same. Indeed, depending on what indicators one believes are relevant, Park and DuBois had much in common in the early twentieth century as well. See Alice O'Connor, *Poverty Knowledge: Social Science, Social Policy, and the Poor in Twentieth-Century U.S. History* (Princeton, N.J.: Princeton University Press, 2001).

2. Gilbert Osofsky, *Harlem; The Making of a Ghetto; Negro New York, 1890–1930* (New York: Harper and Row, 1971), 42–43.

3. Nancy J. Weiss, *The National Urban League, 1910–1940* (New York: Oxford University Press, 1974), 17–20.

4. Ibid., 17–20.

5. Frances A. Kellor, *Out of Work: A Study of Unemployment* (New York: Arno Press and the New York Times, 1971), 227–35.

6. Weiss, *National Urban League*, 17–20.

7. Ibid., 21–23, 27–28.

8. Ibid., 23.

9. Ibid.

10. None of this is to suggest that the committee did not attract the disciples of the Wizard of Tuskegee. A number of Washington's friends and allies, including William H. Baldwin Jr., Charles W. Anderson, and T. Thomas Fortune and Fred Moore of the *New York Age*, were involved with the CIICN. Nevertheless, the committee's activities and philosophy would, as historian Jesse Moore has argued, appear to have been in line with guiding principles of social work. The ties between Bulkley's organization and the social sciences are further highlighted by his efforts to court support from social scientists. When Bulkley first attempted to establish the CIICN he initially sought the assistance of the Charity Organization Society, a social work association. The committee's members would, moreover, include many influential social workers and social scientists. Paul Kellogg, editor of *Charities*, Mary White Ovington, Lilian Brandt, and black sociologist George E. Haynes were all active participants in the organization. See Jesse T. Moore, *A Search for Equality: The National Urban League, 1910–1961* (University Park: Pennsylvania State University Press, 1981); and Weiss, *National Urban League*, 24–27.

11. Weiss, *National Urban League*, 29, 32–33.

12. George E. Haynes, *The Negro at Work in New York City* (New York: Longmans, Green & Co., 1912), 41.

13. Ibid., 84–85.

14. Ibid., 147.

15. Weiss, *National Urban League*, 42–43.

16. Ibid., 40–45.

17. Ibid., 29.

18. NLUCAN Bulletin, "Report 1911–12" (October 1912) NUL Papers, Series 13, Box 1.

19. Guichard Parris and Lester Brooks, *Blacks in the City: A History of the National Urban League* (Boston: Little, Brown, 1971), 36–37.

20. Ibid., 65–67.

21. Ibid., 76–79.

22. Ibid., 80–82.

23. Ibid., 191–93.

24. Ibid., 188, 194.

25. Arvarh Strickland, *History of the Chicago Urban League* (Columbia: University of Missouri Press, 2001), 21, 114–15, 144–45; "The Story of the New York Urban League, 1919–1979: Sixty Years of Service," pamphlet published by the New York Urban League.

26. Weiss, *National Urban League*, 30–31.

27. Ibid., 43.

28. Parris and Brooks, *Blacks in the City*, 65; Weiss, *National Urban League*, 181–82, 299.

29. Patrick J. Gilpin and Marybeth Gasman, *Charles S. Johnson: Leadership Beyond the Veil in the Age of Jim Crow* (Albany: State University of New York Press, 2003), 6–10.

30. Weiss, *National Urban League*, 217.

31. The New York Urban League was established in December 1919 and officially began its program as a separate organization on January 1, 1920.

32. Weiss, *National Urban League*, 217; "Program of the New York Urban League," NUL Papers, Series 4, Box 32.

33. Parris and Brooks, *Blacks in the City*, 125–27; Strickland, *History of the Chicago Urban League*, 30–37, 262–63.

34. Strickland, *History of the Chicago Urban League*, 42–44.

35. Ibid., 27–33, 40–42.

36. Ibid., 88–89, 106.

37. Alice O'Connor, *Poverty Knowledge: Social Science, Social Policy, and the Poor in Twentieth-Century U.S. History* (Princeton, N.J.: Princeton University Press, 2001), 47.

38. Dennis Smith, *The Chicago School: A Liberal Critique of Capitalism* (New York: St. Martin's Press, 1988), 3–4. Sociologist Dennis Smith has argued that between 1890 and 1918, Chicago's "first generation" sociologists, including Albion Small, maintained a kind of activist posture that led them to develop strong relationships with civic reformers and social workers. Smith argued that the so-called second and third generations would not share this interest in social activism. An advocate of scientific detachment, Robert Park, for example, actively embraced the creation of social work as a separate discipline from sociology.

39. O'Connor, *Poverty Knowledge*, 53–54.

40. Ibid., 45–49.

41. Ibid., 45.

42. Stow Persons, *Ethnic Studies at Chicago, 1905–45* (Urbana: University of Illinois Press, 1987), 30–37, 45–46.

43. Ibid., 30–35.

44. Herbert Blumer, *Critiques of Research in the Social Sciences: An Appraisal of Thomas and Znaniecki's "The Polish Peasant in Europe and America"* (New Brunswick: Transaction Books, 1979), 22, 62–66.

45. William I. Thomas and Florian Znaniecki, *The Polish Peasant in Europe and*

America (Urban: University of Illinois Press, 1984), 191–203, 205–7, 230–35; Persons, *Ethnic Studies at Chicago*, 50–52; Blumer, *Critiques of Research in the Social Sciences*, 62–66.

46. Thomas and Znaniecki, *Polish Peasant in Europe and America*, 287–90, 293–310; Dennis Smith, *Chicago School*, 94–95, 106.

47. O'Connor, *Poverty Knowledge*, 49; Dennis Smith, *Chicago School*, 137; Robert E. Park, "The Urban Community as a Spatial Pattern and Moral Order," in Ralph H. Turner, ed., *Robert E. Park on Social Control and Collective Behavior* (Chicago: University of Chicago Press, 1967), 55–56.

48. Persons, *Ethnic Studies at Chicago*, 60–61; O'Connor, *Poverty Knowledge*, 49.

49. Robert E. Park, "Racial Assimilation in Secondary Groups," in Turner, ed., *Robert E. Park on Social Control and Collective Behavior*, 120–32.

50. Persons, *Ethnic Studies at Chicago*, 61, 64–67, 74–75.

51. Ibid., 86–89.

52. Park, "Urban Community," 56–63, 65–68; O'Connor, *Poverty Knowledge*, 49.

53. Persons, *Ethnic Studies at Chicago*, 132–34.

54. E. Franklin Frazier, *The Negro Family in Chicago* (Chicago: University of Chicago Press, 1932), 244, 249–52.

55. O'Connor, *Poverty Knowledge*, 45, 53.

Chapter Two

1. Between 1820 and 1865, the percentage of Afro-American New Yorkers fell from 9.4 percent to 1.5 percent. While European immigration had much to do with this relative decline, by the 1840s New York's black population decreased in absolute number as well. Economic instability, hostility from white ethnics, and a general sense of restlessness inspired thousands of Afro-Americans to flee Manhattan for the greener pastures of the surrounding boroughs and hinterlands throughout the mid-1800s.

2. Gilbert Osofsky, *Harlem; The Making of a Ghetto; Negro New York, 1890–1930* (New York: Harper and Row, 1971), 128.

3. Because of low wages and residential segregation, Afro-Americans were generally confined to the least desirable sections of the city. Although segregation and discrimination were pervasive prior to World War I, black New York was too small to result in a distinct black belt. Instead, the city contained a number of Afro-American enclaves that gradually migrated uptown. The northward shift of New York's black community was already under way by the Civil War. While 55.2 percent of blacks in New York lived south of Houston Street in 1860, only 41.5 percent lived there a decade later. In 1900 only about 10 percent of blacks in Manhattan lived below 14th Street. Conversely, between 1870 and 1900, the percentage of blacks living between 14th Street and 86th Street increased steadily from 36 percent to 65 percent.

The moves uptown from Greenwich Village to Tenderloin (1860–80), and from Tenderloin to Columbus Hill—a.k.a. "San Juan Hill"—(1900–1910) were simply migrations from one set of "bad neighborhoods" to another. In the 1910s, however, black New Yorkers were provided the opportunity to move into one of Manhattan's more fashionable districts, Harlem. Thanks to wild real estate speculation, desperate developers opened Harlem up to New York's rapidly expanding Afro-American community. Although the district's homes were generally superior to those previously available to blacks, indifference among landlords and developers quickly contributed to the area's physical decline. Overcrowding further eroded conditions in Harlem.

4. By 1930, Afro-Americans comprised 12 percent of Manhattan's population, whereas they accounted for less than 5 percent of New York City's total.

5. Osofsky, *Harlem*, 128, 130; Kenneth Jackson, *Encyclopedia of New York City* (New Haven: Yale University Press, 1995), 524.

6. Thomas L. Philpott, *The Slum and the Ghetto: Neighborhood Deterioration and Middle-Class Reform, Chicago, 1880–1939* (New York: Oxford University Press, 1978), 115–16.

7. Allan Spear, *Black Chicago: The Making of a Ghetto* (Chicago: University of Chicago Press, 1967), 13. According to Spear, "as early as 1859, 82 percent of the Negro population lived in an area bounded by the Chicago river on the north, Sixteenth Street on the south, the south branch of the river on the west, and Lake Michigan on the east" (ibid.).

8. Philpott, *Slum and the Ghetto*, 123. If black Chicagoans had been distributed equally throughout the city at this time they would have comprised about 1 to 2 percent of the population in each of the thirty-five wards. Yet census data for 1900 revealed that only five wards maintained percentages in this range.

9. More importantly, the number of wards 99.5 to 100 percent black had increased from sixteen in 1900 to twenty-two in 1910. See ibid.

10. Ibid., 123–27.

11. The organization went by the name National League for Urban Conditions Among Negroes (NLUCAN) until it changed its name to the National Urban League (NUL) in 1917.

12. NLUCAN Bulletin, "Report 1913–14 and 1914–15" (November 1915), NUL Papers, Series 13, Box 1; Guichard Parris and Lester Brooks, *Blacks in the City: A History of the National Urban League* (Boston: Little Brown, 1971), 41.

13. NLUCAN Bulletin, "Report 1912–13" (November 1913), NUL Papers, Series 13, Box 1; Parris and Brooks, *Blacks in the City*, 46.

14. NLUCAN Bulletin, "Report 1913–14 and 1914–15" (November 1915), NUL Papers, Series 13, Box 1; "Planning to Solve Negro Housing Problems," *New York Times*, December 19, 1915; Parris and Brooks, *Blacks in the City*, 47.

15. CUCAN Minutes (September 1910), NUL Papers, Series 11, Box 1.

16. NLUCAN Bulletin, "Report 1912–13" (November 1913), NUL Papers, Series 13, Box 1; Parris and Brooks, *Blacks in the City*, 46–47.

17. George E. Haynes, *The Negro at Work in New York City* (New York: Longmans, Green & Co., 1912), 85–89, 99–102.

18. Ibid., 99–102.

19. Seth M. Scheiner, *Negro Mecca: A History of the Negro in New York City, 1865–1920* (New York: New York University Press, 1965), 26–27, 48–50.

20. The bombers' activities intensified in pace with the city's population growth. From March 1918 to August 1919, "twenty-five bombs exploded at the homes of blacks"

who had moved into "white neighborhoods." By the spring of 1919, two bombs a month were detonated on the steps of black homes. By late June, bombs were going off every week in the Windy City. See Philpott, *Slum and the Ghetto*, 169.

21. Chicago Commission on Race Relations, *The Negro in Chicago: A Study of Race Relations and a Race Riot* (Chicago: University of Chicago Press, 1922), 1.

22. Scheiner, *Negro Mecca*, 26–27. This perspective was not unique to those opposing the integration of blacks into the American mainstream, for the dominant strain of reform targeting blacks rested on a version of this view. Mary White Ovington—one of the founding members of the NAACP and friend to the Urban League—argued that "the [black] people on the hill" were generally "known for their rough behavior, their readiness to fight, their coarse talk." Ovington asserted that the riot was triggered by a "fracas between a colored boy and a white peddler." Although she was empathetic and acknowledged that both blacks and whites contributed to the melee, Ovington ultimately argued that racist police officers goaded the short-tempered residents of "the Hill" into conflict. See Mary White Ovington, *Half a Man: The Status of the Negro in New York* (New York: Schocken Books, 1911), 39–41, 199–200.

23. CCRR, *Negro in Chicago*, 534, 529–32.

24. Ibid., 118–21. Many whites were concerned that blacks' presence, irrespective of their behavior, would undermine neighborhood property values. For example, after his house was bombed continuously through 1919, Charles Davis, a black homeowner, finally died of a heart attack. Upon Mr. Davis's death, one of his neighbors explained the concerns fueling the community's less than neighborly response. He asserted: "I could tell the minute I saw him that Davis was an honorable man." "The residents of the block," he asserted, "never had any hard feelings against him personally, we assured him." Nevertheless, the community "feared the presence of Negroes on the block would lower real estate values." See Philpott, *Slum and the Ghetto*, 169.

25. NYUL, "2400 Negro Families in Harlem," 6–8, Schomburg Collection.

26. CUL, Annual Report, 1917, CUL Papers.

27. Ibid., 1927.

28. These sentiments were reiterated in the CUL's 1923 Report, which also urged black Chicagoans to refuse to pay exorbitant rents. See ibid., 1923.

29. CCRR, *Negro in Chicago*, 193.

30. CUL, Annual Report, 1923, CUL Papers.

31. Ibid., 1926.

32. James Grossman, *Land of Hope: Chicago, Black Southerners and the Great Migration* (Chicago: University of Chicago Press, 1989), 151–53; Chicago *Defender*, September 24, 1921.

33. CCRR, *Negro in Chicago*, 1.

34. Charles S. Johnson, "Blacks Workers and the City," *Survey Graphic* 53 (1924–25): 642–43.

35. George E. Haynes, "The Church and the Negro Spirit," *Survey Graphic* (1924–25): 697.

36. Earl Moses' dissertation was eventually published as a report for the Washington, D.C., Public Schools Department of Research.

37. Earl R. Moses, "The Negro Delinquency in Chicago" (Washington, D.C.: Washington Public Schools Department of Research Division X–XIII, 1936), 69.

38. Between 1905 and 1930, the percentage of black males among those arrested for misdemeanors increased from 8.3 percent to 21.2 percent. Blacks accounted for 5.5 percent and 19.1 percent of the total number of men convicted of misdemeanor offenses in 1913 and 1930, respectively. More alarming was that while black women accounted for only 17.1 percent of those arrested for misdemeanors in 1913, they comprised more than 60 percent of those convicted of misdemeanors in 1930.

39. Moses, "Negro Delinquency in Chicago," 31–34, 37–40.

40. Ibid., 130–32.

41. Ibid., 20–23.

42. Ibid., 24–26.

43. Ibid., 117, 122, 138.

44. Ibid., 121–23.

45. Ibid., 115.

46. Ibid., 57, 114–16, 122–24, 194. Statistics appeared to support the claim that familial and communal influences impacted black delinquency. Moses noted that 60 percent of black delinquents' mothers worked outside of the home. Furthermore, he found that 49 percent of all black delinquents brought before juvenile court in 1929 changed addresses two or more times in the space of a year. In contrast, only 9.7 percent of white delinquents did so.

The connection between community life and youth misconduct was reaffirmed by the distribution of crime and delinquency across the black belt. Taking their cues from the works of William Burgess and E. Franklin Frazier, Moses and the CUL claimed that black Chicago consisted of three distinct zones—"I. Disorganized," "II. Transitionary," and "III. Organized"—extending outward from the central business district. The Organized zone had little physical deterioration and was largely absent "of pathological social conditions." Moreover, the populations of neighborhoods in this area were fairly "stable," thanks to high rates of homeownership, shared "common traditions," and "stabilizing community institutions." In contrast, the League described both the Transitionary and Disorganized zones as "area[s] where life is free." Due partially to the prevalence of dilapidated homes in these areas, the populations of both were extremely mobile. Perhaps as a consequence of this mobility, the CUL claimed, the Disorganized zone had "no censors of behavior." In fact, the League claimed "a common body of tradition and stabilizing community institutions are negligible."

Although the Organized zone was not free of youth misconduct, Moses found that rates of serious delinquency and crime were more pronounced in the less stable areas. The Disorganized and Transitionary zones were beset by disproportionately large share of the Black Belt's thefts, muggings, violent crimes, and acts of sexual misconduct. Interestingly, "specialized delinquencies"—acts requiring special skills such as automobile theft—were most common in the Transitionary zone. See Moses, "Negro Delinquency in Chicago," 20–26.

47. Ibid.

48. Earnest T. Attwell, "Community Recreation and the Negro," *Opportunity*, May 1923, 7.

49. Perhaps the black belt's most glaring deficiency was its absence of parks. When compared with all of Chicago, the black belt had an appalling lack of park space. Moses noted that citywide, the Windy City contained more than 5,912 acres of park land. This translated into an average of one acre of park space for just over 500 people. In contrast, the black wards contained a paltry 102.5 acre total, providing one acre of park space for 1,871 people. See Moses, "Delinquency in Chicago," 152.

50. Ibid., 131, 38, 152.

51. Ibid., 13–19.

52. NYUL Report, 1927, NUL Papers, Series 5, Box 10.

53. Ibid.

54. NLUCAN Bulletin, "Report 1912–13" (November 1913), NUL Papers, Series 13, Box 10.

55. NLUCAN Bulletin, "Report 1911–12" (October 1912); NLUCAN Bulletin, "Report 1912–13" (November 1913); NLUCAN Bulletin, "Report 1913–14 and 1914–15" (November 1915), NUL Papers, Series 13, Box 1.

56. NLUCAN Bulletin, "Report 1913–14 and 1914–15" (November 1915), NUL Papers, Series 13, Box 1.

57. CUL, Annual Report, 1926, CUL Papers.

58. NLUCAN Bulletin, "Report 1912–13" (November 1913); NLUCAN Bulletin, "Report 1913–14 and 1914–15" (November 1915), NUL Papers, Series 13, Box 1.

59. "Neighborhood Union," *Opportunity*, June 1925, 178.

60. NLUCAN Bulletin, "Report 1912–13" (November 1913); NLUCAN Bulletin, "Report 1913–14 and 1914–15" (November 1915); NLUCAN Bulletin, "Report 1916–17" (November 1917), NUL Papers, Series 13, Box 1.

61. NLUCAN Bulletin, "Report 1914–15" (November 1915), NUL Papers, Series 13, Box 1.

62. The records of the CUL for this period reveal little about its efforts to attract investment in black belt housing. The Chicago Urban League's work with the providers of both private and public housing is an important element of the second half of this study.

63. NYUL, "2400 Negro Families in Harlem," 5–6, Schomburg Collection.

64. Ibid., 12–13.

65. In 1927, blacks paid $8 more than whites for three rooms; $10 more for four rooms; and $7 more for five rooms.

66. NYUL, "2400 Negro Families in Harlem," 18–19, Schomburg Collection. When combined with the low wages Afro-Americans commanded, exorbitant rents led black women to participate in the paid labor force at rates higher than whites. The decreased presence of black mothers in the home was of interest to Leaguers because it reduced both household efficiency and parental controls over children.

67. In a study of 2,326 Afro-American families, the NYUL found that an alarming 47 percent remained in their apartments for just one year or less. Sixty-eight percent of residents occupied their homes for no more than three years, while 75 percent remained in the same home for no more than five years. See NYUL, "2400 Negro Families in Harlem," 8–9, Schomburg Collection.

68. NYUL, "2400 Negro Families in Harlem," 8, Schomburg Collection.

69. Only 43 percent of the apartments sampled housed families in which the number of rooms exceeded the number of residents, while the number of persons equaled the number of rooms in 19 percent of apartments studied. More significantly, 9.5 percent of apartments sampled had two to three times as many people as rooms, and .4 percent of them had more than three times as many residents as rooms.

70. NYUL, "2400 Negro Families in Harlem," 10–11, Schomburg Collection. Overcrowding was frequently a consequence of the design of the apartments themselves. Leaguers argued that an apartment's size and layout greatly influenced the comfort, privacy, and moral health of renters. According to the NYUL, the number of residents living in an apartment should ideally be equal to the number of rooms. On average, apartments in Harlem met this criterion. More than 50 percent of units in Harlem had four or five rooms, the former being the most common. Since the median family size in the district was five members, quite a few black New Yorkers could obtain relatively spacious accommodations. On the other hand, 18 percent of Harlem's apartments had three or fewer rooms and more than 50 percent of families had more than five members, 52.1 percent of families had five to ten members, and 2 percent had ten or more.

71. "Second-hand houses" were defined as homes that had "not been kept up, have been allowed to go to pieces," and were originally "built for one family" but housed "two, three, or more" (Minutes of the Eleventh Annual Meeting of the NYUL, January 8, 1930, NUL Papers, Series 5, Box 10).

72. NYUL, "2400 Negro Families in Harlem," 12–14, Schomburg Collection.

73. Ibid., 11.

74. Extended family members such as uncles, aunts, and cousins were thus grouped into the same category as family friends and total strangers.

75. NLUCAN Bulletin, "Report 1913–14" (November 1914), NUL Papers, Series 13, Box 1; NYUL "2400 Negro Families in Harlem," 5, Schomburg Collection.

76. Minutes of the Eleventh Annual Meeting of the NYUL, January 8, 1930. One of the most disturbing forms of lodging identified by the NYUL was the "hot bed system." This arrangement required that two boarders share a room and a bed in shifts. It was most frequently used to rent a room to both a day and a night worker, one of whom slept during the day and the other at night, "or to a Pullman Porter who simply desires to maintain a room as a residence in the city." Perhaps what was most startling was that the New York League found that it was not uncommon for families to rent their children's rooms to night workers. Urban Leaguers believed that the "hot bed system," as these arrangements were called, and lodgers in general undermined the health of families. See NYUL, "2400 Negro Families in Harlem," 5, Schomburg Collection.

77. James H. Hubert, "Harlem—Its Social Problems" (reprinted from *Hospital Social Service*, XXI, 1930, 43), 45, NUL Papers, Series 5, Box 10. Though the records of the New York Urban League do not explicitly discuss how such arrangements threatened the family, the Chicago Commission of Race Relation's report on black housing—which was assisted by the Chicago Urban League—did explore this issue in clear terms. As in New York, most of Chicago's boarders lived in large apartments that would have otherwise been beyond the means of the families renting them. While taking in boarders may

have been expedient, the CCRR alleged that the presence of lodgers in homes that were "originally intended for single family use" undermined family privacy. This was especially problematic since it was rarely possible to investigate a lodger's character, "making a difficult situation for families with children" (CCRR, *The Negro in Chicago*, 158).

78. "Steps in Social Progress: Memorandum on the NYUL for 1926," NUL Papers, Series 5, Box 10; Report of the Executive Secretary of the NUL (February 2, 1927), 9, NUL Papers, Series 11, Box 1; "Progress in Racial Adjustment," *Opportunity*, March 1927, 79.

79. NYUL Report, 1931, NUL Papers, Series 13, Box 19.

80. It also seems that in requiring residents to save their earnings to make down payments for the apartments' stock, Rockefeller attempted to impress upon Afro-Americans the importance of taking personal responsibility for one's finances. In a discussion about the difficulties blacks experienced in acquiring mortgages, for example, the managing director of the Dunbar National Bank asserted that the bank's thrift accounts were ultimately designed to "help the Negro help himself" by providing Afro-Americans the opportunity to save for their future. Savings helped to insulate blacks from poverty, by equipping them with the means to own and maintain property while simultaneously providing for life's necessities. See "The Cooperative a Very Present Help in Time of Trouble," *Dunbar News*, March 9, 1932.

81. Ibid.

82. "Rockefeller's Resident Manager in Address to Interracial Conference Tells How Apartments Helped Harlem," New York *Age*, January 26, 1929.

83. Alfred Alexander, "The Housing of Harlem," *Crisis* 35 (October 1928): 335.

84. NYUL, "2400 Negro Families in Harlem," 8, Schomburg Collection.

85. Executive Board Members of NYUL, Newsletter, September 1926, NUL Papers, Series 13, Box 19.

86. Roscoe C. Bruce, "The Dunbar Apartment House: An Adventure in Community Building," *Southern Workman* 60 (October 1931): 420, 423.

87. Ibid., 418–19.

88. Ibid., 420–21.

89. Ibid., 419.

90. Ibid., 426.

91. Alexander, "Housing of Harlem," 335, 351.

92. Hubert, "Harlem—Its Social Problems," 44.

93. Ad for the Paul Laurence Dunbar Apartments, *Dunbar News*, January 28, 1928, 8.

94. Bruce, "Dunbar Apartment House," 421.

95. NYUL, "2400 Negro Families in Harlem," 16, Schomburg Collection.

96. Bruce, "Dunbar Apartment House," 424–25.

97. "Steps in Social Progress: Memorandum on the NYUL for 1926," NUL Papers.

98. "The New Philanthropy," *Opportunity*, January 1929, 5.

99. New York *Age*, January 26, 1929.

100. Even these programs reflected the limits of the League's self-help agenda. As I discuss in Chapter 3, the job training programs offered by the Dunbar Apartments

reflected the Urban League's class anxieties about the poor, and the unemployed in particular.

101. Ad for the Paul Laurence Dunbar Apartments, *Dunbar News*, August 26, 1931.

Chapter Three

1. NLUCAN Bulletin, "Report 1912–13" (November 1913), NUL Papers, Series, 13, Box 1.

2. Though no specific information regarding the scope of this work is available, vocational guidance for young people continued to play a significant role in the League's programs through the Depression.

3. NLUCAN Bulletin, "Report 1912–13" (November 1913), NUL Papers, Series 13, Box 1.

4. NLUCAN Bulletin, "Report 1913–14 and 1914–15" (November 1915) and "Report 1915–16" (November 1916), NUL Papers, Series 13, Box 1.

5. NLUCAN Bulletin, "Report 1914–15" (November 1915), NUL Papers, Series 13, Box 1. The workshop accommodated 774 workers at a time, with an aggregate attendance of 12,739.

6. NLUCAN Bulletin, "Report 1915–16" (November 1916), NUL Papers, Series 13, Box 1.

7. NUL Bulletin, "Annual Report 1917–18" (January 1919), NUL Papers, Series 13, Box 1.

8. As I shall discuss, the NYUL used its vocational work as a means of insuring that workers—both underemployed and employed—comported themselves in a fashion that reflected positively on the race.

9. Because of the nature of the sources, this section draws from the reports of the National, New York, and Chicago Urban Leagues, as well as the writings of prominent League members. Unfortunately the records of the two locals are patchy, making it impossible to follow the development of the affiliates year by year. Instead, one can only piece together the industrial work of the Chicago League from 1917 through the late 1920s, and the New York League's endeavors after 1925. Furthermore, since local Leagues did not exist as such prior to 1917—the year when the National League for Urban Conditions Among Negroes both renamed itself the National Urban League and subdivided into local branches—discussion of local activities prior to this year requires examination of the National League's records. Although the early records of the National League are not particularly rich, they do provide some material with which to make a loose sketch of the League's history.

10. Seth Scheiner, *Negro Mecca: A History of the Negro in New York City, 1865–1920* (New York: New York University Press, 1965), 48–50.

11. Ibid., 48–50; George E. Haynes, *The Negro at Work in New York City* (New York: Longmans, Green & Co., 1912), 73.

12. Allan H. Spear, *Black Chicago: The Making of a Negro Ghetto, 1890–1920* (Chicago: University of Chicago Press, 1967), 29–35; James Grossman, *Land of Hope: Chi-

cago, Black Southerners, and the Great Migration (Chicago: University of Chicago Press, 1989), 197–99.

13. Spear, *Black Chicago*, 29, 151.

14. Grossman, *Land of Hope*, 184.

15. Afro-Americans comprised 4 percent of workers in manufacturing and 4.9 percent of trade workers.

16. Spear, *Black Chicago*, 29, 151.

17. Ibid., 29, 151.

18. Ibid., 29–35.

19. Chicago Commission on Race Relations, *The Negro in Chicago: A Study of Race Relations and a Race Riot* (Chicago: University of Chicago Press, 1922), 381–89. Seventy-one out of 93 respondents believed that blacks were as efficient as whites. Regarding the matter of reliability, 33 employers believed that black workers required no more supervision than whites, as compared with just 28 offering an opposing view; 57 claimed that absenteeism was no more common among Afro-Americans, while only 36 believed it more common; but on the issue of turnover, only 24 respondents claimed that black turnover was equal to white, while 28 asserted that black turnover was higher.

20. CCRR, *Negro in Chicago*, 385–89.

21. CUL, Annual Report, 1920, and CUL, Annual Report, 1923, CUL Papers.

22. CUL, Annual Report, 1920, CUL Papers.

23. Ibid.; CUL, Annual Report, 1923, and CUL, Annual Report, 1926, CUL Papers; CCRR, *Negro in Chicago*, 382–89.

24. It is not clear that the CUL actually employed a worker at this company; however, it did claim credit for the termination of this foremen through its behind-the-scenes work with the employer.

25. CCRR, *Negro in Chicago*, 389; CUL, Annual Report, 1923, and CUL, Annual Report, 1926, CUL Papers. The League's efforts to improve working conditions extended beyond industrial work. In a number of cases of employer abuse of domestic workers who had been hired under false pretenses, the League mediated between workers and their bosses and contacted the appropriate government agencies for additional assistance when necessary.

26. Helen Sayre, "Making Over Poor Workers," *Opportunity*, February 1923, 17.

27. Ibid., 17–18.

28. CUL, Annual Report, 1920, CUL Papers.

29. Daniel T. Rodgers, *The Work Ethic in Industrial America, 1850–1920* (Chicago: University of Chicago Press, 1978), 51–57. The problems with piecework were so widespread that even one of its most infamous proponents, Frederick Winslow Taylor, admitted the tendency among workers to resist the system through sabotage, malingering, and collective antagonism. In his testimony before the U.S. House of Representatives, Taylor claimed to have waged a three-year-long battle with employees of Midvale Steel Works to increase productivity through revision of piece-rates. Employed initially as a workman at the Midvale machine shop, Taylor claimed that he and his coworkers had limited output to about one-third of its potential. Eventually Taylor was promoted to gang boss, at which point he attempted to increase output to a "fair days work." The

workers resisted, but after three years of sabotage, slowdowns, and protests to Taylor's bosses, Taylor succeeded in increasing output. See Harry Braverman, *Labor and Monopoly Capital: The Degradation of Work in the Twentieth Century* (New York: Monthly Review Press, 1974), 92–96.

30. CUL, Annual Report, 1926, CUL Papers. The League's concerns about the problems at the lampshade company revolved around the impact black workers' poor performance at the plant might have on future employment opportunities there.

31. CCRR, *Negro in Chicago*, 366. The CUL's annual reports for 1918 and 1919 were destroyed.

32. CUL, Annual Report, 1920, CUL Papers. In May of 1920, as the decline in black employment began, the CUL reported requests from employers for 1,000 males and 500 females. That month only 941 males and 739 female job seekers filed applications with the Chicago League, which managed to place 722 males and 371 females. By contrast, the Chicago League's records for November 15–20, 1920—one month after the conclusion of League's report for 1920—showed 1,073 job seekers for only 131 openings. See CCRR, *Negro in Chicago*, 402.

33. From October 1926 to November 1927 the CUL averaged 238 applicants for every 100 openings.

34. CUL, Annual Report, 1917; CUL, Annual Report, 1920; CUL, Annual Report, 1923; and CUL, Annual Report, 1931, CUL Papers.

35. In 1923, the League boasted of creating openings in twelve firms that had previously denied employment to blacks. See CUL, Annual Report, 1923, CUL Papers.

36. CUL, Annual Report, 1917; CUL, Annual Report, 1920; and CUL, Annual Report, 1923, CUL Papers.

37. CUL, Annual Report, 1920, CUL Papers.

38. Ibid., 1926.

39. Ira De A. Reid, NYUL Department of Industrial Relations Report (June 1925), NUL Papers, Series 5, Box 10. Expressing frustration with placing a disproportionately high number of unskilled and domestic and personal service workers, the League declared in 1925, "Because low grade applicants, poor paying jobs, unemployables, casuals, [and] migratory workers comprise the main part of the business [of job placements], the character of work is far from satisfactory" (ibid.).

40. Ibid.

41. NYUL, "A Challenge to New York: Annual Report, 1927," NUL Papers, Series 5, Box 10.

42. NYUL Department of Industrial Relations Report (August 8, 1921), NUL Papers, Series 5, Box 1.

43. "Re-organizing" would entail collective bargaining as well as training sessions for both workers and employees.

44. Ira De A. Reid, NYUL Department of Industrial Relations Report (June 1925), NUL Papers, Series 5, Box 10.

45. T. Arnold Hill and Ira De A. Reid, "Unemployment Among Negroes, Activities of the National Urban League: Data on Twenty-Five Industrial Centers" (November 1930), NUL Papers, Series 4, Box 1.

46. NUL Department of Industrial Relations Report, 1932, "The Program of the National Committee on Employer-Employee Relations in the Home," NUL Papers, Series, Box 6.

47. NYUL, "The Negro in New York: Annual Report, 1931," NUL Papers, Series 13, Box 19 (emphasis added).

48. T. Arnold Hill, "Labor—The Problem Self in Vocational Adjustment," *Opportunity*, April 1932, 118. Hill believed vocational training to be a particularly important task since he claimed that "the vast majority [of unemployed] are maladjusted workers, technically inefficient or socially irresponsible, but heretofore kept at work because industry was short of hands" (ibid.).

49. Ira De A. Reid, "The Negro Goes to Sing Sing," *Opportunity*, July 1932, 215. Reid made a similar argument several years later that divulged that concerns about blacks' use of free time were not limited to the economic crisis of the Depression. In his 1940 American Council of Education (ACE) Study, *In a Minor Key*, Reid argued that urban black youth carried with them a "do nothing" view of leisure time which exacerbated the moral degradation and "disturbed emotions" that were inherent to urban life. See Ira De Augustine Reid, *In a Minor Key: Negro Youth in Story and Fact* (Westport: Greenwood Press, 1971), 75–77.

50. Reid, "Negro Goes to Sing Sing," 217.

51. NYUL, "The Negro in New York: Annual Report, 1931," NUL Papers, Series 13, Box 19. The New York League claimed to share the view advanced by the *Amsterdam News* that youth crime could be attributed to the lack of parental guidance received by many black children. Because of the poor wages and employment prospects commanded by black men possessing even specialized skills, black women were almost without exception forced to seek employment outside of the home, thereby reducing parental controls. Though the League's discussion of criminality did not offer any suggestions to rectify the matter, in a separate section on industrial opportunities, it recommended vocational training along with its own ongoing work to open employment in industry to combat the lodger evil and the problem of women working outside of the home.

52. T. Arnold Hill, "Labor-Comrades in Crime," *Opportunity*, October 1929, 316.

53. T. Arnold Hill, "Picketing for Jobs," *Opportunity*, July 1930, 216.

54. T. Arnold Hill, "After the Depression—What?" *Opportunity*, February 1932, 53.

55. T. Arnold Hill, "The Present Status of Negro Labor," *Opportunity*, May 1929, 144–45.

Chapter Four

1. Nancy Weiss, *The National Urban League, 1910–1940* (New York: Oxford University Press, 1974), 205.

2. Ibid., 204–5.

3. Ibid., 206.

4. "The Way Out: A Suggested Solution of the Problems of Race Relations" (October 15–19), NUL Papers, Series 1, Box 1; Weiss, *National Urban League*, 208.

5. Eugene K. Jones, "The Negro's Future in Industry," February 19, 1920, NUL Papers,

Series 1, Box 1; Guichard Parris and Lester Brooks, *Blacks in the City: A History of the National Urban League* (Boston: Little, Brown, 1971), 178.

6. Parris and Brooks, *Blacks in the City*, 179–80. Rockefeller's job placement project entailed compiling national statistics on available employment opportunities in order to direct Afro-American laborers from towns, states, and regions where their particular talents were abundant to locations where they might be in greater demand.

7. Although Hill is generally credited as the architect of the NUL's labor program in this period, many Leaguers expressed similar interest in black trade unionism. George E. Haynes, Eugene K. Jones, Charles S. Johnson, and Ira De Augustine Reid each asserted the importance of black participation in the union movement.

8. T. Arnold Hill, "Prospective Immediate Program," Memorandum (June 24, 1925), NUL Papers, Series 4, Box 1; Parris and Brooks, *Blacks in the City*, 181–83.

9. According to Parris and Brooks (*Blacks in the City*), the National Urban League shifted its focus from job placements to trade unionism by its 1924–25 activity year.

10. Weiss, *National Urban League*, 203–5.

11. Ellis W. Hawley, *The Great War and the Search for a Modern Order* (New York: St. Martin's Press, 1979), 25, 49.

12. Victoria C. Hattam, *Labor Visions and State Power: The Origins of Business Unionism in the United States* (Princeton, N.J.: Princeton University Press, 1993), 9–10.

13. "The A.F. of L. and the Negro," *Opportunity*, November 1929, 335–36.

14. NLUCAN Bulletin, "Report 1912–13" (November 1913), NUL Papers, Series 13, Box 1.

15. As discussed previously, John D. Rockefeller Jr. threatened to cease funding the National Urban League's Department of Industrial Relations if it continued to promote blacks' participation in the union movement.

16. Allen Freeman Davis, *Spearheads for Reform: The Social Settlements and the Progressive Movement, 1890–1914* (New Brunswick, N.J.: Rutgers University Press, 1984), 103–5.

17. Elliot D. Smith, "Potent Leisure," *Survey* 17, no. 2 (May 1930): 134–37.

18. David Brody, *Workers in Industrial America: Essays on the Twentieth Century Struggle* (New York: Oxford University Press, 1993), 22–23; Marc Karson, *American Labor Unions and Politics, 1900–1918* (Boston: Beacon Press, 1958), 39.

19. Charles S. Johnson, "Labor and Race Relations," *Opportunity*, January 1925, 4–5.

20. Patrick J. Gilpin and Marybeth Gasman, *Charles S. Johnson: Leadership Beyond the Veil in the Age of Jim Crow* (Albany: State University of New York Press, 2003), 12.

21. As I discuss later in this chapter, Johnson explored the connection between social disorganization and the reorganization of blacks' lives in his own work.

22. Charles S. Johnson, Associate Executive Secretary, Chicago Commission on Race Relations, "Causes of Misunderstanding," Report to the NUL (n.d.), 1, 14, NUL Papers, Series 9, Box 12.

23. Johnson made this same point in his separate report to the National Urban League.

24. Chicago Commission on Race Relations, *The Negro in Chicago: A Study of Race Relations and a Race Riot* (Chicago: University of Chicago Press, 1922), 393.

25. Ibid., 398.

26. Ibid., 398–99.

27. Urban Leaguers frequently complained that black men's low wages forced black women of all classes to seek employment outside of the home in greater numbers than whites. As I discuss in Chapter 2, Earl R. Moses, like Charles S. Johnson and Ira De A. Reid, argued that this unfortunate reality reduced parents' ability to control their children, resulting in higher rates of delinquency than might otherwise be experienced. Black women were likewise said to have had greater exposure to unsavory influences due to their need for paid employment.

Other ways that deprivation increased black families' exposure to unwholesome influences included taking in boarders, throwing rent parties, and living in "vicious" neighborhoods. In the worst cases, marginal Afro-Americans either augmented or gave up legitimate employment in favor of illicit pursuits.

28. CCRR, *Negro in Chicago*, 398–99.

29. Ibid., 412.

30. Ibid., 399. The League also claimed that it had received no such complaints from blacks employed in larger industries. Industries without unions and small businesses were therefore alleged to have been most likely to pay blacks less than whites for the same work.

31. Ibid., 399–400.

32. James R. Barrett, *Work and Community in the Jungle: Chicago's Packinghouse Workers, 1894–1922* (Urbana: University of Illinois Press, 1987), 39, 48–49; Rick Halpern, *Down on the Killing Floor: Black and White Workers in Chicago's Packinghouses, 1904–54* (Urbana: University of Illinois Press, 1997), 47.

33. CCRR, *The Negro in Chicago*, 412–14.

34. James Grossman, *Land of Hope: Chicago, Black Southerners, and the Great Migration* (Chicago: University of Chicago Press, 1989), 222.

35. Halpern, *Down on the Killing Floor*, 49–52. The CCRR may have attributed efforts to organize blacks to the AMC because of the evolving relationship between it and the SLC.

36. Halpern, *Down on the Killing Floor*, 51–53, 57–59.

37. Ibid., 67. Other working-class community groups followed the SLC's lead. A number of immigrant clergyman expressed empathy for Afro-Americans' plight during the upheaval. Perhaps the most notable was the highly respected Father Louis Grudzinski, who was so bold as to term the riot "the black pogrom." Polish American associations were particularly active in their calls for amity. This was quite significant, given the prevalence of Eastern Europeans in the yards. The Polish press consistently urged restraint, and, as Rick Halpern points out, one publication even printed an article on black history that asked rhetorically, "Is it not right they should hate whites?" At the same time, settlement house workers and the Polish National Alliance worked assiduously to stem violence in Packingtown.

38. Ibid., 66–67.

39. Ibid., 68–69.

40. Ibid., 68–72.

41. Chicago *Defender*, May 13, 1922.

42. In the latter half of 1920, the Chicago branch estimated that some 20,000 Afro-American workers were unemployed. As a result, the CUL's job placements declined from about 15,000 workers in its 1919–20 activity year to fewer than 5,000 one year later. See CUL Report, 1920, CUL Papers; and Grossman, *Land of Hope*, 239.

43. William Evans, "The Negro in Chicago Industries," *Opportunity*, February 1923, 15–16; Grossman, *Land of Hope*, 239.

44. Evans, "Negro in Chicago Industries," 15; Grossman, *Land of Hope*, 239.

45. Program of the NUL, March 15, 1925–December 31, 1927, NUL Papers, Series 4, Box 1. The impact of discrimination in the building trades was of special interest to Leaguers. In a 1928 report, the League noted that while a great many employment opportunities were created by the construction of office buildings in cities such as Chicago and New York, "union labor regulations, always so noticeably effective in the building trades, serve to limit the number of colored craftsmen employed in them" ("Urban League Reports Workers Plentiful in the North," NUL Papers, Series 5, Box 33).

46. NUL Department of Industrial Relations, "Extract from Public Statement of the Fifteenth Annual Conference of the NAACP," NUL Papers, Series 4, Box 1.

47. NUL Department of Industrial Relations, "Prospective Immediate Program" (June 24, 1925), NUL Papers, Series 4, Box 1.

48. "Summary of the NUL's Department of Industrial Relations' Work, 1928," NUL Papers, Series 5, Box 33.

49. Karson, *American Labor Unions and Politics*, 39.

50. Ira De A. Reid, "Lily-White Labor," *Opportunity*, June 1930, 170–71.

51. The NUL's most notable detractors included not only Marcus Garvey but also Urban League apostate Chandler Owens and his partner A. Philip Randolph. Owens's opposition was especially jarring to Leaguers, as he had been one of the first recipients of the Urban League's scholarship to the New York School of Philanthropy.

52. Judith Stein, *The World of Marcus Garvey: Race and Class in Modern Society* (Baton Rouge: Louisiana State University Press, 1986), 4–6; E. David Cronon, *Black Moses: The Story of Marcus Garvey and the Universal Negro Improvement Association* (Madison: University of Wisconsin Press, 1969), 206. The Garvey movement's size was a hotly debated issue. Just three years after his arrival in the United States, Garvey claimed the UNIA had two million members. A year later Garvey declared his membership had doubled. These estimates were likely gross exaggerations. In 1923 W. E. B. DuBois estimated the UNIA had roughly between 10,000 and 20,000 members. At other times DuBois speculated that as many as 80,000 blacks belonged to Garvey's organization. The records of the New York City branch of the UNIA, reviewed during the 1923 Black Star trial, claimed about 30,000 members. Locals in other major cities had less impressive but nonetheless significant memberships. The UNIAs of Chicago and Philadelphia, for example, claimed 9,000 and 6,000 members, respectively.

53. Ira De Augustine Reid, *The Negro Immigrant: His Background, Characteristics and Social Adjustment, 1899–1937* (New York: Columbia University Press, 1939), 159. For Reid the presence of these speakers was indicative of both integration in process and "a conflict phase in the immigrant-native adjustment." Reid asserted: "The social disor-

ganization that attends migration must be replaced by a social reconstruction that will enable harmonious functioning." The "process of organized reconstruction," he argued, tended "to develop new leaders and new movements" (ibid., 159).

54. Ibid., 152–55.

55. Charles S. Johnson, "After Garvey—What?" *Opportunity*, December 1923, 231–33.

56. A. F. Elmes, "Garvey and Garveyism—An Estimate," *Opportunity*, May 1925, 139–41.

57. Charles S. Johnson, "Black Workers and the City," *Survey Graphic* 53 (1924–25): 642–43, 719.

58. Ibid., 721. Johnson also called for the "deliberate training for the new work to come."

59. Ibid.

60. Reid also argued that disorganization was exacerbated by women working outside of the home.

61. Reid, *Negro Immigrant*, 119–22.

62. Ibid. He noted that even militant protest could inspire more reasonable forms of collective action. Referring to a Panamanian labor strike of 1918–19, for example, he claimed Garveyism demonstrated to these workers "that wages need not be determined solely by the company's needs for their individual services." Instead he offered that these employees "discovered the possibility of developing collective bargaining power" (ibid., 154–55).

63. As he argued in the cause of vocational guidance, commercialized recreation and improper use of free time led to immoral behavior and juvenile delinquency. See Ira De A. Reid, "Some Aspects of the Negro Community," *Opportunity*, January 1932, 19.

64. Ibid.

65. Ibid.

66. T. Arnold Hill expressed similar concern about discrimination's impact on blacks' interest in cooperating with whites. In correspondence with the AFL in 1925, Hill asserted that blacks' apprehensions about organized labor were partially attributable to a knee-jerk aversion to groups dominated by whites. To counter this tendency, Hill suggested that the Federation appoint "a capable, industrious and tactful Negro to take general charge . . . of your colored work" in order to "insure the needed confidence of his race in the personnel and integrity of the AF of L" (Letter from T. Arnold Hill to William Green, 1925, NUL Papers, Series 5, Box 33).

67. Mark Naison, *Communists in Harlem during the Depression* (New York: Grove Press, 1983), 13.

68. Ibid., 37, 41.

69. T. Arnold Hill and Ira De A. Reid, "Unemployment Among Negroes, Activities of the NUL: Data on 25 Industrial Centers" (November 1930), NUL Papers, Series 4, Box 1.

70. T. Arnold Hill, "Labor—Communism," *Opportunity*, September 1930, 278.

71. Hill asserted that while the increase in blacks' political activism in 1930 may not have been indicative of communist influence, it was evidence of "a more unified and purposeful discontent which is fertile soil for the communists" (ibid.).

72. T. Arnold Hill, "Labor—Communism," 278. Hill was vexed by the labor movement's initial indifference to radicalism's appeal among Afro-Americans. He claimed that when he had "called the attention of one of the conservative labor groups to the probability of the growing sentiment of communism among Negroes," he was met with the retort, "You need not bother about that, Negroes will never be communist." Nevertheless, he argued that unions provided an important staging ground for a direct assault on communist influence. See ibid.

73. T. Arnold Hill, "Help for the Unemployed," *Opportunity*, November 1930, 340.

74. Letter from Robert Isaacs to the NUL, NUL Papers, Series 6, Box 89.

75. In identifying participation in the labor movement as a means of shaping black workers' attitudes to conform to both mainstream habits and political practices, the Urban League revealed the shortcomings of the politics of respectability. Evelyn Brooks Higginbotham has argued that black churchwomen's attempts to undermine racist stereotypes through respectable behavior had subversive and even radical implications. Such endeavors enabled Afro-American women to create a political sphere of their own while demonstrating blacks' humanity, and by extension their worthiness of full citizenship. Yet as the history of the Urban League illustrates, efforts to secure blacks' assimilation through demonstrations of their acceptance of normative values were hardly radical. In fact, respectability could countenance neither poor work performance nor radical politics. See Evelyn Brooks Higginbotham, *Righteous Discontent: The Women's Movement in the Black Baptist Church, 1880–1920* (Cambridge: Harvard University Press, 1993), 181, 190–93, 195–97, 213–15.

Chapter Five

1. Over the previous few years the Gross National Product had fallen by about 30 percent, construction fell by 78 percent, manufacturing dropped by more than 50 percent, and investment plummeted by 98 percent. See Nelson Lichtenstein, *State of the Union: A Century of American Labor* (Princeton, N.J.: Princeton University Press, 2002), 24.

2. Harvard Sitkoff, *A New Deal for Blacks: The Emergence of Civil Rights as a National Issue* (New York: Oxford University Press, 1978), 37; Anthony J. Badger, *The New Deal: The Depression Years, 1933–1940* (Chicago: Ivan R. Dee, 1989), 18–19.

3. Nelson Lichtenstein, *State of the Union*, 25–38.

4. T. Arnold Hill, "Labor—Settings in New Settings," *Opportunity*, March 1934, 88.

5. Ira De A. Reid, "Black Wages for Black Men," *Opportunity*, March 1934, 73.

6. NYUL, Report of the Industrial Secretary, Annual Meeting (January 10, 1934), NUL Papers, Series 4, Box 32.

7. Nancy Weiss, *The National Urban League, 1910–1940* (New York: Oxford University Press, 1974), 269.

8. As historians Nancy Weiss and Jesse Moore have noted, Hill's tenure as head of the National Urban League was bumpy. Hill's popularity with local Leagues exacerbated his already complex relationship with Jones, leading the acting executive secretary to resign from the NUL in 1940. See Weiss, *National Urban League*, 299–301, and Jesse T.

Moore, *A Search for Equality: The National Urban League, 1910–1961* (University Park: Pennsylvania State University Press, 1981), 82–83.

9. A Report of the NYUL (August 2, 1935), 57, NUL Papers, Series 4, Box 32.

10. NUL Department of Industrial Relations, "Memorandum on Experience of Negroes in Connection with the Program of the NRA," 1933, NUL Papers, Series 4, Box 1; "The Negro Working Population and National Recovery: A Special Memorandum Submitted to Franklin Delano Roosevelt," Prepared by the National Urban League (January 4, 1937), NUL Papers, Series 1, Box 1.

11. While the League supported the Social Security Act and Fair Labor Standards Act, officials were alarmed by the exclusion of domestic and agricultural workers from purview of both pieces of legislation. As Leaguers noted at the time, the exemptions ensured that most Afro-American workers would not benefit from these important initiatives. See *Workers' Council Bulletin*, No. 21, July 1, 1938, 10; and *Workers' Council Bulletin*, No. 4, July 24, 1935, 1–2.

12. Cheryl Lynn Greenberg, *Or Does It Explode?: Black Harlem in the Great Depression* (New York: Oxford University Press, 1991), 160–61.

13. Ibid., 90.

14. Weiss, *National Urban League*, 277–78.

15. CUL, Annual Report, 1936, CUL Papers.

16. Ibid., 1933.

17. Ibid.; CUL Report, "Two Decades of Service, 1916–1936," CUL Papers.

18. NUL Department of Industrial Relations, "The Forgotten Tenth: An Analysis of Unemployment Among Negroes in the United States and Its Social Costs, 1932–1933," *Color Line Series*, no. 1 (May 1933): 13–15.

19. NUL Department of Industrial Relations, "5,000,000 Jobs: The Negro at Work in the United States," *Color Line Series*, no. 2 (May 1933): 26–27.

20. Program of the NYUL, NUL Papers, Series 4, Box 32.

21. Ibid.; Report of the Industrial Secretary (January 10, 1934), NUL Papers, Series 4, Box 32.

22. League records do not divulge what percentage of job seekers this figure represents. However, given that fewer than 1,400 applicants visited the League's placement office the previous year, it is likely that the majority of those seeking the League's assistance were subjected to medical examinations.

23. The clinic listed 6 percent of individuals examined in 1933 as having "defects."

24. Program of the NYUL, NUL Papers, Series 4, Box 32; Report of the Industrial Secretary (January 10, 1934), NUL Papers, Series 4, Box 32.

25. Program of the NYUL, NUL Papers, Series 4, Box 32.

26. Ibid.

27. Ibid.

28. Ibid.

29. Arvarh Strickland, *History of the Chicago Urban League* (Columbia: University of Missouri Press, 2001), 117–20.

30. Ibid., 119.

31. Greenberg, *Or Does It Explode?*, 66.

32. NUL Department of Industrial Relations, "5,000,000 Jobs."

33. Ibid., 26–27.

34. NUL Department of Industrial Relations, "Forgotten Tenth," 55.

35. CUL, Annual Report, 1937, CUL Papers.

36. Although training and job proficiency may have enhanced the job prospects of some Afro-Americans, skill and diligence were hardly sufficient. Human capital's impact on black life was necessarily limited. Afro-American high school and college graduates generally faired better in the labor market than their less educated brethren; however, racism ensured that they possessed neither the job security nor the mobility attained by many of their white counterparts.

37. Richard Sterner, *The Negro's Share: A Study of Income, Consumption, and Public Assistance* (New York: Harper and Brothers, 1943), 44.

38. Greenberg, *Or Does It Explode?*, 66.

39. NUL Department of Industrial Relations, "Forgotten Tenth," 54–55.

40. The NUL Department of Industrial Relations ("5,000,000 Jobs," 22) asserted in 1933 that blacks "would display maladjustments in all relationships of life, directly traceable to unemployment."

41. NUL Department of Industrial Relations, "He Crashed the Color Line!," *Color Line Series*, no. 3 (May 1933) (emphasis added).

42. Program of the NYUL, Series 4, Box 32.

43. CUL Report for 1937, CUL Papers.

44. "NUL's Work in 1939," contained in Report of NUL Executive Secretary Eugene K. Jones, NUL Papers, Series 13, Box 1.

45. Moore, *Search for Equality*, 80–81.

46. Weiss, *National Urban League*, 282–83; letter from T. Arnold Hill to William Green, 1925, NUL Papers, Series 5, Box 33.

47. Lester Granger, "Negro Workers and Recovery," *Opportunity*, May 1934, 153.

48. T. Arnold Hill, "Labor—Workers to Lead the Way Out," *Opportunity*, June 1934, 183.

49. "'Where the Trouble Really Lies,' Worker Labor Leaflets: For Workers Who Think," *Labor Leaflet*, No. 2, 1936; Granger "Negro Workers and Recovery," 153.

50. *Workers' Council Bulletin*, No. 21, July 1, 1938, 5.

51. Weiss, *National Urban League*, 284–85.

52. Ibid.; Moore, *Search for Equality*, 80; *Workers' Council Bulletin*, No. 21, July 1, 1938, 11.

53. Granger, "Negro Workers and Recovery," 153.

54. Weiss, *National Urban League*, 273.

55. Ira De A. Reid, "The Negro Riddance Act," *Social Work Today* (March/April 1934): 13–14.

56. Labor benefited significantly from proscriptions against the yellow-dog contract and the right to establish a "closed shop." The yellow-dog contract had long posed a major obstacle to union organizing drives. Prior to the Wagner Act, employers often required employees to agree to neither join nor form a union as a condition of employment. Since management used yellow-dog contracts to intimidate workers, thereby

thwarting organizing drives, the elimination of this practice was a real boon to organized labor. The closed shop further bolstered labor's standing. This provision of Wagner required all workers at a unionized firm to join the NLRB-sanctioned union. In other words, once a union won recognition as the collective bargaining agent for employees at particular firm, all workers—excluding management—were bound to the union contract and were thus subject to both the benefits and the duties of union membership. By mandating employee participation in NLRB-recognized collective bargaining units, the closed shop institutionalized labor solidarity.

57. Lichtenstein, *State of the Union*, 35–38.

58. *Workers' Council Bulletin*, No. 2, April 26, 1935, 3–4; T. Arnold Hill, "Labor: Labor Marches On," *Opportunity*, April 1934, 120; T. Arnold Hill, "Labor: . . . And So-on to 1935," *Opportunity*, January 1935, 26; "Negro Working Population and National Recovery."

59. Weiss, *National Urban League*, 274–75; National Labor Relations Board, *Legislative History of the National Labor Relations Act, 1935* (Washington, D.C., 1949), 1058–60.

60. Paul D. Moreno, *From Direct Action to Affirmative Action: Fair Employment Law and Policy in America, 1933–1972* (Baton Rouge: Louisiana State University Press, 1997), 78–80, 86.

61. *Workers' Council Bulletin*, No. 14, November 18, 1936, 2.

62. Weiss, *National Urban League*, 287–88; *Workers' Council Bulletin*, No. 4, July 24, 1935, 2–3; *Workers' Council Bulletin*, No. 7, Dec. 11, 1935, 1–2; NUL Publicity Service, "URBAN LEAGUE OFFICIALS STORM A.F. OF L. Convention: Fight to Defeat Color Line" (n.d.), NUL Papers, Series 4, Box 1.

63. *Workers' Council Bulletin*, No. 4, July 24, 1935, 3–4.

64. The circulars' titles offer some insight as to the militancy of the content. They included "FOOLS AND COWARDS CUT THEIR OWN THROATS—Are American Workers Fools or Cowards?" and "EXPEL THE TRAITOR! KICK OUT JIM CROW!" in *Workers' Council Bulletin*, No. 6, October 30, 1935, 2; "Fools and Cowards—Which? Urban League Wants to Know of AF of L," NUL Papers, Series 4, Box 1; and "Organized Labor Moves Toward Wiping Out Jim Crow," NUL Papers, Series 4, Box 1.

65. Robert Zieger, *The CIO, 1935–1955* (Chapel Hill: University of North Carolina Press, 1995), 22–30.

66. *Workers' Council Bulletin*, Special, May 28, 1936, 2.

67. Ibid.

68. *Workers' Council Bulletin*, No. 7, December 11, 1935, 1–2; *Workers' Council Bulletin*, No. 8, January 22, 1936, 1–2.

69. The battle for recognition in Little Steel proved far more arduous than the CIO had initially imagined. Indeed, SWOC would not secure a firm footing in these plants before World War II. Nevertheless, after little more than a year of operation, SWOC represented some 300,000 workers.

70. As historian Robert Zieger has shown in *CIO*, blacks employed at U.S. Steel, for example, generally accepted the legitimacy of the company's ERP, as it had imposed some semblance of job stability on the mills. Afro-Americans' experience with the racist

practices of the Association of Amalgamated Iron Workers further compounded their ambivalence about independent labor unions.

71. Zieger, *CIO*, 34–39, 54–64; Jonathan Rees, *Managing the Mills: Labor Policy in the American Steel Industry during the Nonunion Era* (Lanham, Md.: University Press of America, 2004), 218–24.

72. While the ERP's proponents claimed that it provided adequate representation, the Workers' Bureau demonstrated that the company union had done nothing to address either wage differentials or labor market segmentation. The AA had likewise failed to extend the advantages of union affiliation to black mill workers.

73. *Workers' Council Bulletin*, No. 12, August 7, 1936, 2–5.

74. Horace R. Cayton and George S. Mitchell, *Black Workers and the New Unions* (Chapel Hill: University of North Carolina Press, 1939), 407.

75. Ibid., 411.

76. Jonathan Scott Holloway, *Confronting the Veil: Abram Harris Jr., E. Franklin Frazier, and Ralph Bunche, 1919–1941* (Chapel Hill: University of North Carolina Press, 2002), 4–19; John P. Jackson, *Social Scientists for Social Justice: Making the Case against Segregation* (New York: New York University Press, 2001), 6–7, 17–27.

77. Holloway, *Confronting the Veil*, 11.

78. Ibid., 92–93, 97–98, 101.

79. "'Where the Trouble Really Lies,' Worker Labor Leaflets: For Workers Who Think."

80. Johnson made this same point in his separate report to the National Urban League; see Charles S. Johnson, Associate Executive Secretary, Chicago Committee on Race Relations, "Causes of Misunderstanding," Report to the NUL (n.d.), 1, 14, NUL Papers, Series 9, Box 12.

81. NUL Department of Industrial Relations, Prospective Immediate Program, June 24, 1925, NUL Papers, Series 4, Box 1.

82. T. Arnold Hill, *The Negro and Economic Reconstruction* (Washington, D.C.: Associates in Negro Folk Education, 1937), 71–75.

83. *Workers' Council Bulletin*, No. 18, September 23, 1937, 2–3.

84. Alfred B. Lewis, "The Negro Worker and His Union," *Opportunity*, October 1939.

85. NUL Department of Industrial Relations, "Forgotten Tenth," 44, 52–55.

86. Ibid., 54–55.

87. Correspondence between T. Arnold Hill and Lester Granger, October 7, 8, 1935, Department of Industrial Relations, NUL Papers, Series 4, Box 1.

88. T. Arnold Hill, *Negro and Economic Reconstruction*, 67–72.

Chapter Six

1. Andrew Kersten, *Race, Jobs, and the War: The FEPC in the Midwest, 1941–46* (Urbana: University of Illinois Press, 2000), 10.

2. Paula Pfeffer, *A. Philip Randolph, Pioneer of the Civil Rights Movement* (Baton Rouge: Louisiana State University Press, 1990), 46. The employment prospects for blacks in Chicago and New York were consistent with national trends. A 1941 survey of

358 Chicago-area defense industries revealed that two-thirds of employers in these fields refused to hire blacks. Similarly, more than half of New York City's war industries declared that they would not offer employment to Afro-Americans. See Kersten, *Race, Jobs, and the War*, 26.

3. In 1940, for example, only 240 of the nation's 107,000 aviation industry workers were black. The fifty-six St. Louis firms that were awarded war contracts that same year employed on average just three black workers.

4. Pfeffer, *A. Philip Randolph*, 46, 96; Lee Finkle, "The Conservative Aims of Militant Rhetoric: Black Protest during World War II," *Journal of American History* 60, no. 3 (December 1973): 700.

5. Kersten, *Race, Jobs, and the War*, 11. The plight of skilled and semiskilled black labor was further exacerbated by discrimination in jobs training programs sponsored by the federal government. In December 1940, blacks accounted for just over 1,900, or 1.6 percent, of the students enrolled in preemployment "refresher" courses offered by the U.S. Department of Education and the Employment Service. Between July 1, 1941, and April 30, 1942, the percentage of blacks enrolled in these programs had grown to just 4.4 percent, a far cry from their proportion of the general population. These courses were intended to endow workers with marketable skills, which would ultimately benefit both labor and management. Blacks, however, were generally denied equal access to federal training programs on the grounds that they were unemployable as skilled and even semiskilled workers. Afro-Americans were, therefore, not allowed to take full advantage of such projects since they were rarely referred to public preemployment or refresher defense courses.

6. Cheryl Lynn Greenberg, *Or Does It Explode?: Black Harlem in the Great Depression* (New York: Oxford University Press, 1991), 199; Gunnar Myrdal, *An American Dilemma: The Negro Problem and Modern Democracy* (New York: Harper and Row, 1962), 360, 412.

7. Pfeffer, *A. Philip Randolph*, 46.

8. Finkle, "Conservative Aims of Militant Rhetoric," 701.

9. Pfeffer, *A. Philip Randolph*, 68–71.

10. Pfeffer, *A. Philip Randolph*, 45–82; Beth Tompkins Bates, *Pullman Porters and the Rise of Protest Politics in Black America, 1925–1945* (Chapel Hill: University of North Carolina Press, 2001), 148–65.

11. Finkle, "Conservative Aims of Militant Rhetoric," 694–97, 701–3, 711.

12. Executive Order 8802 did not address Randolph's demand for integration of the military.

13. Kersten, *Race, Jobs, and the War*, 17–18. Though a valuable initiative, the Fair Employment Practices Committee's powers were limited. Since the committee was established by executive order, it could not subpoena, fine, or jail violators of the directive. Instead, the FEPC relied on what it termed "quiet persuasion" to convince employers to hire workers regardless of race, religion, or nationality. These constraints notwithstanding, Urban Leaguers, like Afro-Americans generally, perceived it as a significant step forward.

14. Ibid., 18–19; Bates, *Pullman Porters*, 148.

15. Though Lester Granger was clear that Executive Order 8802 had the potential to enhance black life, as I discuss below, he and other Leaguers consistently pressed federal officials to ensure effective enforcement of the president's order. See "Verbatim Transcript of the Conference on the Scope and Powers of Fair Employment Practices" (February 19, 1943), NUL Papers, Series 1, Box 16.

16. Merl E. Reed, *Seedtime for the Modern Civil Rights Movement: The President's Committee on Fair Employment Practice, 1941–1946* (Baton Rouge: Louisiana State University Press, 1991), 34.

17. The committee refused Dickerson's requests for reappointment because of allegations that he was a political radical. A number of government officials, including U.S. Attorney General Biddle, expressed suspicion that Dickerson was a radical. Consequently, the FBI launched an investigation of Dickerson in 1942. The FBI ultimately found that these charges were unfounded. Nevertheless, Dickerson's "career as a person in public life" was damaged. See Kersten, *Race, Jobs, and the War*, 42.

18. Report by Lester Granger, "Action Forward: A View from the National Office" (August 30, 1941), NUL Papers, Series 1, Box 168; Kersten, *Race, Jobs, and the War*, 43.

19. Granger, "Action Forward." The NUL and its locals also established close ties with public and state employment services so the League might interpret racial problems and impart professional techniques to agency administrators.

20. Kersten, *Race, Jobs, and the War*, 21–23.

21. Ibid., 25–26; CUL, Annual Report, 1942, CUL Papers. The Chicago Relief Administration found that in spite of a general decline in the city's relief population between November 1939 and November 1940, blacks' share of relief actually increased by 5 percent. Whites' share of the relief population, on the other hand, declined by 5 percent.

22. CUL, Annual Report, 1942, CUL Papers; Kersten, *Race, Jobs, and the War*, 26–27.

23. In the first few days of the hearings, Stewart-Warner, Studebaker, and Buick each claimed to be in compliance with Executive Order 8802. When confronted with statistical evidence to the contrary, however, Stewart-Warner—which employed some 8,000 workers, none of whom were black—pledged to comply with the executive order. Majestic Radio and Television immediately followed Stewart-Warner's lead and likewise asserted its intentions to adhere to the president's dictate.

24. Kersten, *Race, Jobs, and the War*, 29–31. H. H. Curtice, the Melrose plant's general manager, denied this implication in a less than compelling fashion, stating that Melrose required applicants to indicate their race and religion merely to get "a picture of the men" applying for work at the plant. The committee's suspicion that Buick was engaged in prejudicial hiring practices was reaffirmed when Curtice asserted that the company's failure to employ IIT's best graduate, who was Afro-American, was "just one of those things that could happen" in a large hiring pool. See ibid., 29–31.

25. Ibid., 29–31.

26. Ibid., 33–35.

27. The testimony of black craftsmen such as Edward Doty revealed the strength of the local building trades' opposition to black plumbers and steamfitters. Doty, a plumber, testified that in 1939 the Chicago PTC offered to open its ranks to Afro-Americans only if

they agreed to work exclusively on buildings owned or rented by blacks. Since black landlords were few and far between, the American Consolidated Trades Council immediately rejected the PTC's proposal.

28. Kersten, *Race, Jobs, and the War*, 33–35; Reed, *Seedtime for the Modern Civil Rights Movement*, 42–45.

29. Kersten, *Race, Jobs, and the War*, 33–35; Reed, *Seedtime for the Modern Civil Rights Movement*, 42–45.

30. Granger, "Action Forward."

31. Kersten, *Race, Jobs, and the War*, 33–35; Reed, *Seedtime for the Modern Civil Rights Movement*, 44–45.

32. Leaguers were so enthusiastic about the FEPC's capacity to increase employment opportunities for the race that, as early as 1943, officials such as Lester Granger began calling for the creation of a permanent Fair Employment Practices Committee, which would operate even following the conclusion of the war. See Lester Granger, "Techniques in Race Relations," *Survey Mid Monthly* (December 1943), NUL Papers, Series 1, Box 173.

33. CUL, Annual Report of the Executive Secretary, period ending December 13, 1942, CUL Papers.

34. Brooklyn Urban League Department of Industrial Relations, "Moving Toward an Equitable Distribution of Negroes in War Production—June, 1942 to August, 1942" (August 28, 1942), NUL Papers, Series 13, Box 19.

35. Ibid.

36. Kersten, *Race, Jobs, and the War*, 37–38.

37. Moreover, when the committee referred the Chicago plumbers and steamfitters' case to McNutt, he refused to take direct action to force the union to comply with Executive Order 8802.

38. A. Heninburg, NUL Department of Industrial Relations, Memorandum (December 30, 1943), NUL Papers, Series 1, Box 16.

39. Granger had already officially withdrawn his membership from the MOWM in late 1942. Though he indicated to Randolph that pressing duties with the NUL precluded his continued involvement with the March on Washington Movement, he was always uncomfortable with the group's policy of racial exclusion. Granger's decision to depart the MOWM may have therefore been influenced by Randolph's decision to limit membership to Afro-Americans. See letter from Lester Granger to A. Philip Randolph (September 1942), NUL Papers, Series 1, Box 28; and Herbert Garfinkle, *When Negroes March: The March on Washington Movement in the Organizational Politics for FEPC* (Glencoe, Ill.: Free Press, 1959), 122–23, 141–43.

40. Kersten, *Race, Jobs, and the War*, 41; Garfinkle, *When Negroes March*, 141–43.

41. "American Council on Race Relations" (n.d.), NUL Papers, Volume 1, Series 1, Box 3; Julius A. Thomas, NUL Department of Industrial Relations, "The Negro in the National Economy, 1941–45" (February 1946), NUL Papers, Series 5, Box 30; Philip A. Klinkner and Rogers Smith, *The Unsteady March: The Rise and Decline of Racial Equality in America* (Chicago: University of Chicago Press, 1999), 168–69.

42. Letter from William Baldwin to Paul McNutt (January 13, 1943), NUL Papers, Series 1, Box 16.

43. "Verbatim Transcript of the Conference on the Scope and Powers of the Committee on Fair Employment Practices." Granger likewise voiced his concerns directly to McNutt as early as 1942. In fall 1942, the NUL's executive secretary and McNutt discussed the implications of the reorganization of the FEPC. See letters from Lester Granger to Paul McNutt (September 29 and October 8, 1942), NUL Papers, Series 1, Box 16.

44. "Verbatim Transcript of the Conference on Scope and Powers of the Committee on Fair Employment Practices."

45. Kersten, *Race, Jobs, and the War*, 17; Klinkner and Smith, *Unsteady March*, 158–60; Bates, *Pullman Porters*, 157–61.

46. Granger, "Action Forward."

47. Thomas, "Negro in the National Economy."

48. Reed, *Seedtime for the Modern Civil Rights Movement*, 45.

49. Brooklyn Urban League Industrial Relations Department Semi-Annual Report, "Negro War Worker—Asset or Liability? America Must Decide Now" (August 23, 1943), NUL Papers, Series 13, Box 19.

50. As the Chicago League noted, the successful personnel manager drew comparisons between black and white workers that highlighted their similarities rather than their differences. See CUL Department of Industrial Relations Bulletin, "An Informational Service for Management and Labor," June—v. 2, no. 2, NUL Papers, Series 13, Box 6.

51. Ibid.; CUL Report, "1943 . . . A Critical Year," NUL Papers, Series 13, Box 6; CUL Labor Relations Bulletin, "An Informational Service for Labor Unions: Wanted—Your comments Pro or Con" (September 1944), NUL Papers, Series 13, Box 6.

52. Even at the height of FEPC activity, many Leaguers claimed that the Urban League's voluntarist efforts to adjust the attitudes of Afro-American workers had much to do with blacks' changing economic fortunes. As Lester Granger argued, employers' satisfaction with the more than 12,000 Afro-Americans the CUL placed in 1942 created opportunities for perhaps "60,000 others who have moved in behind the wedge by the League's efforts." Howard Gould echoed these sentiments when he concluded that the League's "efforts to secure new work opportunities for Negroes have been more successful than ever before," thanks to employer satisfaction with black labor. See Annual Report of the Executive Secretary of the CUL, period ending December 31, 1942, CUL Papers.

53. Reed, *Seedtime for the Modern Civil Rights Movement*, 112; Granger, "Techniques in Race Relations."

54. CUL Report, "1943 . . . A Critical Year." Black women made especially significant employment gains in this period. The NUL reported that between 200,000 and 300,000 black women acquired employment during the war. Though black women were still overrepresented among domestic and personal service workers, wartime labor shortages enabled them to find jobs as assemblers, operators, welders, and riveters in both the aircraft and the communication industries. Afro-American women also made impressive gains in the textile industry. Just prior to the war, the NUL reported that the 252 textile firms it surveyed employed only 2,500 black women. By late 1943, these same

companies employed 28,531 black women. Although most of these women worked as unskilled laborers, more than 11,000 were employed as either skilled or semiskilled workers.

55. Ibid. The League also received requests from 116 commercial and retail employers, 135 requests from hotels and restaurants, 37 requests from laundries and cleaning facilities, and 37 from government and private employment agencies. Requests included appeals for assistance in selecting personnel, settling disputes, and introducing black workers into jobs in which they had not previously been employed.

56. As late as 1943, Julius A. Thomas, the NUL's director of industrial relations, attributed higher retention rates among black industrial workers at certain plants to the use of aptitude tests.

57. Brooklyn Urban League Department of Industrial Relations, "Moving Toward an Equitable Distribution in War Production."

58. Thomas, "Negro in the National Economy." Though many of the more than 300,000 black federal employees employed in 1944 worked in unskilled jobs such as custodial service, a large number were employed as white-collar workers.

59. Granger, "Techniques in Race Relations." Though the League's records do not divulge how often it used its unskilled placements to break into skilled positions, it is likely that this was done frequently, especially in the aircraft industry. Both management and organized labor ardently opposed the introduction of blacks into the aircraft industry, particularly in skilled and semiskilled trades. The National and Brooklyn Urban Leagues reported that companies such as Curtiss-Wright, Bell Aircraft, and Glenn L. Martin had initially resisted attempts to integrate their skilled and semiskilled production jobs. Many personnel managers were apprehensive about Afro-Americans' capabilities and were thus reluctant to hire blacks for anything but unskilled work. Though the Brooklyn League claimed to have eventually secured the cooperation of management in such companies, its records do not reveal how. Lester Granger's discussion of the integration of Bell Aircraft in Buffalo may provide some insight into how the League acquired some support for integrating some of the better jobs in the aviation industry. See Report of Executive Secretary Lester Granger, "Towards Victory for Democracy," Thirty-Second Annual Meeting of the NUL (February 18, 1943), NUL Papers, Series 11, Box 4.

60. CUL Industrial Relations Bulletin (August–September 1944), NUL Papers, Series 13, Box 6.

61. "American Council on Race Relations," Report, NUL Papers, Series 1, Box 3; Thomas, "Negro in the National Economy." The League had reason to believe that failure to ease black workers' introduction to new areas of employment had great potential for upheaval. When the city of Philadelphia hired blacks for the first time on its transit line, for example, the so-called City of Brotherly Love was rocked by riots that were quelled only by the threat of federal intervention. Julius A. Thomas believed that Philadelphia's failure to launch preemptive measures to stave off opposition was largely responsible for the turmoil that gripped the city.

62. CUL Department of Industrial Relations Bulletin, "An Informational Service for Management and Labor" (September 1944), NUL Papers, Series 13, Box 6.

63. CUL Department of Industrial Relations Bulletin (September 1944), CUL Papers.

64. Brooklyn Urban League Department of Industrial Relations, "Moving Toward an Equitable Distribution of Negroes in War Production."

65. Granger, "Techniques in Race Relations"; CUL Department of Industrial Relations Bulletin, "An Informational Service for Management and Labor" (April 1945), NUL Papers, Series 13, Box 6. Two years later, the Chicago League expressed a similar perspective that not only demonstrated the League's concern about blacks' postwar employment prospects but also revealed its appreciation of Afro-American women's role in the better occupations. The CUL implored local employers to consider keeping on black women in skilled and semiskilled work rather than replacing them with men after the war. The Chicago branch argued that while black women were not generally suited for "heavy manual labor jobs," they proved to be every bit as capable as men in fields "requiring manual dexterity, intelligence, and the ability to acquire skills." Employers' positive experience with black women workers in skilled, semiskilled, and white-collar work thus warranted management's consideration. See CUL Department of Industrial Relations Bulletin, "An Informational Service for Management and Labor" (April 1945), NUL Papers, Series 13, Box 6.

66. NYUL Report, 1944, NUL Papers, Series 13, Box 19.

67. Floyd Reeves and Robert Sutherland, "The Special Problems of Negro Youth," *Opportunity*, March 1940. Reeves and Sutherland focused on a middle-class black teen whom the authors dubbed John X. Reeves and Sutherland described John, the son of a professor and a social worker, as well-mannered, intelligent, and driven to go to college and perhaps graduate school. But, the authors believed, while many youth like John were gifted young men, the difficulties they had acquiring employment in occupations for which they were credentialed discouraged them from pursuing professional and skilled lines of work. This led some to engage in criminal and immoral activities. Reeves and Sutherland argued that the success of individuals like John, however, held the potential to counteract the pernicious effects of social isolation and race discrimination.

68. Thomas, "Negro in the National Economy." Reasoning that blacks' greatest gains in white-collar employment stemmed from the growth of federal agencies during the war and Executive Orders 8802 and 9346, the NUL asserted that "it is safe to conclude that without strong intervention on the part of top policy-making officials in government, the displacement of Negroes and the reduction of their numbers in the federal service will be a distressing aftermath of the war's end" (ibid.).

69. Granger, "Action Forward."

70. "Employment Security and the Negro Worker," abstract of remark by Lester Granger at the Race Relations Institute, Fisk University (July 20, 1944), NUL Papers, Series 1, Box 6.

71. Lester Granger, ". . . to the Unfinished Struggle: Three Addresses to American College Youth" (November 1944 to December 1944), NUL Papers, Series 1, Box 168.

72. Thomas, "Negro in the National Economy." Though blacks were able to take full advantage of the GI Bill's education grants, the bill's housing provisions were not actually "color blind." Blacks were unable to acquire mortgages offered through the GI Bill for housing in white communities.

73. Granger ". . . to the Unfinished Struggle."

74. William Julius Wilson, *The Declining Significance of Race: Blacks and Changing American Institutions* (Chicago: University of Chicago Press, 1978), 90–91.

75. Thomas, "Negro in the National Economy."

76. Urban League of Greater New York (October 4, 1948), NUL Papers, Series 13, Box 19; Report of Executive Secretary to Annual Meeting of the NUL (March 9, 1949), NUL Papers, Series 1, Box 6.

77. Report of the NUL Department of Industrial Relations (January 7, 1948), NUL Papers, Series 1, Box 61.

78. Ibid.; letter from LeRoy Jeffries to Julius A. Thomas (February 24, 1948), NUL Papers, Series 1, Box 61; CUL, Annual Report, 1950, "Together," CUL Papers.

79. Letter from LeRoy Jeffries to Julius A. Thomas (February 17, 1948), NUL Papers, Series 1, Box 61; Report of the Executive Secretary to Annual Meeting of the NUL (March 9, 1948), NUL Papers, Series 1, Box 6.

80. NUL, "A Report of Democracy Advancing," 1949, NUL Papers, Series 13, Box 19.

81. CUL, Annual Report, 1950, "Together," CUL Papers.

82. Ibid.

83. These gains notwithstanding, black women continued to lag behind white women in the better female occupations. In 1947, only 3 percent of gainfully employed white women worked as domestics, while 45 percent worked in clerical and sales.

84. Report of the Urban League of Greater New York (October 4, 1948), NUL Papers, Series 13, Box 19. This is not to argue that the League's clerical and sales placements were limited exclusively to women. For example, when the Chicago Urban League discontinued basic domestic service and unskilled placements in favor of "skilled, semi-skilled, technical, professional, managerial, and clerical," it boasted that it managed to secure positions for two young Afro-Americans, one man and one woman, as bank tellers. The young man was a college graduate and was pursuing an accounting degree at Northwestern University under the GI Bill. The woman was an experienced secretary with an "accounting background." Both the Urban Leagues of Greater New York and Chicago actively engaged in efforts to secure openings for Afro-Americans in these fields, through work with department stores, banks, and offices. See ibid.

85. CUL, Annual Report, 1949, CUL Papers.

86. The CUL's Pilot Placement Project was inaugurated in 1950 thanks to a $15,000 grant from the Rosenwald Fund.

87. NUL, "A Report of Democracy Advancing: End of the Summary, 1949," NUL Papers, Series 13, Box 19.

88. Report of the Executive Secretary to Annual Meeting of the NUL (March 9, 1948); CUL, Annual Report, 1948, "American Teamwork—Works," CUL Papers.

89. CUL, Annual Report, 1949, CUL Papers.

90. Urban League of Greater New York, "Reports to Its Friends," 1948 NUL Papers, Series 13, Box 19.

Chapter Seven

1. Michael Homel, *Down from Equality: Black Chicagoans and the Public Schools, 1920–1941* (Chicago: University of Chicago Press, 1984), 29; NYUL Report, "Program Direction Conference of the Urban League of Greater New York," NUL Papers, Series 1, Box 112.

2. See discussion in Chapter 6.

3. Reginald A. Johnson, NUL director of Field Services and Housing Coordinator, "Testimony Before the Joint Committee on Housing" (January 19, 1948), NUL Papers, Series 3, Box 10; Arnold Hirsch, *Making the Second Ghetto: Race and Housing in Chicago, 1940–1960* (Cambridge: Cambridge University Press, 1985), 16–17.

4. As the New York Urban League argued in 1941, "Unemployment and poor housing are the most dangerous . . . enemies to good community living, for in their presence sound neighborhood standards and moral values wither away and disappear" (Lester Granger, "Address Before the Dinner Meeting of the West Harlem Council of Social Agencies at the YMCA" [December 4, 1941], NUL Papers, Series 1, Box 168).

5. CUL Annual Report, 1930–31, CUL Papers; Arvarh Strickland, *History of the Chicago Urban League* (Urbana: University of Illinois Press, 1966), 106; "A Report of the NYUL," Addressed to T. Arnold Hill (August 2, 1935), NUL Papers, Series 4, Box 32; Program of the NYUL, NUL Papers, Series 4, Box 32.

6. Granger, "Address Before the Dinner Meeting."

7. Lester Granger, "Manhattan and Beyond," *Amsterdam News*, August 6, 1949, 16.

8. CUL, "CUL Names Officers of the Board and Executive of Agencies," NUL Papers, Series 13, Box 6; CUL, Annual Report, 1936, CUL Papers; CUL, Annual Report, 1937, CUL Papers.

9. Urban League of Greater New York, "Program of the NYUL" (n.d.), NUL Papers, Series 4, Box 32.

10. NUL *Color Line Series*, No. 7, NUL Papers, Series 5, Box 32.

11. "The Story of the City-Wide Citizens Committee on Harlem" (May 23, 1943), NUL Papers, Series 1, Box 38.

12. NUL *Color Line Series*, No. 7, NUL Papers, Series 5, Box 32.

13. Urban League of Greater New York, "Program of the NYUL" (n.d.), NUL Papers, Series 4, Box 32.

14. Ibid. The League also called for reform of correctional facilities and penalties for first-time offenders and more low-income housing.

15. Urban League of Greater New York, "Report of the Review Committee to the Board of Directors of the Urban League of Greater New York" (October 1947), NUL Papers, Series 13, Box 19.

16. Ibid. As the NYUL stated in this 1947 report, "The Urban League program has been shaped to the end of enabling Negro people to make available community service; serving in an advisory and consultative role in planning additional community services and stimulating community action in attaining of vital services they need."

17. Twentieth Annual Report, 1935, Part II, CUL Papers; Strickland, *History of the Chicago Urban League*, 124.

18. Granger, "Manhattan and Beyond," 16.

19. Ibid., 16.

20. Gail Radford, *Modern Housing for America: Policy Struggles in the New Deal Era* (Chicago: University of Chicago Press, 1996), 89–91.

21. Ibid., 150.

22. Mark Naison, *Communists in Harlem during the Depression* (New York: Grove Press, 1983), 19–24, 66–67; Radford, *Modern Housing for America*, 150–51.

23. Hirsch, *Making the Second Ghetto*, 18.

24. Ibid., 10–13, 18; Strickland, *History of the Chicago Urban League*, 126–28.

25. Strickland, *History of the Chicago Urban League*, 126–28.

26. Ibid.

27. Ibid.

28. Radford, *Modern Housing for America*, 153–54.

29. Urban League of Greater New York, "Program Direction Conference of the Urban League of Greater New York" (n.d.), NUL Papers, Series 1, Box 112.

30. Ibid.

31. Radford, *Modern Housing for America*, 66–69.

32. Weaver asserted that fully three-fifths of all families "earned below figures necessary to afford respectable living quarters without undue skimping on other necessities" (Robert Weaver, "The Negro in a Program of Public Housing," *Opportunity*, July 1938).

33. Ibid.

34. Publicly funded projects also offered the potential for new employment opportunities in construction and related fields. Weaver and the League were especially pleased that many of the jobs created were in the better occupations. Weaver reported that blacks were already employed in management in nineteen completed projects. Three projects employed blacks as architects, while the USHA in Washington employed blacks as clerical and technical workers as well as lawyers and other professionals in policymaking decisions. See "Want a Job in Housing?," *Opportunity*, March 1939.

35. Radford, *Modern Housing for America*, 160–61, 165.

36. Ibid., 162–65.

37. Ibid., 166–68. The Housing Authority preferred renters in "traditional" family units as opposed to those headed by a single parent or comprised of extended kin. Boarders were generally excluded from the building. See Weaver, "The Negro in a Program of Public Housing."

38. In an assessment of the situation for blacks in New York, for example, Lester Granger attributed the high rates of "social disorganization" among blacks in the city to many landlords' failure to properly screen tenants during the application process, resulting in the commingling of disreputable and respectable tenants. See Lester Granger, "The Race Question and Housing" (November 14, 1945), NUL Papers, Series 1, Box 168.

39. Urban League of Greater New York, "The Urban League of Greater New York: Its Background and Its Future—1944," NUL Papers, Series 13, Box 19; Weaver, "The Negro in a Program of Public Housing."

40. Urban League of Greater New York, "The Urban League of Greater New York: Its Background and Its Future—1944," NUL Papers, Series 13, Box 1.

41. Radford, *Modern Housing for America*, 166–67. Initial rents at Harlem River Houses ranged from $19.16 to $31.35 a month, depending on the size of the unit.

42. Ibid.

43. Granger, "Race Question and Housing."

44. Ibid.

45. Chicago *Defender*, November 28, 1936; Strickland, *History of the Chicago Urban League*, 128–29.

46. Chicago *Defender*, February 19, 1938; *Chicago Defender*, February 26, 1938; Strickland, *History of the Chicago Urban League*, 129.

47. Strickland, *History of the Chicago Urban League*, 129.

48. Hirsch, *Making the Second Ghetto*, 40–42, 45–48, 52–57. The housing situation in Chicago in general was quite volatile. Though restrictive covenants hemmed blacks into segregated areas, slum clearance pushed many to explore housing options beyond the boundaries of the South Side. Consequently, the city was the site of scores of race riots during the mid-1940s.

49. Ibid., 88–91; Strickland, *History of the Chicago Urban League*, 159–61.

50. Strickland, *History of the Chicago Urban League*, 167–69.

51. Hirsch, *Making the Second Ghetto*, 13–14.

52. Reginald A. Johnson, NUL director of Field Services and Housing Coordinator, "Testimony Before the Joint Committee on Housing" (January 19, 1948), NUL Papers, Series 3, Box 10.

53. Ibid.

54. David Bartelt, "Housing the Underclass," in *The Underclass Debate: Views from History*, ed. Michael B. Katz (Princeton, N.J.: Princeton University Press, 1993), 145–49; R. Allen Hays, *The Federal Government and Urban Housing: Ideology and Change in Public Policy* (Albany: SUNY Press, 1995), 85–91.

55. Granger, "Race Question and Housing."

56. Ibid. A related account can be found in NUL Report, "Negroes and the Housing Crisis, 1947" (February 1948), Series 3, Box 10.

57. Granger, "Race Question and Housing."

58. Ibid.; Program Direction Conference of the Urban League of Greater New York, "Working Papers for Housing," n.d., NUL Papers, Series 1, Box 112.

59. Program Direction Conference of the Urban League of Greater New York, "Working Papers for Housing," n.d., NUL Papers, Series 1, Box 112.

60. Granger, "Race Question and Housing."

61. Ibid.

62. Ibid.

Conclusion

1. Nancy Weiss, *Whitney M. Young, Jr., and the Struggle for Civil Rights* (Princeton, N.J.: Princeton University Press, 1989), 57–63, 99–104.

2. Dennis Smith, *The Chicago School: A Liberal Critique of Capitalism* (New York: St. Martin's Press, 1988), 7–9.

3. Stow Persons, *Ethnic Studies at Chicago, 1905–45* (Urbana: University of Illinois Press, 1987), 60–61; Alice O'Connor, *Poverty Knowledge: Social Science, Social Policy, and the Poor in Twentieth-Century U.S. History* (Princeton, N.J.: Princeton University Press, 2001), 49.

4. For example, staffers such as Charles S. Johnson and T. Arnold Hill subscribed to ethnic cycle theory but rejected the notion that amity between blacks and whites would occur organically. Believing racial animus toward blacks retarded the natural mechanisms of assimilation, these and other officials sought to engineer mutually satisfactory interactions between the races. Likewise, when the New Deal and World War II opened new avenues for employment and housing, League officials expanded their course of action beyond the bounds of voluntarism to include the welfare state as a battleground for advancing Afro-American equality.

5. O'Connor, *Poverty Knowledge*, 99–123.

6. In its effort to demonstrate the social damage wrought by segregation, the NAACP contended in both *Sweatt v. Painter* (1950) and *Brown v. Board of Education* (1954) that forced separation of the races posed a threat to civic order. As Columbia University–trained social psychologist Kenneth B. Clark alleged in a statement accompanying the association's brief in *Brown*, the "blockage in communications and interaction between" segregated groups tended "to increase mutual suspicion, distrust, and hostility." Signed by more than thirty social scientists, including Ira Reid, Clark's report, much like Charles S. Johnson's 1922 CCRR study, insinuated that integration would foster racial harmony while soothing the psychic wounds inflicted upon both blacks and whites.

Although there is some question as to the rigor of the science behind *Brown*, the work of Clark and others helped provide a rationale for social engineering. In this sense, the NAACP's victories in *Brown* and *Sweatt* highlight the value of Chicago School theories in an era of growing racial liberalism. Still, Chicago sociology's emphasis on behavior apart from consideration of broad political and economic issues had clear limitations. With regard to school desegregation, progressive social scientists' emphasis on personality and culture downplayed the impact of political economy on American race relations. Having devoted insufficient attention to the function of racial hierarchy in southern economic life, *Brown's* social scientists would not anticipate the ferocity of white resistance to integration. See John P. Jackson, *Social Scientists for Social Justice: Making the Case against Segregation* (New York: New York University Press, 2001), 95–98, 164–66; Daryl Michael Scott, *Contempt and Pity: Social Policy and the Image of the Damaged Black Psyche, 1880–1996* (Chapel Hill: University of North Carolina Press, 1997), 125–36; and Kenneth B. Clark et al., "The Effects of Segregation and the Consequences of Desegregation: A (September 1952) Social Science Statement in Brown v. Board of Education of Topeka Supreme Court Case," *American Psychology* 59, no. 6. (September 2004): 497.

7. As the civil rights movement adopted a more aggressive posture in the 1960s, activists turned up pressure on government officials to address blacks' economic frustrations. In the wake of World War II changes in production practices and the quest for cheap labor led manufacturers to relocate from central cities to the suburbs and eventually the so-called Sunbelt. While federally subsidized mortgages enabled white work-

ers to follow decent-paying jobs to the nation's hinterlands, discriminatory housing policies confined Afro-Americans to central cities in the midst of economic transition. As a result, black poverty and unemployment soared throughout the Rust Belt and the nation's other historic manufacturing centers. To counter the deleterious effects of deindustrialization, many civil rights activists demanded a domestic Marshall Plan. Leaders ranging from A. Philip Randolph to the National Urban League's Whitney Young petitioned elected officials to create jobs programs on the scale of the WPA. Political and fiscal concerns ensured that neither the Kennedy nor the Johnson administration would pursue such an agenda. Instead, Democrats in Washington launched an unsuccessful War on Poverty as part of the president's Great Society.

Though the name would imply a serious effort to curb gross income inequality, the War on Poverty was anything but. Formally initiated by the Economic Opportunity Act of 1964, the Johnson administration's crusade against deprivation was the ultimate expression of postwar Keynesianism. Policymakers rejected proposals to redistribute wealth, choosing instead to combat poverty via a growth agenda. President Johnson attempted to create jobs through tax-and-spend policies rather than targeting government works projects. For those who failed to catch the rising wave of prosperity catalyzed by fiscal stimulus, the federal government would mitigate the harshest aspects of poverty through the expansion of public welfare programs and federally sponsored job training and civic mobilization projects such as Community Action. Projects of this sort, it was hoped, not only would provide hardcore unemployed minorities skills that might prepare them for decent-paying jobs but also would use the power of government to integrate these individuals into mainstream society. See Paula F. Pfeffer, *A. Philip Randolph, Pioneer of the Civil Rights Movement* (Baton Rouge: Louisiana State University Press, 1990), 246; O'Connor, *Poverty Knowledge*, 139–45; and Michael K. Brown, *Race, Money, and the American Welfare State* (Ithaca: Cornell University Press, 1999), 224–32, 235–38.

8. O'Connor, *Poverty Knowledge*, 125–29; Brown, *Race, Money, and the American Welfare State*, 226, 231–32.

9. O'Connor, *Poverty Knowledge*, 124–36; Jill Quadagno, *The Color of Welfare: How Racism Undermined the War on Poverty* (New York: Oxford University Press, 1994), 34–37, 40–47, 52–56.

10. Wilson's research has not only followed in the footsteps of that of the likes of E. Franklin Frazier and Robert Park, but he was also the chair of the Department of Sociology at the University of Chicago from 1975 to 1996. He is currently the Lewis P. and Linda Geyser University Professor at Harvard University.

11. William J. Wilson, *The Truly Disadvantaged: The Inner City, the Underclass, and Public Policy* (Chicago: University of Chicago Press, 1987), 7–8, 33–37, 49–56, 60–76.

12. Larry Bennet and Adolph L. Reed Jr., "The New Face of Urban Renewal: The Near North Redevelopment Initiative and the Cabrini-Green Neighborhood," in *Without Justice for All: The New Liberalism and our Retreat from Racial Equality*, ed. Adolph L. Reed Jr. (Boulder, Colo.: Westview Press, 1999), 178–94.

Bibliography

Archives and Manuscript Collections

Chicago, Ill.
  Chicago Historical Society
    Welfare Council of Metropolitan Chicago
    YMCA of Chicago
  Joseph Regenstein Library, University of Chicago
    Ernest W. Burgess Papers
    Robert E. Park Papers
    Julius Rosenwald Papers
  University of Illinois
    Chicago Urban League Papers
    Metropolitan Housing and Planning Council Papers
    Wendell Phillips Settlement House Papers
Madison, Wisc.
  Wisconsin Historical Society
New York, N.Y.
  Columbia University
    Edwin Seligman Papers
    James Phelps Stokes Papers
  Schomburg Center for Research in Black Culture Collections,
      New York Public Library
Washington, D.C.
  Library of Congress
    National Urban League Papers

Newspapers and Magazines

Age
Amsterdam News
Broad Ax
Crisis
Defender
Messenger
Negro World
New York Times

Opportunity
Social Work Today
Survey Graphic
Whip

Government Documents

Negroes in the United States. U.S. Bureau of the Census. Washington, D.C.: Government Printing Office, 1935.

Books and Articles

Allen, Robert L. *Black Awakening in Capitalist America.* Trenton, N.J.: Africa World Press, Inc., 1990.

Anderson, James D. *The Education of Blacks in the South, 1860–1935.* Chapel Hill: University of North Carolina Press, 1988.

Anderson, Jervis. *A. Philip Randolph: A Biographical Portrait.* Berkeley: University of California Press, 1986.

———. *This Was Harlem.* New York: Noonday Press, 1981.

Anderson, Terry H. *The Pursuit of Fairness: A History of Affirmative Action.* New York: Oxford University Press, 2004.

Archdeacon, Thomas. *Becoming American: An Ethnic History.* London: Collier Macmillan Publishers, 1983.

Arnesen, Eric. *Brotherhoods of Color: Black Railroad Workers and the Struggle for Equality.* Cambridge, Mass.: Harvard University Press, 2001.

———. "Following the Color Line of Labor: Black Workers and the Labor Movement Before 1930." *Radical History Review* 55 (Winter 1993): 53–87.

Badger, Anthony J. *The New Deal: The Depression Years, 1933–1940.* Chicago: Ivan R. Dee, 1989.

Barrett, James R. *Work and Community in the Jungle: Chicago's Packinghouse Workers, 1894–1922.* Urbana: University of Illinois Press, 1987.

Bates, Beth Thompkins. "A New Crowd Challenges the Agenda of the Old Guard in the NAACP, 1933–1941." *American Historical Review* 102, no. 2 (April 1997): 340–77.

———. *Pullman Porters and the Rise of Protest Politics in Black America, 1925–1945.* Chapel Hill: University of North Carolina Press, 2001.

Berg, Manfred. *"The Ticket to Freedom": The NAACP and the Struggle for Black Political Integration.* Gainesville: University of Florida Press, 2005.

Blumer, Herbert. *Critiques of Research in the Social Sciences: An Appraisal of Thomas and Znaniecki's "The Polish Peasant in Europe and America."* New Brunswick: Transaction Books, 1979.

Braverman, Harry. *Labor and Monopoly Capital: The Degradation of Work in the Twentieth Century.* New York: Monthly Review Press, 1974.

Brazeal, Brailsford Reese. *The Brotherhood of Sleeping Car Porters: Its Origins and Development.* New York: Harper and Brothers, 1946.

Binkley, Alan. *The End of Reform: New Deal Liberalism in Recession and War*. New York: Vintage Press, 1995.

Brody, David. *Labor in Crisis: The Steel Strike of 1919*. Philadelphia: Lippincott, 1965.

——. *Workers in Industrial America: Essays on the Twentieth Century Struggle*. New York: Oxford University Press, 1993.

Brown, Michael K. *Race, Money, and the American Welfare State*. Ithaca: Cornell University Press, 1999.

Carter, Dan T. *Scottsboro: A Tragedy of the American South*. 2d ed. Baton Rouge: Louisiana State University Press, 1984.

Cayton, Horace R., and George S. Mitchell. *Black Workers and the New Unions*. Chapel Hill: University of North Carolina Press, 1939.

Chafe, William H. *Civilities and Civil Rights: Greensboro, North Carolina, and the Black Struggle for Freedom*. New York: Oxford University Press, 1980.

Chicago Commission on Race Relations. *The Negro in Chicago: A Study of Race Relations and a Race Riot*. Chicago: University of Chicago Press, 1922.

Cohen, Lizabeth. *Making a New Deal: Industrial Workers in Chicago, 1919–1939*. New York: Cambridge University Press, 1990.

Cronon, E. David. *Black Moses: The Story of Marcus Garvey and the Universal Negro Improvement Association*. Madison: University of Wisconsin Press, 1969.

——, ed. *Great Lives Observed: Marcus Garvey*. Englewood: Prentice Hall, 1973.

Davis, Allen Freeman. *Spearheads for Reform: The Social Settlements and the Progressive Movement, 1890–1914*. New Brunswick, N.J.: Rutgers University Press, 1984.

Drake, St. Clair, and Horace R. Cayton. *Black Metropolis: A Study of Negro Life in a Northern City*. New York: Harcourt, Brace and Company, 1945.

DuBois, W. E. B. *The Philadelphia Negro: A Social Study*. Philadelphia: University of Pennsylvania Press, 1996.

——. *The Souls of Black Folk*. Chicago: A. C. McClurg and Company, 1903.

Dudziak, Mary. *The Cold War and Civil Rights: Race and the Image of American Democracy*. Princeton, N.J.: Princeton University Press, 2000.

Fauset, Jessie Redmon. *The Chinaberry Tree*. New York: G. K. Hall & Co., 1995.

——. *Plum Bun: A Novel Without a Moral*. Boston: Beacon Press, 1990.

Ferguson, Karen. *Black Politics in New Deal Atlanta*. Chapel Hill: University of North Carolina Press, 2002.

Fischer, Rudolph. *The Walls of Jericho*. Ann Arbor: University of Michigan Press, 1994.

Foner, Eric. *Nothing but Freedom: Emancipation and Its Legacy*. Baton Rouge: Louisiana State University Press, 1983.

Foner, Philip S. *Organized Labor and Black Workers, 1619–1973*. New York: Praeger, 1974.

Franklin, John Hope, and August Meier, eds. *Black Leaders of the Twentieth Century*. Urbana: University of Illinois, 1982.

Frazier, E. Franklin. *Black Bourgeoisie*. New York: Macmillan Publishing Company, 1962.

——. *The Negro Family in Chicago*. Chicago: University of Chicago Press, 1932.

——. *The Negro Family in the United States*. Chicago: University of Chicago Press, 1966.

Gaines, Kevin K. *Uplifting the Race: Black Leadership, Politics, and Culture in the Twentieth Century.* Chapel Hill: University of North Carolina Press, 1996.

Garfinkle, Herbert. *When Negroes March: The March on Washington Movement in the Organization Politics for FEPC.* Glencoe, Ill.: Free Press, 1959.

Gatewood, Willard B. *Aristocrats of Color: The Black Elite, 1880–1920.* Bloomington: Indiana University Press, 1990.

Giddings, Paula. *When and Where I Enter: The Impact of Black Women in Race and Sex in America.* New York: Bantam Books, 1984.

Gilmore, Glenda. *Gender and Jim Crow: Women and the Politics of White Supremacy in North Carolina, 1896–1920.* Chapel Hill: University of North Carolina Press, 1996.

Gilpin, Patrick J., and Marybeth Gasman. *Charles S. Johnson: Leadership Beyond the Veil in the Age of Jim Crow.* Albany: State University of New York Press, 2003.

Goluboff, Risa L. *The Lost Promise of Civil Rights.* Cambridge, Mass.: Harvard University Press, 2007.

Gosnell, Harold F. *Negro Politicians: The Rise of Negro Politics in Chicago.* Chicago: University of Chicago Press, 1935; reprinted, 1967.

Gottlieb, Peter. *Making Their Own Way: Southern Blacks' Migration to Pittsburgh, 1916–1930.* Urbana: University of Illinois Press, 1987.

Greenberg, Cheryl Lynn. *Or Does It Explode?: Black Harlem in the Great Depression.* New York: Oxford University Press, 1991.

Grimshaw, William J. *Bitter Fruit: Black Politics and the Chicago Machine, 1931–1991.* Chicago: University of Chicago Press, 1992.

Grossman, James. "Blowing the Trumpet: The *Chicago Defender* and Black Migration During World War I." *Illinois Historical Journal* 78, no. 2 (Summer 1985): 82–96.

——. *Land of Hope: Chicago, Black Southerners, and the Great Migration.* Chicago: University of Chicago Press, 1989.

Gutman, Herbert G. *Work, Culture, and Society in Industrializing America.* New York: Vintage Books, 1976.

Halpern, Rick. *Down on the Killing Floor: Black and White Workers in Chicago's Packinghouses, 1904–54.* Urbana: University of Illinois Press, 1997.

Harlan, Louis R. *Booker T. Washington: The Wizard of Tuskegee, 1901–1915.* New York: Oxford University Press, 1983.

Harris, Abram L., and Sterling Spero. *The Black Worker: The Negro and the Labor Movement.* New York: Columbia University Press, 1931.

Harris, William H. *Keeping the Faith: A. Philip Randolph, Milton P. Webster, and the Brotherhood of Sleeping Car Porters, 1925–1937.* Urbana: University of Illinois Press, 1977.

Hattam, Victoria C. *Labor Visions and State Power: The Origins of Business Unionism in the United States.* Princeton, N.J.: Princeton University Press, 1993.

Hays, R. Allen. *The Federal Government and Urban Housing: Ideology and Change in Public Policy.* Albany: SUNY Press, 1995.

Haynes, George E. *The Negro at Work in New York City.* New York: Longmans, Green & Co., 1912.

Hawley, Ellis W. *The Great War and the Search for a Modern Order: A History of the American People and Their Institutions, 1917–33*. New York: St. Martin's Press, 1979.

Higginbotham, Evelyn Brooks. *Righteous Discontent: The Women's Movement in the Black Baptist Church, 1880–1920*. Cambridge, Mass.: Harvard University Press, 1993.

Higham, John. *Strangers in the Land: Patterns of American Nativism, 1860–1925*. New Brunswick, N.J.: Rutgers University Press, 1994.

Hill, Herbert. *Black Labor and the American Legal System*. Madison: University of Wisconsin Press, 1985.

Hill, T. Arnold. *The Negro and Economic Reconstruction*. Washington, D.C.: Associates in Negro Folk Education, 1937.

Hirsch, Arnold. *Making the Second Ghetto: Race and Housing in Chicago, 1940–1960*. Cambridge: Cambridge University Press, 1983.

Holloway, Jonathan Scott. *Confronting the Veil: Abram Harris Jr., E. Franklin Frazier, and Ralph Bunche, 1919–1941*. Chapel Hill: University of North Carolina Press, 2002.

Homel, Michael. *Down from Equality: Black Chicagoans and the Public Schools, 1920– 1941*. Chicago: University of Chicago Press, 1984.

Horne, Gerald. *Black and Red: W. E. B. DuBois and the Afro-American Response to the Cold War, 1944–1963*. Albany: SUNY Press, 1986.

Huggins, Nathan Irvin. *Harlem Renaissance*. London: Oxford University Press, 1971.

Jackson, John P. *Social Scientists for Social Justice: Making the Case against Segregation*. New York: New York University Press, 2001.

Jackson, Walter A. *Gunnar Myrdal and America's Conscience: Social Engineering and Racial Liberalism, 1938–1987*. Chapel Hill: University of North Carolina Press, 1990.

Johnson, Charles S. *Growing up in the Black Belt: Negro Youth in the Rural South*. New York: Schocken Books, 1941.

——. *The Negro in American Civilization: A Study of Negro Life and Race Relations in the Light of Social Research*. New York: Henry Holt and Co., 1930.

——. *In the Shadow of the Plantation*. Chicago: University of Chicago Press, 1934.

Johnson, James W. *Black Manhattan*. New York: De Capo Press, 1991.

Jones, Jacquelin. *Labor of Love, Labor of Sorrow: Black Women, Work, and the Family from Slavery to the Present*. New York: Basic Books, 1985.

Karson, Marc. *American Labor Unions and Politics, 1900–1918*. Boston: Beacon Press, 1958.

Katz, Michael B., ed. *The Underclass Debate: Views from History*. Princeton, N.J.: Princeton University Press, 1993.

Katznelson, Ira. *Black Men, White Cities: Race, Politics, and Migration in United States, 1900–1930, and Britain, 1948–1968*. London: Oxford University Press, 1973.

Kelley, Robin D. G. *Hammer and Hoe: Alabama Communists during the Great Depression*. Chapel Hill: University of North Carolina Press, 1990.

Kellor, Frances A. *Out of Work: A Study of Unemployment.* New York: Arno Press and the New York Times, 1971.

Kersten, Andrew. *Race, Jobs, and the War: The FEPC in the Midwest, 1941–46.* Urbana: University of Illinois Press, 2000.

Kessler-Harris, Alice. *Out to Work: A History of Wage-earning Women in the United States.* New York: Oxford University Press, 1982.

Klinkner, Philip A., and Rogers Smith. *The Unsteady March: The Rise and Decline of Racial Equality in America.* Chicago: University of Chicago Press, 1999.

Kornweibel, Theodore, Jr. *No Crystal Stair: Black Life and the Messenger, 1917–1928.* Westport, Conn.: Greenwood Press, 1975.

Lasch-Quinn, Elisabeth. *Black Neighbors: Race and the Limits of Reform in the American Settlement House Movement, 1890–1945.* Chapel Hill: University of North Carolina Press, 1993.

Lawson, Steven F. *Running for Freedom: Civil Rights and Black Politics in America Since 1941.* Philadelphia: Temple University Press, 1991.

Leamann, Nicholas. *The Promised Land: The Great Black Migration and How It Changed America.* New York: Vintage Books, 1992.

Lewis, David L. *W. E. B. DuBois: Biography of a Race, 1868–1919.* New York: Henry Holt & Company, 1993.

——. *When Harlem Was in Vogue.* Oxford: Oxford University Press, 1981.

Lichtenstein, Alex. *Twice the Work of Free Labor: The Political Economy of Convict Labor in the South.* London: Verso Press, 1996.

Lichtenstein, Nelson. *Labor's War at Home: The CIO in World War II,* Cambridge: Cambridge University Press, 1982.

——. *State of the Union: A Century of American Labor.* Princeton, N.J.: Princeton University Press, 2002.

Lichtenstein, Nelson, and Howell J. Harris, eds. *Industrial Democracy in America: The Ambiguous Promise.* Cambridge: Cambridge University Press, 1993.

Locke, Alain, ed. *The New Negro.* New York: Atheneum, 1992.

Logan, Rayford W., ed. *What the Negro Wants.* Chapel Hill: University of North Carolina Press, 1944.

Lyman, Stanford M. *Militarism, Imperialism, and Racial Accommodation: An Analysis and Interpretation of the Early Writings of Robert E. Park.* Fayetteville: University of Arkansas Press, 1992.

Martin, Tony. *Race First: The Ideological and Organizational Structure of Marcus Garvey and the UNIA.* New York: Majority Press, 1976.

Meier, August. *Negro Thought in America, 1880–1915.* Ann Arbor: University of Michigan Press, 1963.

Moore, Jesse T. *A Search for Equality: The National Urban League, 1910–1961.* University Park: Pennsylvania State University Press, 1981.

Moreno, Paul. *From Direct Action to Affirmative Action: Fair Employment Law and Policy in America, 1933–1972.* Baton Rouge: Louisiana State University Press, 1997.

Morris, Aldon D. *The Origins of the Civil Rights Movement: Black Communities Organizing for Change.* New York: Free Press, 1984.

Moses, Earl. "The Negro Delinquent in Chicago." Washington, D.C.: Washington Public Schools Department of Research Divisions X–XIII, 1936.

Moses, Wilson Jeremiah. *The Golden Age of Black Nationalism, 1850–1925.* New York: Oxford University Press, 1978.

Myrdal, Gunnar. *An American Dilemma: The Negro Problem and Modern Democracy.* New York: Harper and Row, 1962.

Naison, Mark. *Communists in Harlem during the Depression.* New York: Grove Press, 1983.

Northrup, Herbert R. *Organized Labor and the Negro.* New York: Harper and Brothers, 1944.

O'Connor, Alice. *Poverty Knowledge: Social Science, Social Policy, and the Poor in Twentieth-Century U.S. History.* Princeton, N.J.: Princeton University Press, 2001.

Osofsky, Gilbert. *Harlem; The Making of Ghetto; Negro New York, 1890–1930.* New York: Harper and Row, 1971.

Ottley, Roi. *The Lonely Warrior: The Life and Times of Robert S. Abbott.* Chicago: Henry Regnery Company, 1955.

Ovington, Mary White. *Half a Man: The Status of the Negro in New York.* New York: Schocken Books, 1911.

Park, Robert E., and Herbert A. Miller. *Old World Traits Transplanted.* New York: Arno Press, 1969.

Parris, Guichard, and Lester Brooks. *Blacks in the City: A History of the National Urban League.* Boston: Little, Brown, 1971.

Persons, Stow. *Ethnic Studies at Chicago, 1905–45.* Urbana: University of Illinois Press, 1987.

Pfeffer, Paula F. *A. Philip Randolph, Pioneer of the Civil Rights Movement.* Baton Rouge: Louisiana State University Press, 1990.

Philpott, Thomas L. *The Slum and the Ghetto: Neighborhood Deterioration and Middle-Class Reform, Chicago, 1880–1930.* New York: Oxford University Press, 1978.

Quadagno, Jill. *The Color of Welfare: How Racism Undermined the War on Poverty.* New York: Oxford University Press, 1994.

Radford, Gail. *Modern Housing for America: Policy Struggles in the New Deal Era.* Chicago: University of Chicago Press, 1996.

Reed, Adolph L., Jr. *W. E. B. DuBois and American Political Thought: Fabianism and the Color Line.* New York: Oxford University Press, 1997.

——, ed. *Race, Politics, and Culture: Critical Essays on the Radicalism of the 1960s.* New York: Greenwood Press, 1986.

——. *Without Justice for All: The New Liberalism and Our Retreat from Racial Equality.* Boulder, Colo.: Westview Press, 1999.

Reed, Christopher R. *The Chicago NAACP and the Rise of Black Professional Leadership, 1910–1966.* Bloomington: Indiana University Press, 1997.

Reed, Merl E. *Seedtime for the Modern Civil Rights Movement: The President's Committee on Fair Employment Practice, 1941–1946.* Baton Rouge: Louisiana State University Press, 1991.

Rees, Jonathan. *Managing the Mills: Labor Policy in the American Steel Industry during the Nonunion Era.* Lanham, Md.: University Press of America, 2004.

Reid, Ira De Augustine. *In a Minor Key: Negro Youth in Story and Fact.* Westport, Conn.: Greenwood Press, 1971.

———. *The Negro Immigrant: His Background, Characteristics and Social Adjustment, 1899–1937.* New York: Columbia University Press, 1939.

———. *Negro Membership in American Labor Unions.* New York: Alexander Press, 1930.

Robertson, David Brian. *Capital, Labor, and State: The Battle for American Labor Markets from the Civil War to the New Deal.* Lanham, Md.: Rowman and Littlefield, 2000.

Rodgers, Daniel T. *The Work Ethic in Industrial America, 1850–1920.* Chicago: University of Chicago Press, 1978.

Roediger, David R. *The Wages of Whiteness: Race and the Making of the American Working Class.* London: Verso Press, 1991.

Ross, Dorothy. *The Origins of American Social Science.* Cambridge: Cambridge University Press, 1991.

Ross, E. A. *The Old World in the New: The Significance of Past and Present Immigration to the American People.* New York: Century, 1914.

Scheiner, Seth M. *Negro Mecca: A History of the Negro in New York City, 1865–1920.* New York: New York University Press, 1965.

Scott, Daryl Michael. *Contempt and Pity: Social Policy and the Image of the Damaged Black Psyche, 1880–1996.* Chapel Hill: University of North Carolina Press, 1997.

Scott, Emmett J. *Negro Migration during the War.* London: Oxford University Press, 1920.

Shaw, Stephanie. *What a Woman Ought to Be and Do: Black Professional Women Workers during the Jim Crow Era.* Chicago: University of Chicago Press, 1996.

Sitkoff, Harvard. *A New Deal for Blacks: The Emergence of Civil Rights as a National Issue.* New York: Oxford University Press, 1978.

Smith, Dennis. *The Chicago School: A Liberal Critique of Capitalism.* New York: St. Martin's Press, 1988.

Smith, Preston H. "The Quest for Racial Democracy: Black Civic Ideology and Housing Interests in Postwar Chicago." *Journal of Urban History* 26, no. 2 (January 2000): 131–57.

Spear, Allan H. *Black Chicago: The Making of a Negro Ghetto, 1890–1920.* Chicago: University of Chicago Press, 1967.

Spero, Sterling D., and Abram L. Harris. *The Black Worker: The Negro and the Labor Movement.* New York: Columbia University Press, 1931.

Stein, Judith. *The World of Marcus Garvey: Race and Class in Modern Society.* Baton Rouge: Louisiana State University Press, 1986.

Sterner, Richard. *The Negro's Share: A Study of Income, Consumption, Housing, and Public Assistance.* New York: Harper and Brothers, 1943.

Sternsher, Bernard. *The Negro in Depression and War: Prelude to Revolution, 1930–1945.* Chicago: Quadrangle Books, 1969.

Strickland, Arvarh. *History of the Chicago Urban League*. Columbia: University of Missouri Press, 2001.

Sugrue, Thomas J. *The Origins of the Urban Crisis: Race and Inequality in Postwar Detroit*. Princeton, N.J.: Princeton University Press, 1996.

Sullivan, Patricia. *Days of Hope: Race and Democracy in the New Deal Era*. Chapel Hill: University of North Carolina Press, 1996.

Thomas, William I. "The Mind of Women and the Lower Races." *American Journal of Sociology* 12, no. 4 (January 1907): 435–69.

———. *Old World Traits Transplanted*. New York: Harper, 1921.

———. *Disorganization and Reorganization in Poland*. Vol. 4 of *The Polish Peasant in Europe and America*. Boston: Gorham Press, 1920.

Thomas, William I., and Florian Znaniecki, *The Polish Peasant in Europe and America*. Urban: University of Illinois Press, 1984.

Turner, Ralph H., ed. *Robert E. Park on Social Control and Collective Behavior*. Chicago: University of Chicago Press, 1967.

Vincent, Theodore G., ed. *Voices of a Black Nation: Political Journalism in the Harlem Renaissance*. Trenton: Africa World Press, 1973.

Washington, Booker T. *Up from Slavery*. New York: New American Library, 2000.

Weaver, Robert C. *Negro Labor: A National Problem*. New York: Harcourt, Brace and Company, 1946.

Weinstein, James. *The Corporate Ideal in the Liberal State, 1900–1918*. Boston: Beacon Press, 1968.

Weiss, Nancy J. *Farewell to the Party of Lincoln: Black Politics in the Age of FDR*. Princeton, N.J.: Princeton University Press, 1983.

———. *The National Urban League, 1910–1940*. New York: Oxford University Press, 1974.

———. *Whitney M. Young, Jr., and the Struggle for Civil Rights*. Princeton, N.J.: Princeton University Press, 1989.

Wiebe, Robert H. *The Search for Order, 1877–1920*. New York: Hill and Wang, 1992.

Wilson, William J. *The Truly Disadvantaged: The Inner City, the Underclass, and Public Policy*. Chicago: University of Chicago Press, 1987.

———. *When Work Disappears: The World of the New Urban Poor*. New York: Alfred A. Knopf, 1997.

Wright, Richard. *Native Son*. New York: Harper Perennial, 1993.

Zieger, Robert H. *American Workers, American Unions, 1920–1985*. Baltimore: Johns Hopkins University Press, 1986.

———. *The CIO, 1935–1955*. Chapel Hill: University of North Carolina Press, 1995.

Unpublished Papers

Belfon, Henri A. "A History of the Urban League Movement, 1910–1945." Master's thesis, Fordham University, 1947.

Bolden, Alexander. "The Evolution of the National Urban League." Master's thesis, Columbia University, 1932.

Cooper, Dona H. "The National Urban League during the Depression, 1930–1939: The Quest for Jobs for Black Workers." Ph.D. dissertation, School of Social Work, Columbia University, 1982.

Lewis, Edward S. "The Urban League, a Dramatic Instrument of Social Change: A Study of the Changing Role of the New York Urban League, 1910–1960." Ph.D. dissertation, School of Education, New York University, 1960 (also at the Schomburg Center for Research in Black Culture, New York Public Library).

Smith, Preston H. "The Limitations of Racial Democracy: The Politics of the Urban League, 1916–1940." Doctoral thesis, University of Massachusetts, Amherst.

Index

Bruce, Roscoe C., 49, 51–52, 54
Buffalo Urban League, 154
Bulkley, William H., 13–14, 200 (n. 10)
Burgess, Earnest, 19, 205 (n. 46)

Cabrini-Green Apartments, 196
Carter, Elmer, 131
Chicago Commission on Race Relations
    (CCRR), 32–33, 65, 207–8 (n. 77), 210
    (n. 19); on acculturation of Afro-
    American migrants, 40; on interracial
    unions, 91, 132; on racial tension, 34,
    88–91; on wage standards, 91
Chicago Housing Authority, 184–85,
    196
Chicago Planning Commission, 185
Chicago School of Sociology, 7, 195–96,
    232 (n. 6); influence on NUL, 5–6, 19,
    167, 190–92; on migration, 21; models
    of assimilation, 5, 7, 11, 20, 22, 25–26,
    133, 192, 199 (n. 1); on personal demor-
    alization, 21; support from Rockefeller
    Fund, 19. See also Ethnic cycle theory;
    Gemeinschaft; Gesellschaft; Social dis-
    organization and reorganization; Urban
    ecology
Chicago Urban League (CUL), 3, 4, 8, 17,
    83, 110, 117–18, 162, 164–65, 207–8
    (n. 77); adult education program, 119;
    civic department, 174, 178; on crime
    and delinquency, 172; Department of
    Industrial Relations, 110, 113, 117, 142,
    147, 160, 225 (n. 50); domestic place-
    ment work, 153; on dual wage struc-
    tures, 90; educational work, 35, 64, 66,
    112; on employer-employee relations,
    65–66, 87, 144, 210 (nn. 24–25);
    Employment Bureau, 119; on failures of
    local government, 174; and FEPC, 142–
    46; foundation of, 17–18; funding, 95,
    105, 164, 170, 178; housing efforts, 35–
    37, 170–71, 177–78, 183–84, 204
    (n. 28), 206 (n. 62); Ida B. Wells housing
    project, 177–78, 183, 185; and IEAC,

112–13; industrial education program,
    64–65; on interracial job consciousness,
    90–93, 105, 155–56; intervention in
    stockyard strikes, 94; and Jane Addams
    Houses, 183–84; job placement efforts,
    70–71, 78, 94, 117, 147, 162–65, 211
    (n. 32), 215 (n. 42), 225 (n. 52), 226
    (n. 55), 227 (n. 65), 228 (n. 84); and Lan-
    throp Homes, 183; lobbying for political
    assistance, 178; on maladjustment, 65,
    171; on New Deal recovery efforts, 112,
    117; opposition to AFL campaigns, 130;
    on piece-rate pay, 68–69, 210–11
    (n. 29); Pilot Placement Program, 7,
    160–67; on public employment dis-
    crimination, 113, 158, 165–66; on race
    riots, 34; on social disorganization, 34,
    37, 121, 205 (n. 46); sociologists influ-
    ence on, 6; support for CIO, 129; Trum-
    bull Parks Homes, 183; union efforts,
    87, 90, 92–94, 145, 147, 155; vocational
    guidance, 87, 120; on wage inequality,
    91; and Women's Trade Union League,
    67; work to provide organized activities,
    42, 171; work with employers, 62, 64, 94,
    144. See also National Urban League;
    New York Urban League
Citizens Committee on Harlem, 173
Civilian Conservation Corps (CCC), 109,
    118
Civil Works Administration (CWA), 109,
    119
Clark, John T., 17
Closed shop, 85, 126, 219–20 (n. 56)
Committee for Improving Industrial Con-
    ditions of Negroes in New York
    (CIICN), 12, 14, 200 (n. 10); emphasis
    on vocational guidance, 13; foundation
    of, 13; Vocational Exchange, 59
Committee on Urban Conditions Among
    Negroes (CUCAN), 12; foundation of,
    13; racial uplift project, 14; report on
    rent in Harlem, 31
Communism, 106; and Afro-Americans,

Gemeinschaft, 20–21, 25–26

General Electric Company, 162

General Motors' Buick: Melrose Park plant, 144, 146–47, 223 (nn. 23–24)

Gesellschaft, 20–21, 25–26

GI Bill, 159, 227 (n. 72), 228 (n. 84)

Giddings, Paul, 3

Gilmore, Glenda, 3

Glenn L. Martin, 154, 226 (n. 59)

Gompers, Samuel, 85; on Socialism, 97; on unionism, 82, 87

Gould, Howard, 225 (n. 52); as liaison with FEPC, 142, 144; on racial discrimination in New Deal agencies, 113; on war emergency hiring, 144; work with CUL, 17, 110

Granger, Lester, 3, 23, 126, 135, 225 (n. 43), 225 (n. 52); at AFL Atlantic City Convention, 128; on AFL discrimination, 127–28; on black employment, 151, 153–54, 157, 226 (n. 59); education of, 123–24; as executive secretary of NUL, 175; on failures of local governments, 171; and FEPC, 143, 150, 158, 224 (n. 32); as head of Workers' Bureau, 124, 175; and March on Washington Movement, 141, 148–49, 175, 224 (n. 39); as president of NCSW, 17; on public housing, 183, 186–89; on social disorganization, 171, 174–75, 187, 230 (n. 38); support for CIO, 129; support for Executive Order 8802, 142, 223 (n. 15); support for Full Employment Bill (1945), 159

Great Depression, 4, 19–20, 131, 198 (n. 9); and Afro-American poverty, 107, 110; effects on migration, 11, 169; and housing, 55–56, 175–76; impact on CUL, 70, 117; impact on NUL, 17, 73–75, 77, 118–19, 158, 161, 172; impact on NYUL, 74, 114–17; and social disorganization, 102–3, 135. See also Afro-Americans: during Great Depression

Great Migration, 3, 169, 198 (n. 9); to Chicago, 27–28, 170; effects on unionizing

in AFL, 82; to New York City, 11, 27, 170; skills of migrants, 61. See also Afro-Americans: migration of

Green, William, 85; rebuff of NUL, 125

Grossman, James, 35

Halpern, Rick, 94, 214 (n. 37)

Harlem: Citizens Committee on Harlem, 173; during Great Depression, 107; housing in, 44, 48–56, 58, 171, 182, 202–3 (n. 3), 206 (nn. 65–67), 207 (nn. 69–71); North Harlem Community Council, 179; overpopulation of, 27, 176, 182; rent, 53–54, 182; surveys of, 30–31, 45, 48, 53

Harlem Big Brothers movement, 173

Harlem River Houses, 179–82

Harlem Tenants League, 177

Harris, Abram L., 131–32, 191

Haynes, George E., 3, 13, 32, 51, 196, 200 (n. 10); on blacks' assimilation into society, 31; education of, 13, 17; as founder of CUCAN, 13, 31; as founder of NUL, 5, 17; on maladjustment, 13–14; and National Conference of Social Work, 16; on organized labor, 81–82, 213 (n. 7); on responsibility of churches, 36; and social work training center, 15; tenure at NUL, 14, 16

Higginbotham, Evelyn Brooks, 3, 197–98 (nn. 6–7), 217 (n. 75)

Hillman, Sidney: establishment of CIO, 128–29

Hill, T. Arnold, 3, 23, 161, 175, 196, 232 (n. 4); as acting executive secretary of NUL, 110, 217–18 (n. 8); on AFL, 125; on black unemployment, 77–78, 120; on black unionism, 83–84, 94, 96, 102, 104, 122, 133, 213 (n. 7); and CUL, 18; and Department of Industrial Relations, 74, 83–84, 96, 122; on "Don't Buy Where You Can't Work Campaigns," 77; education of, 18; on integration, 90; on interracial working-class solidarity, 133,

216 (n. 66); on job training, 120, 212
(n. 48); meeting with Robert Wagner,
111; meeting with Roosevelt, 140; on
political radicalism, 103–4, 134–36, 216
(n. 71), 217 (n. 72); on recovery efforts,
109, 111; on social disorganization, 74,
76, 103–4; support for CIO, 136; on
Wagner Act, 126; and Workers' Councils, 122–23, 133

Holloway, Jonathan, 131

Home Relief (HR) and Work Bureau (WB),
109

Hoover, J. Edgar, 172

Hope VI, 196

Horner, Henry, 178

Housing. *See* Afro-Americans: and housing

Howard University, 162

Hubert, James H.: at AFL Atlantic City
Convention, 128; appeals against
employer discrimination, 111–12; on
black representation in PWA, 111;
courtship of real estate, 48; as executive
secretary of NYUL, 17; on lodgers, 48

Ickes, Harold, 111, 176, 179, 183–84

Ida B. Wells housing project, 177–78, 183,
185

Illinois Emergency Advisory Council
(IEAC): involvement with CUL, 112, 117

Illinois Institute of Technology (ITT), 144

Illinois State Employment Service, 144, 164

Industrial democracy, 108, 123, 130

Industrial Health Clinic, 115–16

Inter-Municipal Committee on Household
Research (IMCHR), 12

International Association of Machinists
(IAM), 87, 153

International Brotherhood of Boilermakers, Iron, Shipbuilders and Helpers
of America, 153

International Brotherhood of Electrical
Workers, 126–27

Isaacs, Robert, 104

Ives-Quinn Law, 158

Jackson, Alexander L., 16

James v. Marinship, 126

Jane Addams Houses, 183–84

Jenkins, Charles I., 113

Jim Crow, 11, 23, 82, 91, 126, 134, 136, 196,
198 (n. 7)

Johnson, Charles S., 3, 4, 23, 89, 188, 192, 213
(n. 23), 221 (n. 80), 232 (nn. 4, 6); as associate executive secretary of CCRR, 34, 88;
on church, 36, 100; education of, 18–19;
on interracial job consciousness, 88–90,
101, 132; on migration, 39, 104; on political radicalism, 99, 102; on race riots, 34;
on social disorganization, 88, 100–101,
171, 174, 213 (n. 21), 216 (n. 58); on
unionism, 96, 100–101, 213 (n. 7); work
with CUL, 18; work with NUL, 18

Johnson, Lyndon B., 195, 233 (n. 7)

Jones, Eugene Kinckle, 175; on black
employability, 121; on black unionism,
83, 213 (n. 7); education of, 18; efforts to
organize new construction, 44–45; on
executive board of NCSW, 17; as executive secretary of NUL, 16, 83, 110; as
Haynes's deputy, 15; meeting with
John D. Rockefeller Jr., 83; real estate
investment, 54

Journeymen Plumbers' Union: Chicago,
145–46

Karson, Marc, 97

Kellor, Frances A.: as director of IMCHR,
12; on effects of migration, 12; work
with CUCAN, 14

Ku Klux Klan, 98

Labor unions, 85, 91, 97, 126, 219–20
(n. 56); and acculturation efforts by
NUL, 86, 101; membership in, 85, 92,
125; and political radicalism, 101–6,
135; post–World War I strikes, 85; and
race relations, 87–88, 91–96, 101, 105;
racism in, 100, 109, 125, 127–28, 140,
144–46

La Guardia, Fiorello, 171, 179
Lanthrop Homes, 183
Lend Lease Act, 139
Lewis, Alfred B., 134
Lewis, John L., 128
Lichtenstein, Nelson, 108
Little Steel firms, 129, 220 (n. 69)
Lockheed-Vega, 154

March on Washington Movement
    (MOWM), 191, 224 (n. 39); organiza-
    tion of, 140; "Save the FEPC" rallies,
    148; support for, 141
McNutt, Paul, 148, 224 (n. 37), 225 (n. 43)
Moore, Jesse T., 4–5, 122, 198–99
    (nn. 12–13), 200 (n. 10), 217–18 (n. 8)
Moses, Earl: on ecological reasons for
    delinquency, 38, 41, 206 (n. 49); educa-
    tion of, 19, 204 (n. 36); as secretary of
    research at CUL, 37; on social disorgan-
    ization, 38–40, 171, 205 (n. 46), 214
    (n. 27)
Mumford, Lewis, 179–80

Nachmann Company, 66–69
National Association for the Advancement
    of Colored People (NAACP), 5, 111,
    194, 204 (n. 22), 232 (n. 6); Committee
    on the Future Plan and Program, 131;
    on interracial unionism, 95, 145; lobby-
    ing for government housing assistance,
    179; Second Amenia Conference, 131–
    32
National Committee on Employer-
    Employee Relationships in the Home,
    73
National Conference of Catholic Charities,
    176
National Conference of Social Work
    (NCSW), 16–17
National Heath Service (NHS), 119
National Industrial Recovery Act (NIRA),
    108, 112, 127; Section 7(a), 124–25;
    Title II, 176

Nationalism, 97–98. See also Garvey,
    Marcus
National Labor Relations Act (NLRA). See
    Wagner Act
National Labor Relations Board (NLRB),
    125
National League for the Protection of Col-
    ored Women (NLPCW), 14; foundation
    of, 12; housing and employment ser-
    vices, 12–13
National League on Urban Conditions
    Among Negroes (NLUCAN). See
    National Urban League
National Recovery Administration (NRA),
    109, 112
National Urban League (NUL), 3, 203
    (n. 11), 213 (n. 9), 223 (n. 19); adult edu-
    cation courses, 154; on Afro-American
    criminality and delinquency, 172, 212
    (n. 51), 214 (n. 27); on black employ-
    ability, 110–11, 118, 226 (n. 61); on
    black protest activity, 98, 106, 132, 214
    (n. 27); community development, 40–
    41; concerns about AFL, 125, 127–28;
    creation of EACS, 112; Department of
    Housing, 17; Department of Industrial
    Relations, 17, 74, 83–84, 96, 100, 109,
    114, 118, 120–23, 160–67, 219 (n. 40),
    226 (n. 56); Department of Research,
    17–18; educational work, 59, 96; effects
    of expansion of welfare state on, 9, 166–
    67, 189; embrace of Chicago School of
    Sociology, 6, 19, 26, 167, 190–94; Fel-
    lows Program, 15–17; and FEPC, 142–
    43, 147–48, 150–51, 158, 167, 222
    (n. 13), 224 (n. 32); field studies, 5, 30;
    foundation of, 5, 11, 14; funding, 160–
    61; Harlem Big Brothers movement,
    173; Haynes: development under, 14–
    15; Haynes: dismissal of, 16; high school
    guidance program, 59; housing activ-
    ities, 9, 26, 42–44, 56, 170–71, 175–77,
    179–80, 183, 185–90; Housing Bureau
    of New York, 30, 44, 48; job placement,

62, 74, 77, 79; Industrial Health Clinic, 115–16; job placement efforts, 72, 109–12, 114–17, 166; job registration bureau, 116–17; Juvenile Park Protective League (JPPL), 42–43; lobbying for political assistance, 179; on maladjustment, 41, 134, 171; on Mayor Fiorello La Guardia, 171; mayor's Unemployment Committee, 60; on New Deal recovery efforts, 109, 111–12; and North American Aviation, 154; on overcrowding of ghettos, 47, 187; personnel shortage, 116; Pilot Placement Program, 7, 160–67, 199 (n. 17); providing organized activities, 42, 50, 171–72, 229 (n. 16); on publicly financed housing, 187; research on social disorganization of ghettos, 30–31; social reorganization attempts, 173; sociologists influence on, 6; support for Taft-Ellender-Wagner Act, 187; on technological unemployment, 77; vocational guidance, 73–78, 120

North Harlem Community Council, 179

O'Connor, Alice, 19, 192, 199 (n. 1)
Office of Price Management (OPM), 142–45, 148. *See also* Fair Employment Practices Committee
Office of War Information (OWI), 141
Opportunity, 40, 42, 55, 67, 76, 99, 103, 124, 134, 157, 180–81
Osofsky, Gilbert, 11
Ovington, Mary White, 204 (n. 22)

Packard Motor Company: Detroit, 151
Packinghouses: Chicago, 91–95, 214 (n. 37)
Park, Robert, 11, 18–19, 131, 192, 201 (n. 38); and W. E. B. DuBois, 199–200 (n. 1); and ethnic cycle theory, 22; on southern race relations, 23; on transition between gemeinschaft and gesellschaft, 20; on urban ecology, 20–

23; and Booker T. Washington, 199–200 (n. 1). *See also* Social disorganization and reorganization
Pfeffer, Paula, 141
Philadelphia Negro, The. See DuBois, W. E. B.
Pilot Placement Program, 7, 160–67
Pipe Trade Council (PTC), 145–47, 223–24 (n. 27)
Plessy v. Ferguson, 1
Population, Afro-American. *See* Afro-Americans: population of in Chicago; Afro-Americans: population of in New York
Public Works Administration (PWA): and black employment, 109; effects on housing, 176, 178, 180, 182

Queensboro Project, 183
Quirk, William, 145

Race relations, 25–26, 32–35, 151, 202 (n. 3), 204 (n. 22); in Chicago packinghouses, 92; and Communism, 104; effects of migration on, 11; and Garveyism, 99, 104; impact on hiring, 60, 169, 222 (nn. 2–3, 4); impact on housing, 28–29, 175, 186, 188, 204 (n. 24); in the South, 1, 23; and unionism, 87–88, 91–96, 105, 215 (n. 45), 216 (n. 66); and Urban League, 88–90
Race riots, causes of, 11, 91; in Chicago, 17, 32–33, 87, 91–93, 203–4 (n. 20); in Detroit, 141, 149; in East St. Louis, 91; newspaper coverage of, 33–34, 36, 204 (n. 22); in New York, 11, 17, 32–33, 171
Racial uplift, 3, 6, 25–26, 29, 37, 50, 56, 61, 105, 121, 131, 139, 150, 152, 155, 157–58, 166–67, 170–75, 179–80, 186, 189–91, 193, 196, 197 (n. 6)
Radford, Gail, 179, 182
Radicalism, 97–106, 132, 134–35, 191, 216 (n. 71), 217 (n. 72). *See also* Communism; Socialism